Securing Development in an Unstable World

Annual World Bank Conference
on Development Economics—Europe
2006

Securing Development in an Unstable World

Edited by
François Bourguignon
Boris Pleskovic
Jacques van der Gaag

THE WORLD BANK
Washington, D.C.

1818 H Street NW
Washington DC 20433
Telephone: 202-473-1000
Internet: www.worldbank.org
E-mail: feedback@worldbank.org

1 2 3 4 09 08 07 06

Edited by François Bourguignon, Boris Pleskovic, and Jacques van der Gaag

Professional affiliations identified in this volume are as of the time of the conference, May 23–24, 2005.

ISBN-10: 0-8213-6107-4
ISBN-13: 978-0-8213-6107-8
eISBN: 0-8213-6108-2
DOI: 10.1596/978-0-8213-6107-8
ISSN: 1813-9477

Contents

ACKNOWLEDGMENTS vii

INTRODUCTION AND SUMMARY 1
François Bourguignon, Boris Pleskovic, and Jacques van der Gaag

WELCOME ADDRESS 9
Jean-François Rischard

OPENING ADDRESS
Head above Water 15
Agnes van Ardenne-van der Hoeven

KEYNOTE ADDRESS
Stability, Security, and Development: An Introduction 21
François Bourguignon

KEYNOTE ADDRESS
Development in an Unstable World: A Japanese Experience to Promote Human Security 35
Hisashi Owada

KEYNOTE ADDRESS
The Other Path to Growth: Private Sector Development 45
Gerrit Zalm

KEYNOTE ADDRESS
Trade and Development 53
Ernesto Zedillo

Macroeconomic Vulnerability

Macro Vulnerability in Low-Income Countries and Aid Responses 65
Patrick Guillaumont

COMMENT
Duncan Green 109

Vulnerability: A Micro Perspective

Vulnerability: A Micro Perspective 117
Stefan Dercon

COMMENTS
Paul Mosley 147
Richard Wilcox 157

Health Risks

Scaling Up Access to HIV Prevention, Treatment, and Care in Resource-Poor Settings: Challenges and Opportunities 163
Joep M. A. Lange

COMMENTS
Françoise Ndayishimiye 179
Henk Rijckborst 185

Acknowledgments

The planning and organization of the 2005 conference was a joint effort by the Government of the Netherlands and the World Bank. We wish to thank Jean-Christophe Bas for preparing the conference. We gratefully acknowledge contributions made by all the members of the steering committee, several anonymous reviewers, Aehyung Kim, and Celestin Monga for their useful advice and suggestions. We also thank conference coordinators Leita Jones, Anna Kuznicka, Nina Maqami, and Gaetano Vivo whose excellent organizational skills helped to ensure a successful conference. Finally, we thank the editorial staff for pulling this volume together, especially Aziz Gokdemir and Stuart K. Tucker from the Office of the Publisher and Sherrie Brown, the manuscript editor.

Introduction and Summary

FRANÇOIS BOURGUIGNON, BORIS PLESKOVIC, AND JACQUES VAN DER GAAG

The Annual Bank Conference on Development Economics (ABCDE) is one of the world's best-known series of conferences for the presentation and discussion of new knowledge on development. It is an opportunity for many of the world's finest development thinkers to present their ideas. In 1999, in recognition of Europe's pivotal role in the provision of development assistance and to bring the World Bank's research on development into close contact with European perspectives, the World Bank created a distinctively European platform for debate on development issues.

The seventh Annual Bank Conference on Development Economics in Europe was held in Amsterdam, the Netherlands, May 23–24, 2005. The conference was co-organized by the Government of the Netherlands. The theme of the conference was "Securing Development in an Unstable World."

The conference opened with remarks by Jean-François Rischard, the World Bank's Vice President for Europe, and Agnes van Ardenne-van der Hoeven, Minister for Development Cooperation, the Netherlands. Their remarks were followed by keynote addresses by François Bourguignon, Chief Economist and Senior Vice President of the World Bank; Hisashi Owada, Judge, International Court of Justice, and former Vice Minister for Foreign Affairs, Japan; Gerrit Zalm, Minister of Finance, the Netherlands; and Ernesto Zedillo, former President of Mexico, and Director, Yale Center for the Study of Globalization, Yale University. Three papers—on macroeconomic vulnerability; vulnerability: a micro perspective; and health risks—were then presented.

François Bourguignon is Senior Vice President, Development Economics, and Chief Economist at the World Bank. Boris Pleskovic is Research Manager, Development Economics at the World Bank. Jacques van der Gaag is Professor of Development Economics and Dean of the Faculty of Economics and Business at the University of Amsterdam.

Annual World Bank Conference on Development Economics—Europe 2006

Welcoming Address

Jean-François Rischard notes the Netherlands' steadfast support for development over the past decade. For example, he states that the Dutch have maintained a high level of commitment, contributing over 0.8 percent of GDP for many years, as well as initiating new programs such as the Education for All "Fast Track Initiative" and the Multi-country Demobilization and Reintegration Program around the Great Lakes region of Africa. The Netherlands has thus become one of the most influential actors on the development scene. Minister van Ardenne, in particular, has been an ardent advocate with regard to security issues and their impact on development—a topic that actually represents the umbrella subject that brought us together in Amsterdam. Rischard continues that the ABCDE conference is now a real stakeholders' meeting, and the sort of gathering that goes beyond academic research and debate toward genuinely moving the solutions of development issues and global issues forward. Rischard indicates that this year over 500 participants from 90 countries attended the conference, and that the conference brings together professionals not just from academia, but also from think tanks, government, nongovernmental organizations, and private business. Rischard adds that ABCDE conferences have continuously increased in scope and size over the years. This year's conference focuses on "securing development in an unstable world." It focuses primarily on issues related to vulnerability of the country, household, and individual levels, and the design of strategies for assistance to the vulnerable; second, on issues related to country-based growth and how international financial institutions can help countries achieve it; and third, on issues related to securing development, which encompasses many things, including securing finance for the poor, protecting workers, preventing epidemics, and boosting efforts for Africa.

Opening Address

Agnes van Ardenne-van der Hoeven discusses some of the risks faced by the many who live on the margins—how they cope with vulnerability, and what we in the West can do to help them protect themselves. She looks at vulnerability from both a micro and a macro perspective, saying that poor people and poor countries often lack the resources to deal with insecurity and risk. They stay poor because they cannot afford to take chances on risky but potentially profitable investments. They become even poorer when unexpected price shocks and other setbacks throw them farther down the income ladder. At the micro level, van Ardenne-van der Hoeven considers securing sexual and reproductive health and rights critical for addressing the vulnerability of women. Reproductive rights are human rights. But they are also a key to development. Sexual and reproductive health problems account for nearly one-fifth of the worldwide burden of disease, and one-third of the burden among women of reproductive age. This is a drag on the world economy and on development. At the macro level, van Ardenne-van der Hoeven points out two areas to improve the security of poor countries. One area is international trade liberalization, from which all countries stand to gain, but free trade reshuffles the cards of the international economy—production moves across borders according to comparative advantage. Poor countries need development assistance to adapt to the realities of globalization, including an international "aid for trade" mechanism as part of an ambitious Doha deal. van Ardenne-van der Hoeven points out that low-income, vulnerable countries could draw on this facility to deal with adjustment costs and to build supply and trading capacity. She states that the second macro area is ensuring the security of peace. We cannot free countries from poverty when they are still stuck in the conflict trap. At present, the international community still lacks the tools to deal with postconflict situations in an integrated manner that combines political, security, and development instruments. The UN summit in September 2005 will discuss the establishment of a Peacebuilding Commission to fill this gap. But setting up another commission is not enough. A number of security-related activities with direct relevance to development cannot currently be financed with official development assistance money. Van Ardenne-van der Hoeven indicates that the Netherlands will therefore continue to work with a coalition of the willing to push for a broader definition of official development assistance. She concludes by stating that civil wars in developing countries cost US$100 billion a year—almost twice the annual amount of development assistance provided by the international community in the recent past.

Keynote Addresses

François Bourguignon offers an introduction to the links among stability, security, and development. Over the last few years, the security of persons—security with a capital *S* as it is often called—has become a major source of concern for the world. But there are other definitions of security—with a small *s:* economic security, or the stability of individual standards of living; and social security, including not only insurance against longevity but also issues such as crime and violence, natural disasters such as the 2004 tsunami, or epidemics. Focusing on economic security issues, Bourguignon argues that whatever the definition of security one chooses, there are some basic mechanisms through which risks, insured or uninsured, often cause some damage to economic and social development. At the micro level, uninsured economic risks for poor people or low-income countries tend to create poverty traps, which in turn severely limit income generation and development prospects. While it is generally possible to mitigate these risks, risk mitigation itself has a cost and may reduce long-run income. Both through poverty traps and the negative effects of risk mitigation, insecurity tends to increase poverty and inequality. The same principles apply to macro volatility and macro risks. In macroeconomics, volatility is usually the unpredictable variability of economic aggregates such as GDP, or prices, or productivity. In a negative shock with some permanence—such as the recent increase in oil prices for oil-importing countries—low-income countries first run down their international reserves and then must contract fiscal spending, which in turn produces a drop in GDP. This occurs because they have limited access to international capital markets. However, high-income countries are able to smooth shocks by relying on foreign borrowing when foreign asset sales are insufficient. The amplitude of the effect of negative shocks on GDP and, therefore, crisis volatility thus depends on access to international capital markets, that is, on the long-run solvency of countries, which depends on their levels of income. Bourguignon concludes by suggesting policies to help countries mitigate or cope with macro volatility. On the domestic front, having the right macroeconomic policies, the right domestic institutions, and the right policy regimes (especially in the exchange-rate domain) would provide most countries with adequate protection from crises. On the external front, it is essential for many low-income countries to be able to count on the support of the donor community when they experience major shocks. Foreign aid delivered in ways conditional to the kind of shock experienced by each country, debt sustainability arrangements, and carefully designed export stabilization mechanisms could be key components of the strategy of donor support.

Hisashi Owada discusses a Japanese experience to promote human security. He addresses the historical consequences of the Cold War and argues that the Cold War resulted in a devastation of the economic wealth of many nations and brought about political corruption in many parts of the developing world. However, according to Owada, the end of the Cold War replaced external forces with indigenous ones that tend to disrupt the social fabric of society in many developing countries. He defines the new challenges of development as how to link the freedom from want with the freedom from fear. As an example, Owada describes Japan's experience with East Asia. The essence of this experience has been local ownership combined with external partnership as the new framework of economic cooperation between Japan and the countries of the region. He attributes the success of the "East Asia Economic Miracle" to this framework of cooperation. Owada describes several initiatives, such as the 1993 G-7 Summit in Tokyo and the Tokyo International Conference on the Development of Africa (TICAD), that have been taken by the Japanese government to promote this framework of the twin principles of ownership and partnership. He concludes that the international community needs an integrated strategy for development that focuses on the central theme of how we can promote development effectively through ensuring human security, which should comprise all the elements that can contribute to creating a human society empowered to meet the challenges that hinder development.

Gerrit Zalm focuses on investment climate as a subset of a country's institutions for development. He emphasizes that reducing the risks and costs of doing business and the barriers to entry for new firms should be on the top of the agenda for reaching the Millennium Development Goals. Zalm also argues that private property and competition are essential for economic growth, which ultimately is based on the human nature of "truck, barter, and exchange." In this sense, macroeconomic concern for economic growth rests on micro institutions. He provides the example that institutional quality explains most of the growth difference between Asia and Africa. But, he adds that we need to go beyond recognition of the importance of institutions and ask how to create and maintain effective institutions. Private property rights should be considered the cornerstone of a market economy. Formal property rights substantially expand the size of the market by reducing transaction costs, and secure property rights can significantly increase property values, investment, and productivity. Zalm points out that establishing formal property rights means reforming the law and property system in a way that eases access to formal property and allows informal arrangements to influence law making and play a role in defining property rights. He says that government regulation should reduce or eliminate market failures, thereby increasing social welfare. Heavier regulation is associated with greater inefficiency in public institutions, more unemployment and corruption, and lower productivity. Reducing outmoded or ill-conceived regulations should be a priority. Zalm emphasizes that the potential benefits would be significant, and that the Copenhagen Consensus considers easing start-up to be one of the most cost-effective ways to spur development. He concludes by hoping that cooperation between the World Bank and the European Bank for Reconstruction and Development (EBRD) on this issue will be transformed into a global initiative including all major multilateral development banks.

Ernesto Zedillo argues that upholding an open, equitable, rules-based, predictable, and nondiscriminatory multilateral trading system is of great importance from both the development and security perspectives. He asks what multilateral trading system would best support, first, the attainment of the Millennium Development Goals (MDGs) by 2015, and afterward, the continuation of the fight against poverty until it is effectively eradicated. Trade openness can be a powerful driver of economic growth, which in turn is indispensable to reduce poverty, but trade alone is not a silver bullet for achieving development. There is no way around the other institutional and policy conditions that must also be met to attain development. In moving toward freer trade, adjustment costs also need to be taken into account. In particular, measures to safeguard the poorer individuals who could be negatively affected by more open markets are essential for successful trade liberalization. But, Zedillo maintains, trade openness, if not sufficient, is certainly necessary to boost economic growth and defeat poverty. He argues that the biggest and most costly aberration of the trading system is to be found in agriculture, although trade barriers in nonagricultural products continue to be significant. Developing countries' exports to developed countries face tariffs that are, on average, four times higher than those imposed on the exports of other developed countries. Developing countries' exports suffer from tariff peaks and tariff escalation imposed by rich countries on goods of great export potential. Beyond the numbers, services are fundamental for development, in terms of both the efficiency and growth potential of the economy as a whole, as well as access to basic services to improve the lives of the poor. Zedillo argues that the biggest responsibility for failure so far lies with the biggest players: the European Union, the United States, and Japan, who have failed to honor the core commitments established in the Doha Declaration. Developing countries were told that the only way to solve satisfactorily their pending issues was to launch the new Round. And the pending issue that looms largest by far is agricultural protectionism in rich countries. A good part of the Doha Round's troubles stem from the very same mercantilist logic of reciprocal liberalization that for almost 60 years has driven the evolution of the multilateral trading system. Politicians generally assume that opening one's markets is a necessary evil to get access to others' markets, and therefore they expect their trade negotiators to minimize their country's concessions while maximizing others' concessions. At this point, the question is whether the mercantilist approach to trade liberalization, so effective in the past, can continue to drive the construction of the global public good of open markets. Zedillo outlines 10 elements for a successful conclusion of the Doha Round negotiations, including the recommendation that the WTO focus solely on trade and be relieved of other global economic governance tasks. Zedillo concludes his address by inviting all to consider the benefits of trade for peace and security reflected in Immanuel Kant's assertion in his 1795 work, *Perpetual Peace,* that "The Spirit of Commerce sooner than later takes hold of every people, and it cannot exist side by side with war . . ."

Macroeconomic Vulnerability

Patrick Guillaumont argues that vulnerability matters, particularly for low-income countries. Drawing from the literature and ongoing work, he examines how vulnerability lowers growth and slows down poverty reduction. He also examines how to assess structural vulnerability and presents an index of economic vulnerability that can be used for development cooperation guidance, as it already is for the identification of the Least Developed Countries. Using such an index, he considers the implications for aid policy of the macro vulnerability of poor countries, with a view toward dampening the consequences of the shocks, as well as toward lowering the uncertainty resulting from them. Guillaumont also argues that at the macro level, several analytical issues remain unsolved, and the difference between ex ante and ex post effects of vulnerability are not well understood because threshold effects have not been thoroughly investigated. Pass-through mechanisms are crucial and may have changed over time. Guillaumont also argues that the macroeconomic links between macro vulnerability and poverty must be explored with the help of micro and macro country case studies. The first implication for aid policy is that selectivity principles have to be revisited so that vulnerability becomes one of the main criteria, both because it increases aid effectiveness and because it is a structural handicap to growth. Second, aid can be used as insurance in a new conditionality framework, where a guarantee is offered under the condition that some rules of shock management are agreed upon in advance. Finally, and more difficult, Guillaumont notes that we need to continue to consider how to target aid to reduce the size of the shocks and the exposure of low-income countries.

Vulnerability: A Micro Perspective

Stefan Dercon introduces recent work that has highlighted the crucial role played by risk and vulnerability in determining people's living conditions and opportunities to escape poverty. He states that many development practitioners and researchers have long recognized that individuals, households, and communities face a large number of risks related to, for example, climate, health, or economic shocks. Different disciplines, including economics, geography, and nutritional studies, have analyzed the consequences of life in this risky environment. Dercon continues that specific policies such as preventive health care, safety nets, and famine early-warning systems form a well-established part of the aid and policy efforts in developing countries. High downside risk to income and livelihoods is part of life in developing countries. Climatic risks, economic fluctuations, and a large number of individual-specific shocks leave these households vulnerable to severe hardship. The paper explores the links among risk, vulnerability, and poverty, taking a micro-level perspective. He considers that risk does not just result in variability in living standards. Increasing evidence indicates that the lack of means to cope with risk and vulnerability is in itself a cause of persistent poverty and poverty traps. Risk results in strategies that preclude taking advantage of profitable but risky opportunities. Shocks destroy human, physical, and social capital, thus limiting opportunities further. Dercon concludes that the result is that risk is an important constraint on broad-based growth in living standards in many developing countries. However, risk is relatively ignored in the design of antipoverty policies and efforts to attain the Millennium Development Goals.

Health Risks

Joep M. A. Lange argues that communicable diseases remain the major cause of morbidity and mortality in resource-poor settings. Through both biological and social mechanisms, poverty greatly enhances the vulnerability of people to many infectious diseases. And the major infectious scourges like HIV/AIDS, tuberculosis, and malaria perpetuate poverty and are an important contributor to negative economic and social development. He continues that HIV/AIDS is a case in point, because it primarily affects people in the prime of their lives, leading to losses in productivity and social cohesion. HIV/AIDS also fuels the spread of tuberculosis. The effects of this disease are most dramatic in Sub-Saharan Africa, where the situation is often aggravated by the fact that so many countries are suffering from weak or dysfunctional governance. Weak governance has contributed to a steadily progressive erosion of the public health sector in those countries. Lange declares that on one hand, we are dealing with greatly increasing demands on the public health sector, especially in countries hardest hit by HIV/AIDS; on the other hand, that the health sector is losing already scarce workers to the epidemic. Likewise, the capacity of the education sector is weakened because of increased mortality of HIV-infected teachers. He states that in an era of globalization, the world cannot afford to ignore the health (and other) problems of developing countries. Humanitarian motives aside—which alone should be enough reason for action—the downward spiral of economic and social development in the poorest countries presents a recipe for global insecurity and instability. Lange emphasizes that despite the progress that has been made during the past few years in the closing of the "funding gap," implementation of effective interventions in countries has been lagging behind. Global leadership is greatly needed in the fight against HIV/AIDS, as is a global action plan that takes a pragmatic approach, based upon the best of science and empirical evidence. Lange concludes by noting that the challenge is formidable, but the current momentum for the scale-up of antiretroviral treatment regimens provides a unique opportunity to empower the poor and build sustainable health care systems in Africa and other resource-poor settings.

Welcome Address

JEAN-FRANÇOIS RISCHARD

I am delighted to welcome you on behalf of the World Bank to this ABCDE conference in Europe. It is the seventh such conference that I have participated in since I have been the World Bank's Vice President for Europe and since we took this initiative in 1999.

As those of you who have attended past ABCDE conferences will know, this initiative has continued to increase in scope and size over the years. By now, the ABCDE in Europe conference has grown into a full-fledged global forum on development policy and practice. This year, we have 450 participants from 90 countries. And once again, the conference brings together professionals not just from academia, but also from think tanks, government, NGOs, and private business. The ABCDE conference is now a real stakeholders' meeting—and the sort of gathering that goes beyond academic research and debate toward genuinely moving the solutions of development issues and global issues forward.

Let me now say a few words about our host, the Government of the Netherlands.

From where I sit as the World Bank's VP for Europe, I can tell you with some authority that no country has done more to support development over the past decade than the Netherlands:

- The Dutch have shown the way to the international community with their steadfast commitment to maintaining a high level of aid—over 0.8 percent of GDP for many years.
- They have been pioneers in the decentralization of bilateral assistance, and in their longstanding commitment to harmonization—often pulling even the Bank along, for which we are genuinely grateful.
- The Dutch are often the first to support important new initiatives—like the Education for All "Fast Track Initiative" and the Multi-Country Demobilization and

Jean-François Rischard is World Bank Vice President for Europe.

Annual World Bank Conference on Development Economics—Europe 2006

Reintegration Program around the Great Lakes of Africa. The Dutch government always brings a potent mixture: both constructive criticism and solid, generous financial support to important new causes. The Netherlands has thus become one of the most influential actors on the development scene.
- Minister van Ardenne, in particular, has been an ardent advocate concerning security issues and their impact on development—a topic that actually represents the umbrella subject that brings us together here in Amsterdam today.

This Year's Conference

Under the title of this year's conference, "Securing Development in an Unstable World," you will be probing some of the most significant problems in development today—issues that policy makers are grappling with:

- One set of issues relates to vulnerability on the country, household, and individual levels, and to the design of strategies for assistance to the vulnerable—which can be quite controversial (entanglement with moral hazard issues, and so forth).
- Another set of issues relates to country-based growth and how international financial institutions can help countries achieve it. In that regard, while high growth in Asia clearly has lessons for development policy, it is also clear that there is no single recipe or path to growing out of poverty.
- A third set of issues relates to something we call in the conference title itself "securing development in an unstable world," which encompasses many things, including securing finance for the poor, protecting workers, preventing epidemics, boosting efforts for Africa, and many other topics.

These and many other subjects are the ones you will be looking at over the next few days.

2005: The "Year of Development?"

This ABCDE is taking place during the so-called year of development. The year 2005 has been marked as a year of reckoning in relation to 2015, which is the target year for reaching the Millennium Development Goals (MDGs). As we approach the midpoint of this linchpin year of 2005, it is clear that the glass is half empty, but as I hope this conference will demonstrate, it may also be half full.

Glass Half Empty?

Let us start with the glass half empty points:

- Africa is struggling:
  - Most Sub-Saharan African countries will not achieve the growth levels (per capita income growth of 3–5 percent) needed to move out of poverty.

  - According to current projections, close to 40 percent of Africa's people will remain in poverty (living on less than $1 per day).
  - In 2003, only 59 percent of African children completed primary school, and on current trends, the region will not achieve universal primary completion before 2060 or so.
  - Child mortality remains the highest in the world at 180 deaths per 1,000 children under five years of age—twice the level of South Asia (92 per 1,000) and almost nine times the levels in the Middle East and North Africa region and the East Asia and Pacific region (26 per 1,000 and 20 per 1,000, respectively).
- Trade talks are faltering:
  - Prospects for the Hong Kong (China) Ministerial Conference of the World Trade Organization (WTO) are dim: unless great progress is achieved in the next few months, there will be little change in Organisation for Economic Co-operation and Development country agricultural policies or subsidy levels, or in the matter of reducing trade-restricting effects of nontariff measures, or in lowering of tariffs by developing countries themselves, and expanding their trade in services.
  - If the Hong Kong (China) deadline is missed, the U.S. Fast Track Authority runs out and we're all in deep trouble with respect to the Doha Development Agenda, which is a critical prerequisite for the MDGs to be met.
- Aid levels are too low:
  - At around $68 billion in 2003, aid was still well below urgent requirements—around twice that amount per year may be needed to reach the MDGs.
  - Quality and composition of aid are a problem—much of the $16 billion increment last year went to debt relief or to Iraq or Afghanistan, not to MDG efforts, and too much aid takes the form of expatriate technical assistance.
- Deadly conflict continues around the world, for example, in the Great Lakes region of Africa, the Middle East, and now Central Asia.
- Environmental deterioration continues to receive little serious attention, and even less consensus about action to be taken—in spite of the United Kingdom's commendable attention to climate change during its G-8 presidency.

Glass Half Full?

- Despite the overall picture, there are signs in Africa that accelerated change is possible:
  - Fifteen countries in Africa have accelerated growth to 5 percent or more, including Ghana, Mali, Mozambique, Tanzania, and Uganda.
  - Poverty is falling in many countries, such as Burkina Faso, Ghana, Mozambique, Senegal, and Uganda.
  - African countries are doing more: the New Partnership for Africa's Development and the African Peer Review Mechanism are demonstrating promising developments in governance; the African Union has intervened in civil conflict in Côte d'Ivoire and Togo.

- Undeniably, there has been a global rallying around Africa, including the U.K. G-8 year, during which the United Kingdom strengthened its Commission for Africa; and donors agreeing to a 30 percent increase in the Bank's fund for the poorest countries, the International Development Association, which will translate into a 45 percent increase in concessional and grant funds available to Africa.
- Bilateral donors are ramping up their aid commitments:
  - the European Commission has surpassed its interim commitment of 0.39 percent (average) for 2006 and is talking about a 0.56 percent goal for 2010.
  - France and the United Kingdom are making solid moves toward their 0.7 percent commitment.
  - The United States has begun committing funds from its Millennium Challenge Account.
  - Harmonization and alignment are being pursued with a new momentum after the successful Paris conference on that topic in February, 2005.
- Thanks to the United Kingdom's G-8 climate change initiatives, at least the probable consequences of inaction may get more public attention.
- Elections in Afghanistan, Iraq, and West Bank and Gaza have been in themselves positive events, and may be helping to build momentum for peace and for change.

The ABCDE Conference's Contribution to Building Irreversible Momentum

In the glass half empty and half full context, this ABCDE conference could be a milestone event in a 2005 that cannot and should not be a meaningless anniversary or stocktaking (as in Beijing plus five), but rather, a starting point for accelerated, intensified action toward 2015.

I urge you therefore to think, in each of the sessions, in terms of possible action plans—because action on all of the issues you will be addressing in this conference could have some impact on progress toward the MDGs. You need to ask yourselves, for example,

- What kinds of vulnerabilities represent major constraints to development, and what practical steps can mitigate them or cushion their impact?
- Where should we go from here to improve aid effectiveness: what are the major efforts that need to be made, whether for assisting fragile states, or for accelerating harmonization?
- How can migration contribute to growth and development, and what are the steps that the world should be taking to facilitate development-positive migration?
- How, in a 10-year framework for action, can we scale up anti-retroviral therapy in poor countries?

At the World Bank, we see the task for 2005 as building *irreversible momentum.* As we've been saying in these conferences for several years now, we know what has to be done for development—the problem is how to do it and how fast we can move.

This conference can play a critical role, now and in the years to come—including by making sure that a full chorus of voices is raised, urging policy makers to stay the course.

Its annual deliberations can and must be an integral part of the push to 2015, which all of us must continue to exert. So I wish you an excellent conference.

Opening Address

Head above Water

AGNES VAN ARDENNE-VAN DER HOEVEN

Your Royal Highness, ladies and gentlemen,

We all want to stand on firm ground. Today and tomorrow, you will be looking for answers to important questions, to expand the body of knowledge by reducing ignorance and uncertainty. But, as the philosopher Karl Popper said, "our knowledge can only be finite, while our ignorance must, necessarily, be infinite." According to Popper, in science we can never really find firm ground. Scientists should regard theories as, at best, interesting speculation. We can never drive out uncertainty.

What applies to scientific theory also applies in practice, in the real world. Without firm ground beneath our feet, we drift on an ocean of insecurity. We never know what is around the corner. That is why we have to protect ourselves against these risks. But some are in a better position to do that than others. While all of us are adrift on that same ocean, we are not all in the same boat. The poor and disenfranchised, the billion people who live on less than a dollar a day, can barely keep their heads above water.

Today I will discuss some of the risks faced by the many who live on the margins, how they cope with vulnerability, what we in the West can do to help them protect themselves, and what I want to do. For us, this is not just a matter of taking the moral high ground. Throwing the poor a lifeline is also in our own interests. In today's world, we have a shared vulnerability. As Kofi Annan said in a recent article on the UN summit this September, and I quote: "The misery of people caught in unresolved civil conflicts or of populations mired in extreme poverty, for example, may increase their attraction to terrorism."

Agnes van Ardenne-van der Hoeven is Minister for Development Cooperation, the Netherlands.

Annual World Bank Conference on Development Economics—Europe 2006

Vulnerability and Poverty

As economists often do, I will look at vulnerability from both a micro and a macro perspective. Poor people and poor countries often lack the resources to deal with insecurity and risk. They stay poor because they cannot afford to take chances on risky but potentially profitable investments. They become even poorer when unexpected price shocks and other setbacks throw them further down the income ladder.

I was struck by the story of a young widow in northern Ethiopia. Ten years ago, when a severe drought hit the region, she fell into the poverty trap. She was forced to sell her last cow to buy food and never managed to save enough to buy it back. Now she can no longer sell butter and milk. So she spends all day gathering firewood and selling cattle dung. She and her family can barely keep their heads above water. At the end of the day, all their money is gone. That means the widow cannot join the traditional rotating savings groups. Or the funeral insurance group. She can only dream of saving for a cow or a goat. She is stuck in the black hole of poverty.

This black hole not only affects unfortunate individuals. At the macro level it can suck in entire countries. As Jeffrey Sachs recently emphasized, commodity price shocks and unfavorable weather conditions can push countries over the edge. It took the Ethiopian economy four years to recover from the drought I just mentioned. Developing countries are especially vulnerable because they often rely heavily on the export of primary commodities. Export earnings are much more volatile in commodities such as coffee and cotton than in manufactured products. Research shows that in the 1970s and 1980s, negative terms of trade shocks affected the long-term output of 56 developing countries. Collier and Dehn (2001) calculate that a 40 percent deterioration in terms of trade costs about 20 percent of national income. This is a severe blow to any country, let alone a poor one. Every shock turns back the clock of development.

The economic fallout can destabilize a country and plunge it into violent conflict, leaving it stuck in both a poverty trap and a conflict trap. Once a country is trapped in conflict, it is difficult for it to escape. There is a 50 percent chance of conflict resuming in the first decade after peace has been achieved. And these conflicts are contagious: Liberia's civil war infected all three of its neighbors, while the conflict in the Democratic Republic of Congo destabilized Central Africa.

Addressing Vulnerability by Achieving the Millennium Development Goals

I could go on and on talking about vulnerability, telling heart-wrenching personal stories of lost opportunities, and describing the macroeconomic effects of negative shocks. But that is not my job. My job is to do something about it. And I am not alone. Five years ago, 189 heads of state committed themselves to eight time-bound and quantified targets to meet the needs of the most vulnerable: the Millennium

Development Goals (MDGs). This autumn, these world leaders will convene at the UN to discuss progress. Or rather, the lack of progress. The crisis of extreme poverty is still with us. In recent decades, globalization has improved many lives. But it hasn't helped the poorest of the poor. Globalization is good, but not good enough. In East and South Asia, more than 200 million people have been lifted out of poverty since 1990. By contrast, this year's *Global Monitoring Report* indicates that Sub-Saharan Africa is off track on all the MDGs. And there is a risk that the UN summit in September will focus on Security Council reform, pushing the MDGs into the background. That would be a tragedy. How could we explain to our children that we wasted a historic opportunity to end poverty? That we argued about who sits at a table in New York, while every day 800 million people go to bed hungry? We cannot allow that to happen. All dimensions of freedom are related. It is impossible to secure freedom from fear without securing freedom from want. As the UN Secretary-General wrote in his report to the summit: "A world in which every year 11 million children die before their fifth birthday and three million people die of AIDS is not a world of larger freedom."

We must seize the opportunity to free people and their countries from the prison of poverty. The Netherlands has been in the front lines of the war on poverty for decades. We will certainly rise to the occasion. Together with our EU partners, we will call on developed and developing countries alike to rally around the MDGs and put political and financial commitment on the table. My government insists on ambitious interim funding targets to speed up progress toward achieving the UN's official 0.7 percent.

Addressing Vulnerability at the Micro Level by Securing Sexual and Reproductive Health and Rights

In September we also have an opportunity to correct a major flaw in the MDGs. A few years ago in New York, women's rights were not adequately incorporated into the new development agenda. Diplomats and politicians left out one of the most basic rights of all: the right to choose. A woman's right to control her own body—to take informed decisions on her reproductive and sexual health. Taking away these rights leaves women all too vulnerable. "Too sensitive an issue," most diplomats must have thought. I must give the World Bank credit for arguing vigorously for the inclusion of reproductive health. But for fear of sparking controversy, the international community eventually gave in to the hard-liners: the United States; the Vatican; and conservative, mostly Islamic, developing countries. The failure to take onboard sexual and reproductive health and rights is measured in the rolls of the dead—and on it are written thousands and thousands of new names each year. Still today, in our age of unprecedented prosperity, a woman dies during pregnancy or childbirth every minute in the developing world. Every minute. This is a double tragedy considering the millions of children left without mothers each year.

Reproductive rights are human rights. But they are also key to development. I do not need to convince an audience of economists that freedom of choice breeds economic prosperity. When individuals are allowed to freely determine the number, timing, and spacing of their children, families are smaller and population growth is slower. That contributes to economic growth, sustainable development and poverty reduction. Sexual and reproductive health problems account for nearly one-fifth of the worldwide burden of disease, and one-third of the burden among women of reproductive age. This is a drag on the world economy and on development. Research has shown that investments in reproductive health are extremely cost-effective. A study in Mexico has shown that for every peso spent on family planning services, the government saved nine pesos in expenses for treating complications of unsafe abortion and providing maternal and infant care.

The Netherlands has long been in the front lines of the fight for women's rights. During our EU Presidency, the EU committed itself to universal access to sexual and reproductive health by 2015. During the summit in September, we should try to rally the support of the whole world for this goal and make it a target under the fifth MDG on maternal health. We are not proposing a revolution: the target was already embraced by the international community at the Cairo conference in 1994. Again, how could we explain to our children—especially our daughters—that we wasted this opportunity to save women's lives?

Respecting the right to choose saves both lives and money. But there is still much opposition from cultural, religious, and political quarters. For example, the Bush administration's efforts to spread freedom in the world do not include reproductive freedom. A winning strategy for dealing with such opposition is through dialogue, not confrontation. Nearly all religions share a deep concern for people who cannot keep their heads above water. This is an essential starting point for a meaningful dialogue. As a Catholic myself, I am proud that many Catholic organizations in the field have adopted a pragmatic and compassionate attitude. In *The New York Times,* I read the story of a Brazilian priest who keeps a small framed condom in his office with a sign saying: "In case of emergency, break the glass." It is time to break the glass. Every minute, five adolescents are infected with HIV—that certainly sounds like an emergency to me. A new study by researchers from Columbia and Johns Hopkins Universities clearly challenges the significance of abstinence in Uganda's successful response to HIV/AIDS, while stressing the importance of condoms. I hope that in New York developing countries will join the EU in the fight for women's rights. They have every right and reason to. I also hope that they will get the more conservative countries on board. The opposition to reproductive rights often wraps itself in the flag of family values. And let me stress that a world without family values, values like love, fidelity, and respect for one another and human dignity is unthinkable. But saving women's lives, the lives of mothers, is just as much a part of family values! My message in New York will be: "Let no woman be left behind."

Addressing Vulnerability at the Macro Level by Aid for Trade

Likewise, at the macro level, we should leave no country behind. When it comes to international trade liberalization, all countries stand to gain. In December, a political breakthrough at the World Trade Organization (WTO) summit in Hong Kong (China) could eventually lift 500 million people out of poverty and pour $200 billion a year into developing economies. But we should not forget, that in the short run, free trade can leave poor countries especially vulnerable to adjustment shocks. Free trade reshuffles the cards of the international economy—production moves across borders according to comparative advantage. Developed countries have enough resources to deal with the adjustment costs themselves. Developing countries often do not. They need development assistance to adapt to the realities of globalization: aid for trade. That is why I am in favor of an international "aid-for-trade" mechanism as part of an ambitious Doha deal. Low-income countries, vulnerable countries, could draw on this facility to deal with the adjustment costs and to build their supply and trading capacity. However, success in the world economy also depends on crucial investments in infrastructure, information and communication technologies, and innovation.

Even if they successfully adjust to freer trade, developing countries could face increased risk because of price volatility. Earlier, I mentioned the high volatility of export earnings in primary commodities. The Netherlands has supported vital EU and World Bank research on commodity risk management. It is high time to invest in insurance services against the financial risks of commodity price fluctuations and adverse weather conditions such as droughts, floods, or hurricanes.

The biggest risk to development does not lie in free trade. Far from it. Foreign trade remains, in the words of Irving Kravis, "the handmaiden of growth." The real risk to development is a collapse of the Doha Round, or a flawed compromise. Recent World Bank research, financed by the Netherlands, shows that if developed countries exempt as little as 2 percent of their agricultural products from tariff reductions, the poverty impact of the Doha Round will be zero. Without an ambitious Doha deal, the MDGs will become dead letters.

Addressing Vulnerability at the Macro Level by Integrating Security and Development Policies

In any case, we cannot free countries from poverty when they are still stuck in the conflict trap. Security is a precondition for development. At present, the international community still lacks the tools to deal with post-conflict situations in an integrated manner. This means combining political, security, and development instruments. At the UN summit in September, we will discuss the establishment of a Peacebuilding Commission to fill this gap. But setting up another commission is not enough. A number of security-related activities with direct relevance to development cannot currently be financed with official development assistance (ODA) money. I will therefore continue to work with a coalition of the willing to push for a broader definition of ODA. Steering countries into safer waters is not only the right thing to do. It is also much cheaper. Civil wars in developing countries cost $100 billion a year—almost twice the annual amount of development assistance provided by the international community in the recent past.

Concluding Remarks

After this speech, I'll be leaving for Brussels to attend a meeting of EU ministers. We will be preparing action on the important opportunities this year to lighten the burden of the vulnerable. Here, you will start your discussions and your efforts to throw more light on the issue. You will benefit from the presence of representatives from many sectors of society: academia, the private sector, civil society, international organizations. I am particularly pleased to see so many business people in the room—you have an important role to play, and I work with you whenever I can. For example, together with Dutch leading commercial banks, the Dutch government established the Netherlands Financial Sector Development Exchange, NFX. This public-private partnership aims to improve financial services in developing countries, so that a poor widow in Ethiopia can buy an insurance policy to protect herself and her family from risk, and take out a loan to buy a new cow. Ultimately, only private sector-led growth can light the way to a future without abject poverty.

But then again, growth matters only if it is pro-poor—when it touches the lives of the vulnerable. This also goes to the heart of the World Bank's mission in its threefold role:

- as banker, a major source of development finance;
- as brains, a major source of knowledge on development;
- as broker, spreading this knowledge to those in need.

A major challenge for the Bank is to better align its lending and knowledge activities—the banker and the brains. But without a doubt, under the leadership of Paul Wolfowitz, the World Bank will remain a leader in the war on poverty and will certainly engage the private sector in this more than ever.

Ladies and gentlemen, we cannot win this war without international cooperation—passing each other by like ships in the night. Only by acting together with our shared vulnerability in mind can we save those who are most in need. We must leave no one behind.

Thank you.

Reference

Collier, P., and J. Dehn. 2001. "Aid, Shocks, and Growth," World Bank Working Paper No. 2688, Washington, DC.

Keynote Address

Stability, Security, and Development: An Introduction

FRANÇOIS BOURGUIGNON

Your Royal Highness, Madam Minister, distinguished guests,

It is a real pleasure for me to be here today for this new edition of the Annual Bank Conference on Development Economics (ABCDE) hosted by the Dutch government. My colleague Jean-François Rischard has already mentioned the preeminent role played by the Netherlands on the development front. As the World Bank's Chief Economist, and following the remarks by Minister van Ardenne, the Dutch Minister for Development Cooperation, I would like to acknowledge the very close collaboration we have had with the Dutch government on various research topics, and say how grateful we are for this excellent relationship. This conference in Amsterdam is yet another strong indication of the high quality of our collaboration.

The topic of my address is stability, security, and development. I must say that I am a bit uncomfortable because what Minister van Ardenne said was so profound and to the point. She took away many of the things I wanted to say . . . At this stage, I am afraid that I am condemned to repeat many of her views. However, remembering both my function in the World Bank and my academic past, I will take a more analytical view on these issues, so as to introduce more precisely the various plenary sessions of this conference and reinforce her messages.

As you may remember, the 2000–1 World Development Report titled *Attacking Poverty* pointed to three key areas for action in development and poverty reduction: opportunities, empowerment, and security. The first two areas correspond to what is now known as the twin-pillars strategy of development and poverty reduction, which has underlined all World Bank operations in recent years: improving the investment climate to enhance growth on the one hand, and empowering people through investing in human capital and improving governance on the other hand. Of course, these two pillars are not independent. Both strategies must be followed simultaneously for the development process not to get stalled at some point. At the

François Bourguignon is Senior Vice President, Development Economics, and Chief Economist at the World Bank.

Annual World Bank Conference on Development Economics—Europe 2006

same time, both strategies have common elements. The third item of the 2000–1 World Development Report may be one of these common elements. Security of goods, property rights, and persons is necessary not only for improving the investment climate but also for empowering poor people. Yet, comparatively little has been written and there has been less debate on security than on the other components of the twin-pillar strategy. This edition of the ABCDE, which is entitled *Securing Development in an Unstable World,* is an opportunity to bring this issue back to the forefront.

Over the last few years, the security of persons—security with a capital *S* as it is often called—has become a major source of concern for the world. Several leaders, including Colin Powell in a recent article entitled "No Country Left Behind" (Powell 2005), have expressed the notion that reaching Security at the national, regional, and global levels requires economic development to be faster, and shared more uniformly. In other words, more Security in the world implies a more harmonious development process. But there are other definitions of security—with a small *s:* economic security, or the stability of individual standards of living; and social security, including not only insurance against longevity but also issues such as crime and violence, natural disasters such as the recent tsunami, or epidemics. With this second set of definitions, the relationship between security and development is much clearer and stronger, although we are still far from taking advantage of the good knowledge that we have of the problems at hand. This conference will mostly discuss that relationship between security (with a small *s*) and development, with the goal of drawing lessons on how to improve Security (with the capital *S*). As the title of my address suggests, my presentation will only be a general introduction to these various issues, which will be debated at length in the plenary sessions of the conference. Beyond that goal, however, I would also like to offer a general framework for thinking about the various issues before us.

Whatever the definition of security you choose,[1] there are some basic mechanisms through which risks, insured or uninsured, often cause some damage to economic and social development. We should be able to learn from these patterns, in particular for domestic and international policies that can help mitigate these risks—and cope with them. For the sake of simplicity, I will focus on economic security issues, even though most of what I will say also applies to other types of security. First, I will show that we now have growing evidence of the substantial cost of risk to development, in particular when it is uninsured and in low-income countries. Then, I will review policies available to mitigate these costs, insisting on the need for bold innovations and for coordination between action at the national level and what is being done by the international community.

As a starting point, I would like to show that uninsured economic risks for poor people or low-income countries tend to create poverty traps, which in turn severely limit development prospects, both at the micro and macro levels. Of course, it is generally possible to mitigate these risks. However, even though risks can be reduced, risk mitigation itself has a cost and may reduce long-run income. Then, I would like to show that both through poverty traps and the negative effects of risk mitigation, insecurity tends to increase poverty and inequality. All this applies mostly to *covari-*

ant risks rather than to idiosyncratic risks, which, in theory, may be more easily mutualized, either formally through insurance markets, or informally through other social arrangements. Covariant risks that affect several people at the same time in a community or in a country are not insurable. Those are the types of risks I am focusing on.

Basic Mechanisms through Which Economic Insecurity Negatively Affects Development

To understand why risk affects high- and low-income people differently, consider the upper part of figure 1, where a nonpoor household confronts a negative income shock. The solid line shows the time path of income while the dotted line shows the path of consumption of a nonpoor individual. Initially, the household spends what it earns. Then, the negative income shock negatively affects consumption, but only marginally. At the time of the shock, the household reacts by using savings or borrowing from a bank, while shifting its consumption slightly downward. After the shock, the household keeps consumption below income so as to reconstitute its wealth or to reimburse the loan obtained at the time of the shock. In other words, this nonpoor household is able to "smooth" consumption thanks to its initial wealth or its access to the credit market. Its income path after the shock is unaffected.

FIGURE 1.
Microeconomic Effect of a Large Negative Shock on the Income and Consumption Paths of a Poor and a Nonpoor Household

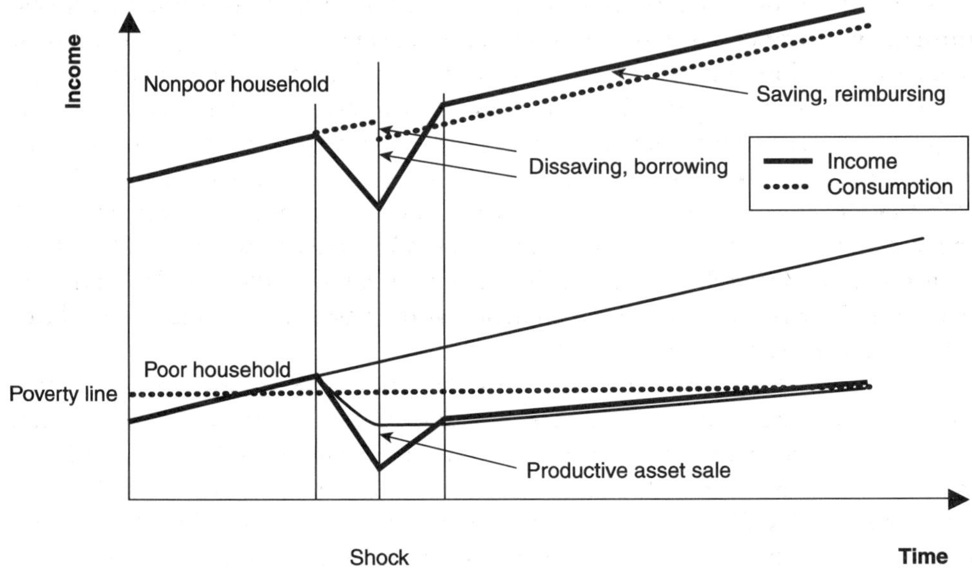

Source: Author.

The lower part of figure 1 shows what usually happens to a poor household going through the same shock, but having no or very little savings, and no possibility of borrowing resources because the credit market does not function properly. Faced with a negative shock and such constraints, the poor household typically drastically reduces consumption and runs down its productive assets. It would sell livestock, for instance, thereby smoothing its consumption a little but also losing some source of future income. Figure 1 shows the implications of this decision: after the shock, the solid line (income) displays a trend much lower than the initial one, reflecting the permanent loss of productive capital by the poor household. As illustrated in the figure, a household in that situation can very well fall below the poverty line, not only momentarily at the time of the shock but for as long as it has not reconstituted its lost productive assets—if it is ever able to do so. That is an illustration of the poverty trap, or of the persistence of the effects of a negative shock on poor households.

I have mentioned the example of a poor household forced to sell its productive assets, such as livestock. Other decisions also contribute to the poverty trap, such as parents taking the children out of school because of a shock, and not sending them back after the crisis (or even when they do, the children have missed important parts of the curriculum and therefore have a permanent handicap). In that case, the income path of the parents would be unaffected by the shock, but, of course, that of the children would be lowered. Figure 1 would then have to be modified to take into account the fact that the loss of income potential is shifted to the next generation.

In principle, there are ways for poor households to avoid these negative shocks. If saving is not a self-insurance option for poor people facing subsistence constraints, there are ways of mitigating risks. Farmers, for instance, may diversify their production. Instead of concentrating on one high value crop, they may produce several crops to mitigate price or weather risks. However, there is a cost to such a mitigating strategy. By diversifying their production, poor farmers do not fully exploit their comparative advantage, which may be in the production of a specific crop. In effect, bearing less risk implies a loss in efficiency and in income.

Figure 2 illustrates this dilemma. On the one hand, a nonpoor farmer who can self-insure through savings enjoys higher levels of income by concentrating in his or her comparative advantage. On the other hand, poor farmers may adopt a risk mitigating strategy, but crop diversification implies less expected income, less efficient investments, and less income growth. One can also observe that such situations generate more poverty, because poor households do not earn as much as they could through insured risk, and more inequality, because the income differential between poor and nonpoor households keeps growing.

This general principle applies, with some variation, to all situations in which markets are imperfect—labor, credit, or even goods and services—and in which economic agents, households or firms, are too poor to self-insure against risks in these markets. It also applies at the macroeconomic level. A poor economy with no access to

FIGURE 2.
The Effect of Risk Mitigation on the Expected Income Path of Poor Households

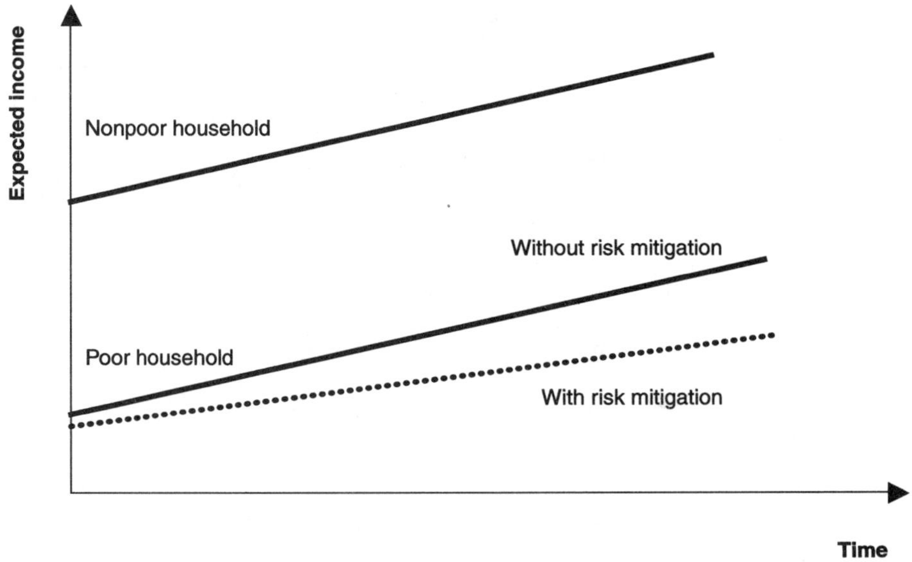

Sources: Author.

international credit markets has to run down consumption and investment when a succession of shocks depletes all the reserves it may have accumulated. It is thus the case that economic insecurity in general negatively affects development prospects in low-income contexts.

Examples of the Negative Effects of Economic Insecurity on Development

This analytical framework is not just another principle in economic theory. Ample empirical evidence in the literature (both in micro and in macro terms) supports it. Let me start with micro evidence. Figure 3 shows the effect of Hurricane Mitch (1998) on the income of poor and nonpoor people in Honduras.[2] During the hurricane, all households were hit in the same proportion, losing on average 31 percent of their productive assets (land, livestock, and plantations). The revealing feature in this figure is the situation of Honduran households three years after the disaster: nonpoor farmers (illustrated with the dark bars) have been able to recover from the shock, whereas poor farmers (white bars) not only have not regained what they lost but have even seen their situation worsened. This is a good example of the basic mechanism discussed above by which uninsured risks lead to the permanence of the effects of shocks and the possibility of poverty traps.

FIGURE 3.
The Effect of Hurricane Mitch on Honduran Households

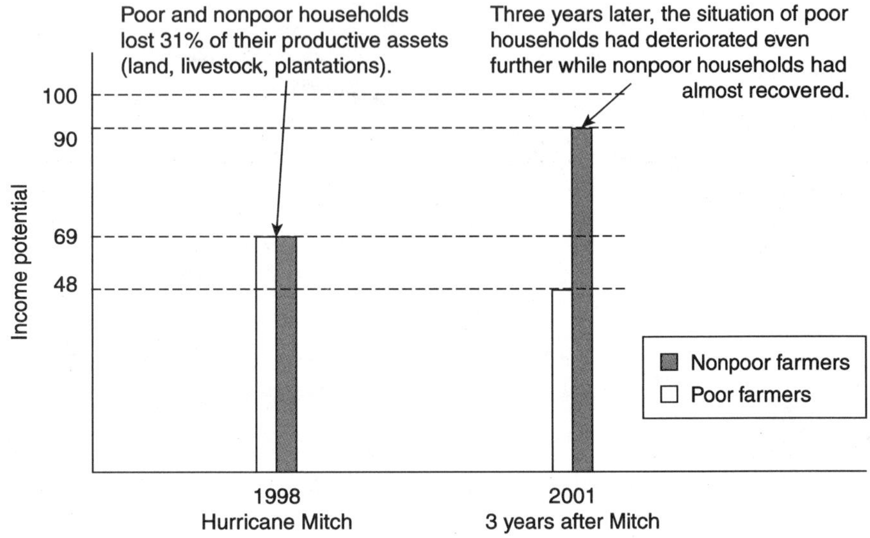

Source: Graph based on study by Carter et al 2005.

I could give other similar examples but will simply refer you to Stefan Dercon's contribution to this volume. I will only stress a point made by Minister van Ardenne that further illustrates the basic mechanism linking economic insecurity and inefficiency. A common explanation of the high fertility behavior in poor households is that parents tend to mitigate the risk of lack of resources when they reach old age and are unable to work by having many children. Of course, parents could self-insure against that risk by saving when they are younger, but subsistence constraints as well as the occurrence of production risks of the type analyzed above prevent them from doing so. Yet, such a strategy has a heavy cost on income and consumption per capita—it leads to families that are too large.

Let me now move to macro volatility and macro risks, and show that the same principles apply. In macroeconomics, volatility is usually the unpredictable variability of economic aggregates such as gross domestic product (GDP), or prices, or productivity. Volatility is generally measured by the standard deviation, that is, the deviation (upward or downward) of these economic aggregates from their long-run trend (Aizenman and Pinto 2005). Figure 4 provides an illustration of GDP per capita volatility in Indonesia.

As shown in figure 4, the growth rate of GDP per capita has been fluctuating significantly over the past three decades in Indonesia. Worldwide volatility, as measured by the standard deviation of per capita GDP growth rate, is 4.1 percent.[3] Figure 4 actually hides two types of volatility. In effect, it is useful to conceptually distinguish "normal" volatility from "crisis" volatility. One type of fluctuation, within a particular band—say, the average of GDP fluctuations in the world—can

FIGURE 4.
Macro Volatility in Indonesia, 1960–2002

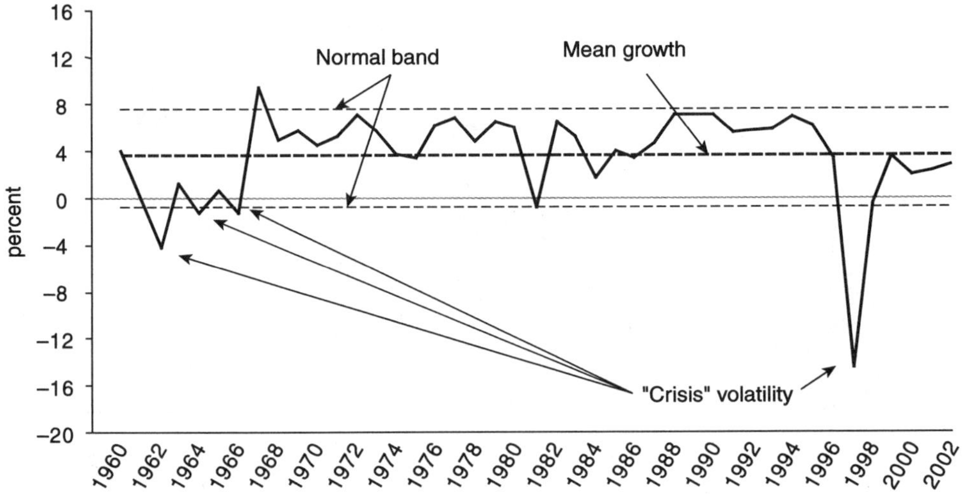

Sources: Based on study by Hnatkovska and Loayza (2005).

be considered normal (this band is represented by the dashed lines in figure 4). Most of the fluctuations in Indonesia's GDP throughout the period under consideration have been within that band. But there have also been some catastrophic events, or "crisis shocks," leading to fluctuations of GDP outside the normal band. They were some occurrences in the 1960s and in the early 1980s and, of course, the country was hit by a big crisis in 1998 (the so-called Asian crisis) when GDP fell by 15 percent. Macroeconomic risks in a country such as Indonesia mostly arise from these crisis shocks. Without these major negative shocks, the volatility of GDP in Indonesia would have been 2 percent, half of what was actually observed.

Figure 5 provides a picture of the level and evolution of volatility in different country groups (high-, middle-, and low-income countries) over four decades (1960–2000). Quite remarkably, volatility has consistently been much higher for low-income countries, averaging 4.5 percent, compared to 2.2 percent for high-income countries. In effect, it can be seen that GDP volatility is quite clearly a decreasing function of income since volatility in middle-income countries lies between that in low- and high-income countries.

The economic interpretation of that relationship follows the basic mechanism analyzed above. In a negative shock with some permanence—such as the recent increase in oil prices for oil-importing countries—low-income countries first run down their international reserves and then must contract fiscal spending, which in turn produces a drop in GDP. This is because they have only very limited access to international capital markets. On the contrary, high-income countries are able to smooth shocks by relying on foreign borrowing when foreign asset sales are insufficient. The amplitude of the effect of negative shocks on GDP and, therefore, the crisis volatility thus

FIGURE 5.
Extent and Evolution of GDP Volatility by Country Income Level

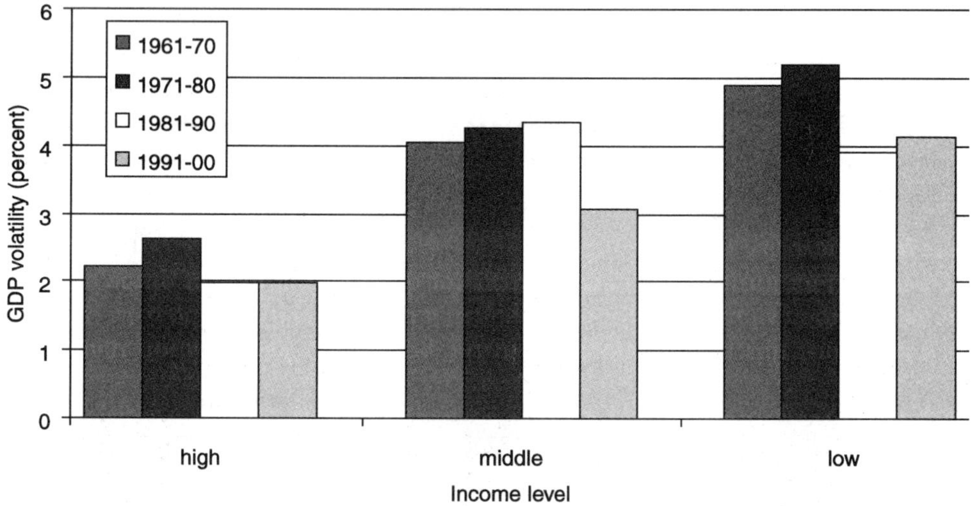

Sources: Based on study by Hnatkovska and Loayza (2005).

depends on access to international capital markets, that is, on the long-run solvency of countries, which depends on their levels of income.

An interesting finding in figure 5 is that volatility tends to decline over time—with the exception of middle-income countries where there were major debt crises in the 1980s. This overall declining trend in volatility in the world may be due to globalization and the efficiency gains of international capital markets.

In low-income countries, crisis volatility usually constitutes the core of volatility. While it represented only 12 percent of total volatility in a big country like India in 1960–2000—meaning that the country suffered relatively few big crises—it amounted to 46 percent in Nicaragua during the same period. What explains such volatility? We tend to associate volatility with exogenous shocks such as terms of trade shocks, commodity price fluctuations, natural disasters such as drought or hurricanes, and so forth. Looking in detail at the sources of crisis volatility, it appears that while such exogenous shocks are often at the core of the problem, poor economic management of these shocks, and sometimes sustained bad policies, contribute as well. Crisis volatility is sometimes the result of shocks that have not been managed adequately, not the sole result of external causes.

In line with this argument, recent research[4] has shown that GDP volatility across countries depends not only on the level of income of a country but also on the strength of its economic institutions, the development of its financial sector (with declining returns), and its ability to implement countercyclical macroeconomic policies. A World Bank study shows that volatility is higher in low-income countries with limited and undiversified exports. Together with the preceding explanatory factors, this confirms the potential role of commodity price shocks in generating volatility (Hnatkovska and Loayza 2005).

As with the previous microeconomic argument, macro volatility affects long-run growth through various channels. First, because of macro uncertainty, investment in physical and human capital is often lower than it could have been. Second, credit constraints in the financial system produce asymmetries between good and bad shocks, and weaken the resilience of the economy. Third, in cases of high volatility, downward wage rigidity negatively affects long-run profits and investments. Fourth, cleansing and countercyclical research and development expenditures do not take place in periods of crisis because of credit constraints (Caballero and Hammour 1994). Fifth, many of the domestic institutions designed to serve as "social automatic stabilizers" are negatively affected by shocks, because they suffer a decline in their resources.

All of these channels lead to a significant impact of volatility on growth. Cross-country data for the period 1960–2000 indicate that increasing volatility in a country by the worldwide standard deviation of 1.07 percent reduces GDP by 1.3 percent a year in the long run (table 1). If we carry out the same experiment only for the 1990s, we find a loss of long-run GDP on the order of 2.2 percent, suggesting that the growth sensitivity to volatility is increasing—at the same time as volatility itself decreases. The message here is quite worrisome, especially given the low growth rate in many low-income countries. In fact, these calculations show that the 1 to 2 percent average growth rate observed is within the band of what could simply be due to fluctuations in volatility rather than due to some autonomous forces. It is worth noting that volatility does not seem to have any impact at all on high-income countries: they are sheltered against shocks because of their easy access to international capital markets—which play some sort of insurance role.

On the basis of these results, there seems to exist a poverty or, more exactly, a "slow growth" trap at the macro level. Low-income countries tend to suffer higher volatility than other countries, which in turn leads to slow growth and keeps income low (figure 6).

Volatility also has heavy social consequences. Major macroeconomic crises have deleterious effects in developing countries. First, they tend to cause a permanent increase in inequality and poverty because the cost of the crisis and adjustment is disproportionately borne by the poorest. Second, these macro crises have the same microeconomic effect on households and firms as the ones that were discussed earlier in this presentation. For instance, when Mexico's GDP per capita fell by almost 8 percent in 1995, gross primary school enrollment rates declined and mortality from anemia increased among children (World Bank 2000). Likewise, the 14.6 percent decline in Indonesia's GDP per capita in 1998 was associated with a higher school dropout rate for children in the poorest fourth of the population, and a higher share of women whose body mass indexes were below the level at which risks of illness and death increase (World Bank 2000). Third, macroeconomic crises almost always lead to a decline in public spending, which is likely to affect key sectors such as infrastructure and human development disproportionately. They also tend to increase the risk of political destabilization, especially in countries with weak institutions.

TABLE 1.
Direct Effect of Volatility on Growth

	Percent
All countries	**–1.3**
All countries during the 1990s	**–2.2**
All countries (crisis volatility only)	–2.1
Low-income countries	**–1.6**
Middle-income countries	–0.9
High-income countries	**0**

Source: Hnatkovska and Loayza 2005.

Note: Effect of a one standard deviation increase of GDP volatility on long-run growth (annual rate).

All estimates are corrected for the possible endogeneity of volatility.

FIGURE 6.
The Slow Growth–High Volatility Trap for Low-Income Countries

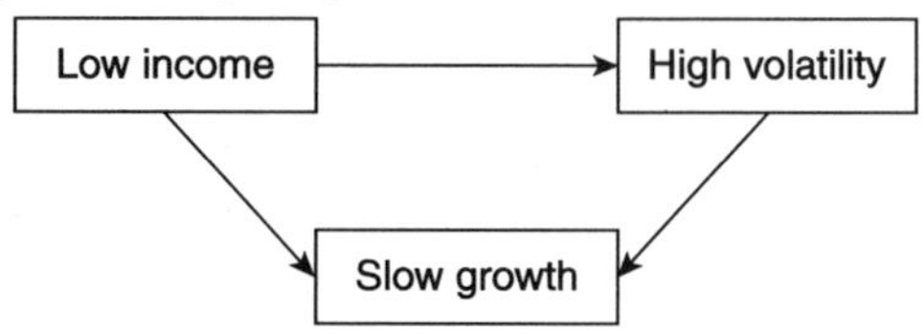

Source: Author.

Conclusion: Policies to Mitigate and Cope with Economic Insecurity

What policies should be implemented to help countries mitigate or cope with macro volatility? On the domestic front, the preceding arguments suggest that having the right macroeconomic policies, the right domestic institutions, and the right policy regimes (especially in the exchange rate domain) would provide most countries with adequate protection from crises. On the external front, it is also essential for many low-income countries to be able to count on the support of the donor community when they experience major shocks. Foreign aid delivered in ways conditional to the kind of shock experienced by each country, debt sustainability arrangements, and carefully designed export stabilization mechanisms could be key components of the strategy of donor support (figure 7).

It is also important to minimize the social consequences of volatility. In general, social spending in developing countries does not provide insurance against shocks. Of course, workfare programs have been implemented in a number of countries where means-tested transfers are developing. However, they are still limited and means-tested programs cannot really be developed without the administrative ability to actually observe individual incomes. It is, therefore, necessary to promote market insurance instruments such as weather insurance, micro credit, saving incentives, and so on. However, it is unlikely that these various safety nets will be able to cover all the population if there is a macro crisis and a need for massive resources, unless

FIGURE 7.
Basic Instruments for Dealing with Macro Volatility and Growth

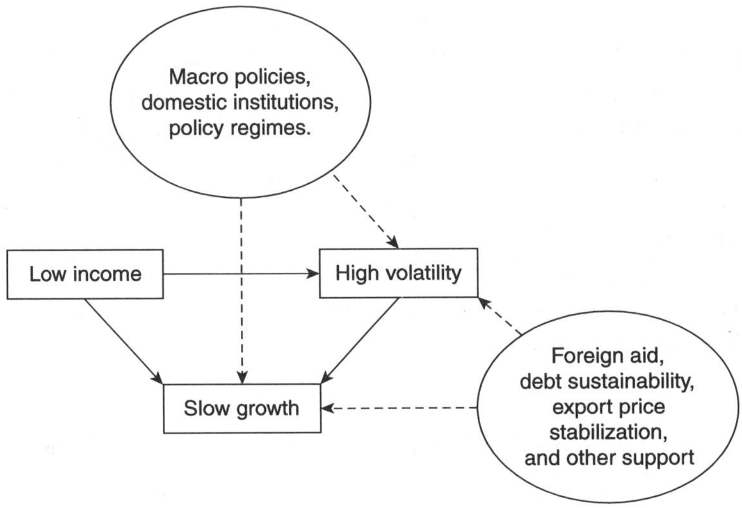

Source: Author.

special budgetary procedures are in place. This may be related to the need to protect the corresponding components of social spending in the government budget (IMF 2003).

There is another aspect of volatility and Security (with a capital *S*), which I will not discuss, as it will be discussed later in this conference. However, an important question to think about is whether it is possible to "buy" more Security with development assistance that would both accelerate development and lower its volatility. James Wolfensohn has often said that the world would perhaps be a better place if, instead of spending $60 billion on aid and $600 billion on defense, it was the opposite.

Let me close with a comment on what all of this implies for the kind of discussion ahead of us for these two days, and for future research. First, increasing evidence points to the large economic and social costs of economic insecurity. These costs are often compounded by the fact that there are close links between the various aspects of security: a permanent loss of income worsens poverty and increases inequality; this in turn can create social disruptions (including crime, violence, health crises, and conflicts) with potential spillover political effects at the national, regional, and global levels.

Second, this is essentially a problem for low-income countries. All the risks I have mentioned and their negative effects on income, people's lives, and economic development are experienced in developing areas of the world. The implication is that economic policies aimed at alleviating economic insecurity should primarily promote growth and development. But countries also need policies that deal specifically with shocks. Economic security and stability issues should be more systematically taken into account in the design and implementation of development strategies. This is an additional argument in favor of stronger and more effective institutions and policy regimes in low-income countries.

On the donors' side, there should be a renewed emphasis on higher levels of aid and the need for innovative modifications in the way aid is delivered. To me, it is a key condition for lifting low-income countries out of the slow growth–high volatility trap. Here I can only join Minister van Ardenne's message for more efforts by the donor community, and call for the strongest support of the international compact signed by the world community at the 2002 International Conference on Financing for Development in Monterrey.

I thank you very much for your attention.

Notes

1. For a review of various definitions of vulnerability, see Kamanou and Morduch (2004).
2. Here I am using data from an empirical study, Carter et al 2004.
3. This number measures the gap between actual GDP and the long-run trend of GDP. It is calculated as follows: first, a volatility measure for each country in the sample is obtained as a standard deviation of GDP per capita growth rate over the 1960–2000 period; second, the average of these volatility measures over the countries in the sample is used to approximate the worldwide volatility. For details on the data and calculations, see Hnatkovska and Loayza 2005.
4. There is a large body of literature on the determinants of volatility. See, for instance, Deaton (1999); Easterly, Islam, and Stiglitz (2001); Furman et al (1998); and Hnatkovska and Loayza (2005).

References

Aizenman, J., and B. Pinto, eds. 2005. *Managing Volatility and Crises: A Practitioner's Guide.* New York: Cambridge University Press.

Caballero, R. C., and M. L. Hammour. 1994. "The Cleansing Effect of Recessions." *The American Economic Review* 84 (5): 1350–68.

Carter, M. R., P. D. Little, T. Mogues, and W. Negatu. 2004. "Shocks, Sensitivity, and Resilience: Tracking the Economic Impact of Environmental Disaster on Assets in Ethiopia and Honduras." Staff paper no. 489, Department of Agricultural and Applied Economics, University of Wisconsin–Madison.

Deaton, A. 1999. "Commodity Prices and Growth in Africa." *Journal of Economic Perspectives* 13: 23–40.

Easterly, W. R., R. Islam, and J. E. Stiglitz. 2001. "Shaken and Stirred: Explaining Growth Volatility." In *Annual Bank Conference on Development Economics,* ed. Boris Pleskovic and Nicholas Stern. Washington, DC: World Bank.

Furman, J., J. Stiglitz, B. Bosworth, and S. Radelet. 1998. "Economic Crises: Evidence and Insights from East Asia." *Brookings Papers on Economic Activity* 2: 1–135.

Hnatkovska, V., and N. Loayza. 2005. "Volatility and Growth." In *Managing Volatility and Crises: A Practitioner's Guide,* ed. Joshua Aizenman and Brian Pinto. New York: Cambridge University Press.

IMF. 2003. *Fiscal Adjustment in IMF-Supported Programs: Evaluation Report.* Washington, DC: IMF.

Kamanou, G., and J. Morduch. 2004. "Measuring Vulnerability to Poverty." In *Insurance Against Poverty,* ed. Stefan Dercon. Oxford: Oxford University Press.

Powell, Colin. 2005. "No Country Left Behind." *Foreign Policy* January/February: 28–35.

World Bank. 2000. *World Development Report 2000/2001: Attacking Poverty.* New York: Oxford University Press.

Keynote Address

Development in an Unstable World: A Japanese Experience to Promote Human Security

HISASHI OWADA

It is an honor as well as a personal pleasure to be invited to this forum of the Annual Bank Conference on Development Economics (ABCDE) and to share with you some of my personal reflections on the issue of development, based on my modest experience in the world of development.

I am sure many of you are wondering why a judge of the International Court of Justice (ICJ) should come to a conference of the World Bank and address the issue of development. Indeed, this is an appropriate moment for me to offer a disclaimer on my part. Today I am not speaking in my professional capacity as a judge of the International Court of Justice.

In fact, before coming to the ICJ, I spent many years in public service in the Government of Japan and had been heavily involved in the formulation and implementation of Japan's policy in the field of development. Also, in my previous incarnation before coming to the Court, I had spent a substantial part of my life in academia and worked on the issues of peace, security, and development in the broader context of contemporary international relations.

It is in those contexts that I am going to speak today about the issue of development as seen from the experience of Japan in this field and especially in relation to the concept of human security, which the Government of Japan identifies as the centerpiece of a "new strategy for development" that she is promoting. I am therefore speaking totally in my personal capacity; nothing that I say reflects the position of the ICJ of which I am a member.

I wish to start my short presentation by commending the organizers of this conference for the opportuneness of the occasion in addressing the subject of "Securing Development in an Unstable World." Indeed, the world today is in the midst of unprecedented uncertainty and instability. And it is my personal conviction that the

Hisashi Owada is Judge of the International Court of Justice. The views expressed here are those of the author in his personal capacity and do not reflect the position of the institution to which he belongs.

Annual World Bank Conference on Development Economics—Europe 2006

issue of development is the most serious of the challenges that we are going to face as a global community in the context of the growing reality of globalization in the 21st century.

I wish also to take advantage of this opportunity to pay a special tribute to my friend, Jim Wolfensohn, who is going to retire soon from the post of President of the World Bank. He is one of those few farsighted people who have understood the importance of a holistic approach to development. I recall with nostalgia the number of evenings that both us spent together in Jackson Hole in the summer of 1995 discussing issues of development. I would like to believe it was out of those brainstorming sessions we had that his famous Comprehensive Development Framework (CDF) Plan of the World Bank emerged. Later, as Senior Adviser to the President of the Bank, I always enjoyed discussions with him, as well as the monthly executive sessions with the senior staff members of the Bank under the chairmanship of Jim Wolfensohn. Sadly, my tenure at the Bank had to be terminated prematurely due to my appointment at the ICJ.

The Changing Environment for Development

What is development? And why is development cooperation necessary? These are questions that have been raised ever so frequently by different people with divergent answers. It is only natural that the answers to these questions have been divergent, reflecting as they did the dominant political, economic, and social environment of the period in which the questions were raised.

While I have no intention of going into the whole history of development studies and development cooperation in the post–Second World War period, I wish to point out, however, that the nature of the issue of development has gone through a major metamorphosis in recent years, especially since the end of the Cold War.

First, I wish to point out that the demise of the "divided world" created by the Cold War confrontation on ideological grounds has had the beneficial effect of liberating the minds of the people engaged in development activities from the spell of Cold War logic.

Throughout the days of the Cold War era, the issue of development used to be styled as the "North-South" problem. It seems undeniable that the denomination of the issue of development as the "North-South" problem, thus juxtaposed with the "East-West" confrontation, succeeded in creating a somewhat distorted framework for dealing with the issue of development. Within this framework, the East tried to argue that the root cause of the problem of the North essentially lay in colonialism, which was the offspring of imperialism. Because imperialism was defined by Lenin as the highest stage of capitalism, the culprit of the plight should be traced to capitalism. Based on this logic, it was easy to argue that there was a natural basis for the formation of alliances between the East, which was fighting against the West, and the South, which was struggling against the North, because both had their common enemy, that is, capitalism, in the West, which is the North.

This logic created an expedient framework for the exploitation of the issue of development for political purposes.

What is more, the Soviet model of development, which attracted a lot of attention in those days for the remarkably speedy growth in industrialization of the Soviet Union, was presented as demonstrating the superiority of this model based on central economic planning by the state that would enable biased allocation of resources for development. In fact, this presentation provided a convenient vehicle for justifying the imposition of a dictatorial system of government in many of the newly born nations, especially in Africa. Moreover, the existence of extreme poverty that came to prevail in these former colonies after the colonial powers had left offered fertile ground for political exploitation by the "revolutionary forces" in these countries.

The subsequent history has, however, unfortunately shown that this ideological alliance results in a devastation of the economic wealth in many nations and in a prevalence of political corruption in many parts of the developing world, with little benefit for the people involved. In this situation, the demise of the Cold War has now come to offer an opportunity to reexamine the whole strategy for development in this changed environment.

Second, however, the end of the Cold War has come to witness another new development going in a less benevolent direction in the developing world, posing a gigantic challenge. The demise of a world divided by the rivalry between two camps in confrontation has ushered in a new era in which exogenous forces that used to work for keeping nations in unity have disappeared and in its stead indigenous forces that tend to work for disrupting the social fabric of society and disintegrating society itself have been unleashed. The result is that the solid basis for fostering the body politic of a nation in cohesion, and for consolidating the system of governance in society, has not been allowed to develop. Thus, in many of the newly created "nation states," social solidarity, to be built on the basis of development in the common consciousness of "belongingness" to a nation, either did not come to flower or collapsed, thus creating a situation of "failed states."

In this new situation, it has become clear that the problem of development can no longer remain in the conventional realm of economic development to be measured by such criteria as the growth in income per capita of individuals, or the wealth of a nation in terms of the size of its GNP. It would seem that the day has now come when development as defined primarily as the issue of freedom from want has to be regarded as being inseparably linked with the issue of freedom from fear. It is through this new development in the situation that the issues relating to human security have to be looked at as part and parcel of the issue of development.

The Japanese Initiative for a New Strategy

It was against this new development in the post–Cold War situation that Japan embarked upon an initiative for rethinking in a fundamental way the issue of development and for formulating a new strategy for development in light of the new factors that I have just described.

Japan's Experience with East Asia

While triggered by the drastic change in the international environment of the post–Cold War era, however, this initiative of Japan in the field of development was motivated by her own reflection on the issue of development, based on her accumulated experience of the post–Second World War period relating to the countries of East Asia. Japanese economic cooperation with the countries of the region had its origin in the execution of the reparations scheme that Japan had assumed under the peace treaties with these countries. These reparations were carried out in the form of contributions in kind through the offer by Japan of goods and services to these countries. This scheme enabled the recipient countries to develop partnership relations for implementation between the local entities and the Japanese participants, while retaining ownership of the whole process in their hands, in accordance with the priorities set by the recipient countries in partnership with Japan.

This basic structure of cooperation, based on the principles of local ownership combined with external partnership, was further pursued in the succeeding period when this reparations scheme was replaced by the new framework of economic cooperation between Japan and the countries of the region. It is my submission that this framework of cooperation thus created in the region was one of the major factors contributing to the remarkable economic and social development that this region has come to achieve, which the World Bank labeled as the "East Asian Economic Miracle" of the 1980s.

Another major factor that contributed to this "miracle" was the fact that throughout this process, most of the countries in the region—with the exception of the Indochinese Peninsula—were comparatively immune from the kind of negative impact of the Cold War that has been sketched out above in relation to Africa. In partnership with Japan, most of these countries of East Asia focused their energy and resources on the task of nation building at the critical nascent stage of their statehood through efforts for strengthening the social fabric of their society as a nation and for constructing the system of governance of their body politic. While these efforts are still under way, the basic orientation adopted by these countries seems to have enabled them to create a solid basis for holistic development of their societies as healthy nation-states.

Japan's Initiative for a New Development Strategy

This picture of the East Asian region makes a striking contrast with the dire picture that one is witnessing in some parts of Africa at present. It is especially noteworthy to recall, as a matter of pure statistics, that as of 1960 Asia had been lagging behind Africa in the average per capita income of the population. It is worth reflecting on the question as to why, after 40 years, the present gap between the countries of these two regions, which had attained their independence about the same time with somewhat the same legacies of colonization, has come to such a remarkable result.

It was on the basis of this experience that Japan, in the wake of the demise of the Cold War, decided in 1993 to embark upon her new initiative, to call for a new common approach to development in the context of the G-7 Summit that Japan was hosting in Tokyo. This new development strategy, according to Japan, was to be based on the twin principles of ownership and partnership, getting out of the then prevailing doctrine of "strategic development assistance," which at one time had been in fashion in the politico-ideological atmosphere of the Cold War period.

As it turned out, however, Japan's initiative unfortunately proved to be simply premature as of that time. Most of the other G-7 members turned a cold shoulder, if not outright hostility, to this initiative, based on their conviction that here was the moment when at last those in the First World could get rid of the political onus of the "North-South" problem forced upon them by the Cold War situation and focus on the issue of a "peace dividend" against the background of the so-called aid fatigue of their domestic constituencies. (It is ironic to find that the most staunch advocates of this negative view among the G-7 at that time are those who are now claiming to be at the forefront of the campaign for poverty eradication, albeit represented by different administrations in their respective countries.)

The TICAD Process

Faced with this environment, Japan decided, through the Tokyo International Conference on the Development of Africa (TICAD), which it organized in the fall of the same year, to test the water by putting into practice on the soil of Africa what Japan had successfully tried through the process of cooperation for nation building in East Asia. TICAD is an ongoing process that has held three major conferences so far at the level of the heads of state or government, in which the major components of the new strategy for development that Japan has been advocating are being set out for implementation.

Thus, at TICAD-I in 1993, consensus was established that while more active assistance efforts for Africa would obviously be needed, mere volume in outside assistance in itself could not solve the problem of Africa. Japan emphasized the importance of the twin principles of ownership and partnership. Equally significant, the critical importance of a holistic approach to development was endorsed. This holistic approach to development should include as its essential ingredients such items as those listed in the "right-hand column of the balance sheet" in Jim Wolfensohn's CDF Plan, that is, the structural, social, and human dimensions of development, such as the issue of democratization and good governance. Another point of particular significance at this conference was the importance attached to the promotion of a new type of "South-South cooperation," based on the possibility of the transfer of Asian experiences to Africa.

In TICAD-II in 1998, where the "Tokyo Plan of Action" was adopted, three major areas, again in line with the spirit of a holistic approach, were picked out as of special importance for attaining comprehensive development. They were the area of social development including education, health, and empowerment; the area of economic development including the increased role of private sectors and agriculture; and the area relating to the consolidation of the sociopolitical basis of development including systems of good governance, conflict prevention, and post-conflict reconstruction.

Another important characteristic of TICAD-II, reflecting one of the essential ingredients in the new development strategy of Japan, was the emphasis placed on the "output-oriented approach," as compared with the "input-oriented approach" that had been in fashion in the earlier period. If what would matter in development was not so much the amount of money put into the efforts as the outcome achieved as the result of such efforts, it was only reasonable to look at the latter, rather than the former. On the basis of this reasoning, an elaborate matrix on some major components of holistic development designating their expected level of achievement by some target date was made up and incorporated in the "Tokyo Plan of Action." It is interesting to recall that the Millennium Development Goals follow the same approach.

It was, however, at TICAD-III in 2003 that the problem of interlinkage, inherent in the present situation surrounding development, between the issue of "freedom from want" centering on the eradication of poverty through economic growth, and the issue of "freedom from fear" geared toward the alleviation of insecurity through consolidation of peace, was squarely taken up. And it is here that the advancement of the concept of "human security" has come to be identified as the unifying theme for the promotion of development through integrating the two freedoms that constitute the essence of development in the contemporary setting.

Introduction of "Human Security" into the Development Debate

The concept of human security consists in the protection of the vital core of all human lives in ways that enhance human freedoms and human fulfillment. Human security can be said "to comprise protecting people from critical (severe) and pervasive (widespread) threats and situations; using processes that build on people's strengths and aspirations; creating political, social, environmental, economic, military, and cultural systems that together give people the building blocks of survival, livelihood, and dignity."

When thus defined, it seems clear that there is a lot in common between this concept of human security and the new philosophy of development as conceived in the present day conditions of human existence. If the essential core of development consists in realizing freedom from fear and freedom from want, as I believe it is, then the promotion of human security should be at the heart of the new strategy for development for meeting the new challenges of the world of today.

As I stated earlier, the collapse of the Cold War order has unleashed forces that have their origin very often in religious, racial, ethnic, and other social tensions, as well as inequity and other grievances in society, including political and social alienation and extreme poverty, giving rise to numerous civil wars and armed conflicts in many parts of the world. Moreover, what is important in this situation is that each of these challenges has complex interlinkages to one another.

To overcome these direct threats to the life and security of people who suffer from such dire conditions, it is not enough to deal with each of these threats separately and on a piecemeal basis, treating some as "developmental issues" in the technical sense, while treating others as "security issues" in the conventional sense. In fact, even the concept of "security" itself is undergoing a major transformation from the traditional concept relating to protection against external threats to a state to a much wider concept relating to the protection of human individuals against threats to their security as individuals. What is required under such circumstances is to build a societal environment in which human individuals are empowered so that they can live free from want and free from fear. For this to be achievable, our responses should consist in addressing those diverse threats in a comprehensive manner, capturing the interlinkages among them from a human perspective. It is for this reason that the approach to the issue of development should be made from the perspective of "human security," by translating such aspirations into concrete action.

With a view to elaborating this concept in the context of peace, security, and development, the Government of Japan proposed the idea of an independent commission for human security on the occasion of the UN Millennium Summit in 2000. The Commission on Human Security, chaired jointly by Mrs. Sadako Ogata, former UNHCR, and Professor Amartya Sen, Nobel Prize Laureate for Economics, produced a major report on this topic in 2003. While I do not intend here to go through this voluminous report crammed with rich material of wise counsel, it is worth remembering that the report, after noting that "human security is concerned with safeguarding and expanding people's vital freedoms," declares that "it requires both shielding people from acute threats and empowering people to take charge of their own lives" (Commission on Human Security 2003, p. iv).

UN Secretary-General Kofi Annan himself specifies this comprehensive aspect of human security. Stressing that human security joins the main agenda items of peace, security, and development, he goes on to say

> Human security, in its broadest sense, embraces far more than the absence of violent conflict. It encompasses human rights, good governance, access to education and health care and ensuring that each individual has opportunities and choices to fulfill his or her potential. Every step in this direction is also a step towards reducing poverty, achieving economic growth and preventing conflict. Freedom from want, freedom from fear, and the freedom of future generations to inherit a health natural environment—these are the interrelated building blocks of human—and therefore—national security. (United Nations 2000)

This, I believe, is what development in the present setting is all about. To achieve such an objective, however, it is clear that we need "integrated policies that focus on people's survival, livelihood, and dignity, during downturns as well as in prosperity" (Commission on Human Security 2003, p. iv).

The Need for an Integrated Strategy

The report of the High-Level Panel on Threats, Challenge and Change, established by the UN Secretary-General, makes a strong case for comprehensive collective security. Noting that "today, more than ever before, threats are interrelated and a threat to one is a threat to all," (United Nations 2004, p. 14) it claims that "poverty, infectious disease, environmental degradation and war feed one another in a deadly cycle" (p. 15). The report convincingly demonstrates by evidence that poverty (as measured by per capita GDP) is strongly associated with the outbreak of civil war.

All this boils down to one theme: in the present situation, the international community badly needs an integrated strategy for development that focuses on how we can promote development effectively through ensuring human security, which should comprise all the elements that can contribute to creating human society empowered to meeting these threats and challenges that hinder development.

For this strategy to be truly effective, certain conditions, such as the following, will have to be met:

The strategy must be holistic.

The strategy has to be holistic in its approach, dealing with all the issues essential for creating society empowered to ensure human security of individual components of this society. From this angle, I have some serious personal misgivings about a somewhat simplistic call for "poverty reduction/eradication" as if it were in itself the goal of development.

On this question, I completely agree with my revered friend Amartya Sen, when he so forcefully declares

> Focusing on human freedom contrasts with narrower views of development, such as identifying development with the growth of gross national product, or with the rise in personal incomes, or with industrialization, or with technological advance, or with social modernization. Growth of GNP or of individual incomes can, of course, be very important as *means* to expanding the freedoms enjoyed by the members of society. But freedom depends also on other determinants, such as social and economic arrangements (for example, facilities for education and health care) as well as political and civil rights (for example, the liberty to participate in public discussion and scrutiny). . . Viewing development in terms of expanding substantive freedoms directs attention to the *ends* that make development important, rather than merely to some of the *means* that, inter alia, play important part in the process. (Sen 2001, p. 3)

This would mean in practical terms that in approaching the issue of development, we should avoid falling into the trap of myopically focusing on some highly visible but only partial segment of the whole picture. We have to look for a strategy that is sufficiently holistic to enable people to build a society where individuals can enjoy human security free from fear, as well as free from want.

The strategy must be comprehensive and global.

For this to be feasible, the strategy has to be worked out on a truly comprehensive and global basis. Given the fact that the world has become so interlinked and global and the concept of development so multifaceted with so many different dimensions, it is essential that all the major players in development activities and all the stakeholders in development be involved in the process of formulating and implementing the strategy.

The strategy must encompass the "twin principles."

This would mean, in particular, that the twin principles of local ownership and external partnership are indispensable for the success of the new development strategy. An approach based on the so-called Washington Consensus simply is not going to work, however rational it may be from a purely macroeconomic point of view, and however well intentioned it may be, as long as it is imposed upon an unpersuaded party on the basis of the pressure of conditionality.

The strategy must encompass an effective division of labor.

This "global approach," however, is easier said than done, because one essential characteristic of the international system as we have it today lies in the compartmentalization of competences on the basis of national sovereignty. This is true even when we are tackling problems belonging to the realm of global public goods, such as development. The conventional wisdom to deal with this situation has been to rely on advocacy and on the call for more effective "coordination" among these different competences and divergent interests on the basis of voluntary cooperation. However, I am afraid that in this instance this will not be sufficient. At the least, a pragmatic but effective mechanism for a genuine division of labor based on an agreed common holistic strategy on a global basis is called for, rather than an ad hoc coalition which at best may aim at coordination on a voluntary basis among several players, but is clearly insufficient for the task.

In this respect, the suggestion made in the report of the High-Level Panel of the United Nations to transform the Economic and Social Council (ECOSOC) into a "development cooperation forum," with a reinforced system of regular meetings between ECOSOC and the Bretton Woods institutions for encouraging collective action, may go some way in the right direction. However, that in and of itself would not seem to be enough. A somewhat more drastic innovative mechanism would seem to be possible as well as desirable, even within the basic framework of the contemporary international system based on compartmentalized national competences.

Conclusion

Given the tight constraints of time, I regret that my brief presentation has evidently fallen short of doing justice to the topic assigned to me. In particular, I fear that as a result, my presentation has been much too general and conceptual, lacking in the degree of specificity and concreteness required for the discussion of a subject such as this. To compensate for whatever lacuna that exists in my presentation, I should like to invite you to the extensive treatment of the subject contained in *Human Security Now,* the report of the Commission on Human Security, submitted in 2003 to the UN Secretary-General.

Thank you for your attention.

References

Commission on Human Security. 2003. *Human Security Now.* New York.

Sen, Amartya. 2001. *Development as Freedom.* Oxford: Oxford University Press.

United Nations. 2000. "Secretary-General Salutes International Workshop on Human Security in Mongolia." Press release SG/SM/7382. May 8.

United Nations. 2004. "A More Secure World: Our Shared Responsibility," Report of the Secretary-General's High-Level Panel on Threats, Challenges and Change. New York.

Keynote Address

The Other Path to Growth: Private Sector Development

GERRIT ZALM

Dear ABCDE participants,

I hope this will be a fruitful conference. I would like to start by discussing the origins of a new trend in development economics. That trend is to analyze how to create and maintain effective institutions for development. As an important subset of a country's institutions, I will focus on the importance of a good investment climate. This is an area where analysis and reform can still have an enormous payoff—up to 2 percent extra economic growth in development countries.[1] Reducing the risks and costs of doing business and the barriers to entry for new firms should be on the top of our agenda for reaching the Millennium Development Goals (MDGs). Securing property rights and reducing red tape, in particular, involve low costs but high benefits. It would be a tragedy if this opportunity to close the gap to attaining the MDGs would not be embraced by all of us.

Generations of Development Economics

But let me start by sharing some observations on development economics. If you could pinpoint an official date of birth for economic science, it would probably be the publication of *Wealth of Nations* by Adam Smith, 230 years ago. For all its diverse coverage of economic topics, the central theme of *Wealth of Nations* is growth. While division of labor ignites the growth process, it is capital accumulation that keeps it going. In Smith's economic system, private property and competition are essential for economic growth, which ultimately is based on the human nature of "truck, barter and exchange." In a sense, Smith's macroeconomic concern for economic growth rests on micro institutions.

Development economics, as a separate discipline, is said to have been born after the Second World War. The so-called first generation of development economists were

Gerrit Zalm is Minister of Finance, the Netherlands. Special thanks go to Ernst van Koesveld and Mark Bezemer.

Annual World Bank Conference on Development Economics—Europe 2006

quite confident in formulating grand models of development strategies. They believed that developing countries did not have a reliable market price system and that the supply of entrepreneurship was limited. Therefore, they turned to the state as the major agent of change. The state was to promote capital accumulation and to utilize surplus labor. The state was to undertake industrialization and import substitution. The state was to coordinate the allocation of resources through programming and planning. At one of the first ABCDEs in 1992, Paul Krugman rightly argued that the first generation was "at first unable, and later unwilling to codify [their insights] in clear, internally consistent models . . . The result was that development economics as a distinctive field was crowded out of the mainstream of economics" (Krugman 1992, p. 15). Moreover, the criticism of the early models was reinforced by bad experience with government intervention. The rationale for public intervention had been to remedy market failure, but the perverse result was only too often government failure. This was due to inadequate information, institutional weaknesses, and failings of the civil service. In fact, Hayek and Friedman among others, raised these issues in the West. Their views hardly trickled down to the poorer parts of the world. To put it more bluntly, it took the breakdown of the Soviet economy to make that happen.

The second generation of development economics in the 1980s and 1990s was no longer visionary, but based on realism of getting prices right. As Dani Rodrik wrote, "The good news here is that we have found homo economicus to be alive and well in the tropics and other poor lands" (Rodrik 1999, p. 1). Private sectors in developing countries, too, responded quickly to favorable price and other incentives. Anne Krueger takes this conclusion one step further. She argued that "once it is recognized that individuals respond to incentives, and that market failure is the result of inappropriate incentives rather than of non-responsiveness, the separateness of development economics largely disappears. Instead, it becomes an applied field [of economics]" (Krueger in Meier and Stiglitz 2001, p. 18).

In accordance with neoclassical theory, the second generation moved from macromodels to microstudies of firms and households. The allocation of capital became more important than its sheer size. The emphasis shifted from physical capital to human capital accumulation, including learning and innovation. The black box of the state was opened by using notions such as public choice, rent-seeking, and state capture. New market failures were recognized—imperfect and costly information, incomplete markets, transactions costs, and the absence of futures markets. These notions were applied to two sectors that had been relatively neglected: agriculture and finance. In this respect, I would like to recommend the workshop on financial sector development organized by the newly established Netherlands Financial Sector Development Exchange (NFX). It was quite long ago that Joan Robinson commented that "where enterprise leads, finance follows," but I feel that this thought is rather persistent.

The consensus in the early 1990s was for the promotion of policy reforms to get prices right. This started with a focus on macroeconomic stabilization, liberalization, and privatization, generally dubbed the Washington Consensus. In my view, these were, intellectually speaking, the relatively easy recommendations of the second generation of development economists, the low-hanging fruit. It took bad experiences in Asia, Latin America, and the transition economies to recognize that to get prices right and get policies right, it is also necessary to get *institutions* right. We have learned that institutional development is a key, if not the only, variable that reliably predicts how successful development in a country is. Institutional quality explains most of the growth difference between Asia and Africa. But we need to go beyond recognition of the importance of institutions and ask how to create and maintain effective institutions. I hope that a third generation of economists will take up this challenging task.

The Need for Institutional Reform

There is at least one crucial area where this task has been taken up seriously, and that is with respect to improving the investment climate. This is about location-specific factors that shape opportunities and incentives for firms to invest, create jobs, and expand. Economic growth is analyzed from a microeconomic perspective, particularly through the lens of a private sector firm. Systematic information from firms gives us fresh insights into how arrangements vary across countries and influence the level and productivity of private investment. This enables governments to shape market-enhancing institutions.

Is it fair to say that the World Bank's recent activities in this area were preceded by good work of the European Bank for Reconstruction and Development (EBRD) for transition economies. Much earlier, Hernando de Soto, the president of the Institute of Liberal Democracy in Peru, undertook pioneering work in this field. In *The Other Path* (de Soto 1989), he exposed the damaging effects of heavy business regulation and weak property rights. With burdensome entry regulations, few businesses bother to register. Instead, they choose to operate in the informal economy. Facing high transactions costs to get formal property title, potential entrepreneurs cannot use informal assets to obtain loans. De Soto calls this "dead capital." This is bad for poor people, who remain outsiders; bad for breaking monopolies; bad for society as a whole.

The World Bank has recently launched two major initiatives in this area: the Investment Climate Surveys and the Doing Business project. The *World Development Report 2005* (World Bank 2005) builds on these studies. Firms assess the package of policies as a whole, focusing on costs, risks, and barriers to competition. I believe these insights are very valuable. After all, private firms create over 90 percent of jobs, supply most of the goods and services necessary to improve living standards, and provide the tax base needed to fund public services. Also, by addressing barriers to entry, the report analyzes ways to bring outsiders into the formal sector. In poor countries, the informal sector amounts to 40 percent of the economy and contains many pockets of poverty. Finally, many features of a good investment climate, such as efficient infrastructure, improve the lives of people directly. I therefore believe that Adam Smith's focus on private property and competition, complemented by strong market-enhancing institutions, are key for pro-poor growth. Indeed, a strong market presupposes a strong state. A strong state, however, should not be confused with a big state. Big is not beautiful.

Let me share some salient findings of the *World Development Report,* related to costs, risks, and barriers to entry. First, policy uncertainty dominates the concerns of firms in developing countries. Some 30 percent of surveyed firms consider policy uncertainty as the main obstacle. Paraphrasing the ABCDE title, being predictable will help secure development. Investment opportunities are abundant, but broken promises are too. Second, the costs of regulation, unreliable infrastructure, contract enforcement difficulties, crime, and corruption can easily amount to over 25 percent of sales. This is more than three times what enterprises are typically paying in taxes. The third main element of the investment climate, barriers to competition, is less likely to be mentioned by incumbent firms as a key constraint. As the saying goes, monopolies are bad, unless you are one. Reducing barriers to competition could stimulate the diffusion of ideas and foster the competitive process of "creative destruction." The report indicates that net market entry can account for more than 30 percent of productivity growth. Strong competitive pressure can increase the probability of innovation by more than 50 percent.

Governments can contribute greatly to competition by fighting collusive behavior and by facilitating market entry and exit. According to the latest Doing Business indicators, the cost of starting a business is often no more than a small percentage of people's annual income. However, in Sub-Saharan Africa it costs on average twice the annual income per capita. Fulfilling the required procedures takes 27 days on average in rich countries. But in Latin America it takes 70 days. A similar picture emerges with regard to the time to go through insolvency. This will take just over a year in various developing countries. However, closing down a business takes an average of some 5 years in South Asia and as many as 10 years in Brazil, India, and Chad. This is business as *un*usual.

There remains ample scope for governments to improve their business climates by reducing risks, costs, and barriers to competition. I would like to highlight two specific areas for reform that deserve more attention: property rights and deregulation. It is rather ironic that both issues were already on John Williamson's list of policy reforms that he considered being the Washington Consensus. With the macro battle increasingly won, attention needs to shift further to such microeconomic aspects of a good investment climate.

Private property rights should be considered the cornerstone of a market economy. Taken for granted in rich countries, secure property rights are still lacking in many other countries. For instance, in Mexico, so-called extra-legally owned property is estimated to have a total value of about US$315 billion, more than double Mexico's outstanding external debt. In developing countries as a whole, about 85 percent of urban parcels and around 50 percent of rural parcels are held *without* official property rights. The total value of this extralegal real estate is estimated at a minimum of US$9.3 trillion dollars. The size of this "dead capital" is close to the cumulative value of all the companies listed on the main stock exchanges in the 20 most developed countries. Unfortunately, poor people are often the owners of this dead capital.

What are the tangible benefits of a clear and secure property rights system? First, formal property rights substantially expand the size of the market by reducing transactions costs. Informal property or business owners can only engage in ad hoc business relationships or trade with people they know and trust. Formal property systems could convert the population of a country into a larger network of individual, identifiable, and accountable business agents.

Second, entrepreneurs can obtain mortgages on their homes or land or use it to guarantee contracts. For instance, a case study shows that farmers in Thailand borrowed between 50 to 500 percent more if they had title to their land.

Third, owners of secure property invest more in homes and land than when they do not have secure titles. In Thailand, farmers with secure titles invested so much more in their land that their output was 14 to 25 percent higher than those without titles.

Given the advantages of secure property rights, it will come as no surprise that titling can significantly increase property values, investment, and productivity. After rural land was titled in Brazil, Indonesia, Thailand, and the Philippines, its value increased between 43 and 81 percent. Moreover, China and Vietnam managed to significantly accelerate rural economic growth in the 1980s by granting farmers greater rights to the use of land. These agricultural reforms played a significant role in reducing poverty in rural areas.

To promote the creation of formal property rights, Hernando de Soto points out that two specific factors need to be taken into consideration. First is to learn from the lessons of the past. The evolution of property fights in the West shows that the present formal property rights system was not simply created by clamping down on informality. It meant reforming the law and property system in a way that eased access to formal property and allowed informal arrangements to influence law making and play a role in defining property rights. Second, this is not just about bringing assets into the formal sector but about keeping them there, too. For instance, many titling programs in Africa have not had a lasting impact. If the formal cost of selling property is too high, titles will eventually become irrelevant by being traded informally. The Doing Business report reveals that in various countries registering property still takes more than 300 days. It is therefore important to simplify and combine procedures for registering.

Regulation and Red Tape

This brings me to the issue of government regulation and administrative burden. Following Pigou's theory, government regulation should reduce or eliminate market failures, thereby raising social welfare (Pigou 1947). Still, countries significantly differ in the intensity and the ways with which they regulate business operations. Regulation can be excessive or be captured by bureaucrats and existing firms, as public choice theory has taught us. In both ways, the overall social welfare is reduced to the benefit of a few privileged groups. This brings me back to the main question: what do right institutions look like and how do we get them?

The World Bank's ongoing Doing Business project has been and will be extremely helpful in finding an answer to this crucial question. This is done by comparing the factual—rather than perceived—differences in the regulatory burden across countries, both in the developing and industrialized worlds. The research shows that heavier regulation is associated with greater inefficiency in public institutions, more unemployment and corruption, and lower productivity. Moreover, excessive regulation often has a perverse effect on the very people it was meant to protect. Too many firms remain in the informal sector without social protection. It is a myth that social protection requires more business regulation.

Considering how much there is to gain from reducing outmoded or ill-conceived regulations, the Dutch government has made it a top priority. We have calculated that the total administrative burden is equivalent to 3.6 percent of our GDP, over US$20 billion. Two years ago, we committed ourselves to cut administrative burdens by 25 percent within four years, to be realized in 2007. It is important to note that we intend to do this without harming essential policy objectives, such as protection of the environment or employees. Meanwhile, the Dutch Cabinet and Parliament have agreed on the package of concrete measures that amount to a 25 percent reduction, an important milestone. Reducing the regulatory burden has also been put high on the EU agenda. The red tape could be as much as US$450 billion for the EU as a whole. Reducing the EU administrative burden by 25 percent could lead to a 1.7 percent increase in real GDP.

I sincerely hope that in the developing world, cutting red tape by simplifying legislation and regulation will become a top priority, too. Businesses in poor countries generally face even larger regulatory burdens than those in rich countries. They face three times the administrative costs, and nearly twice as many bureaucratic procedures and delays associated with them. This is excluding informal payments, which are highly correlated with official procedures and fees. In this respect, it was disappointing that the annual Doing Business report showed that over the past year African countries had reformed the least. This is such a contrast with the opportunities highlighted in the beautiful documentary, “Africa Open for Business,” that we just watched.

The potential benefits are huge. It is estimated that reducing the time and cost of starting a business can add between a quarter and half a percentage point to growth rates in the average developing country. Moreover, a hypothetical improvement in the ease of doing business to the top performers is associated with an increase in annual economic growth of up to 2 percentage points. At the same time, the costs of these reforms are relatively low. Let me take an example from Turkey, which I visited earlier this month. At a one-time cost of no more than US$10 million, Turkey streamlined the process for starting a new business by cutting the time from 38 days to 9 days in 2003 and combining seven procedures into one. The benefits were structural: a strong increase in new business registrations, by some 20 percent in the first year. A similar exercise in Vietnam cost only US$2.5 million dollars, paid for by donor agencies.

World Bank calculations suggest that the benefits of such reforms are about 25 times higher than their costs. Indeed, the Copenhagen Consensus group of eminent economists considered easing start up as one of the most cost-effective ways to spur development. These days, we speak a lot about increasing aid and aid effectiveness to attain the MDGs. Rightly so. But we should also speak and act to reduce the risks and costs of doing business and lower the entry barriers for firms. I, therefore, would like to encourage developing countries to commit themselves to a drastic reduction of the administrative burden, too—perhaps also by 25 percent over the next five years. I strongly believe that this would bring the MDGs closer to realization. Indeed, there is a close correlation between the ease of doing business and human development.

As noted, this will not cost much money, but it will sometimes cost both a lot of energy and courage to attack vested interests and to overcome the tyranny of the status quo. But we have to recognize that all instances of successful development are ultimately the collective result of individual decisions by existing *and* new entrepreneurs. There is no other path to development anymore.

The Role of Aid Organizations

Let me conclude by sharing some general suggestions for aid organizations. First of all, I applaud the role of the World Bank as a catalyst for a better investment climate around the globe. It is very important that things are measured, because what gets measured gets done. I, therefore, encourage the World Bank to further deepen and expand its analytical work to cover more areas and more countries. Based on analysis, the Bank should continue giving technical assistance. It is also positive that World Bank–EBRD cooperation in this field will be transformed into a global initiative of all major multilateral development banks.

Second, it goes without saying that the World Bank and other development banks will also need to internalize the Bank's findings in their own policies. Doing Business considerations are increasingly part of country strategies and results-based management systems. One step further would be to consider Doing Business indicators in a more systematic manner in the performance-based allocation systems of development banks. Progress in institutional reform for a better investment climate will then be rewarded by larger flows of aid. These flows of aid, in turn, will also become more effective.

A third way of promoting private sector development is to employ the private sector directly in programs. An interesting avenue is the ongoing pilot with so-called output-based projects in the fields of infrastructure, health, and education services. Governments delegate service delivery to a firm, which is paid from disbursement of public funding, including World Bank money, only upon the delivery of an agreed service or output to targeted groups. An obvious key advantage is that this promotes the effective use of public funds in ways that leverage private finance. It also transfers performance risk to the service provider, thereby providing incentives to achieve concrete results.

On a fourth and somewhat more critical note, governments and the private sector also face significant costs of doing business with aid agencies, including the World Bank. Especially in middle-income countries, the World Bank's administrative budget and procedures weigh heavily on the Bank's operations. Replacing the Bank's policies with institutions and systems that countries already have in place could reduce transactions costs. Of course, minimum standards should apply. This is already happening in, for example, financial management and procurement, and I welcome the pilot programs for national environmental and social safeguards.

My final remark is addressed to the academics. It may have taken some time, but Hernando de Soto's book shows that research can have a profound impact on policy advice worldwide, and thus on economic development. I believe that interaction among representatives of different economic disciplines and policy makers is fruitful. I, therefore, encourage you to "truck, barter, and exchange" your ideas. After all, we are all sons and daughters of Adam Smith.

Thank you!

Note

1. Hernando de Soto's first book, *The Other Path,* is a too-long-ignored forerunner of the current interest in the microeconomic analysis of the business climate from a private firm perspective.

References

de Soto, Hernando. 1989. *The Other Path: The Economic Answer to Terrorism.* New York: Basic Books.

Friedman, M. 1962. *Capitalism and Democracy.* Chicago: University of Chicago Press.

Hayek, F. A. 1945. *Road to Serfdom.* Chicago: University of Chicago Press.

Krugman, P. 1992. "Toward a Counter-Counterrevolution in Development Theory." In *Proceedings of the World Bank Annual Bank Conference on Development Economics 1992,* 15–61. Washington, DC: World Bank.

Meier, Gerald M., and Joseph E. Stiglitz, eds. 2001. *Frontiers of Development Economics: The Future in Perspective.* Oxford: Oxford University Press.

Pigou, A. C. 1947. *A Study in Public Finance.* London: Macmillan.

Rodrik, D. 1999. "Institutions for High Quality Growth: What They Are and How to Acquire Them." Harvard University, Cambridge, MA.

World Bank. 2005. *World Development Report 2005.* Washington, DC.

Keynote Address

Trade and Development

ERNESTO ZEDILLO

I am very pleased and thankful to participate in this important conference, which brings to the table topics of great relevance at this definitive moment for the future of international cooperation.

The true willingness of pertinent leaders to confront collectively the scourges of poverty and conflict in our world will be crucially tested in what remains of 2005. When the sequence of the July G-8 Summit, the September UN Millennium Review Summit, and the December World Trade Organization (WTO) Ministerial Meeting is completed, we should know whether leaders will continue to gamble on a strategy of business as usual or at last will embark on a bolder strategy—harder in the short term but more promising over the long haul—for the pursuit of international prosperity, peace, and security.

The agenda to pursue such a strategy comprises many and complex issues, some of which are being explored at this meeting. In compliance with the time available I wish to focus on just one of those issues, but one which I, as I am sure many of you also, consider to be of great importance from both the development and security perspectives: upholding an open, equitable, rules-based, predictable, and nondiscriminatory multilateral trading system.

In fact, what I want to do is to present, albeit in a very concise manner, an overview of the *Trade for Development Report* that a task force in which I served as co-coordinator produced for the United Nations Millennium Project. We delivered this report last January to the project coordinators and since then it has been available on the Web; but the print edition is becoming available as of today, on the occasion of this ABCDE conference.

As is common in this kind of endeavor, either because of respectable differences of opinion or to protect the institutions with which authors are professionally affiliated, our publication contains some conventional disclaimers. I can assure you,

---

Ernesto Zedillo is Director of the Yale Center for the Study of Globalization and former President of Mexico.

Annual World Bank Conference on Development Economics—Europe 2006

however, that most members of our task force do endorse what I wish to submit to you this morning.

Our work was driven by a concrete question: what multilateral trading system would best support, first, the attainment of the Millennium Development Goals (MDGs) by 2015, and afterward, the continuation of the fight against poverty until it is effectively eradicated?

In answering this question, we start by arguing, as have many before us, that trade openness can be a powerful driver of economic growth, which in turn is indispensable to reduce poverty. We grant, however, that trade alone is not a silver bullet for achieving development. There is no way around the other institutional and policy conditions that must also be met to attain development. In moving toward freer trade, adjustment costs also need to be taken into account. In particular, measures to safeguard poorer individuals who could possibly be negatively affected by more open markets are essential for successful trade liberalization. But, I maintain, trade openness, if not sufficient alone, is certainly necessary to boost economic growth and defeat poverty.

It is for this reason that our task force thought it important to take very seriously the commitment adopted at the Doha Ministerial for making the new round a true development undertaking. For this commitment to be fulfilled it was, and continues to be, imperative to identify and address effectively in the round's negotiations the core development priorities for the multilateral trading system.

The biggest and most costly aberration of the trading system is to be found in agriculture. The dimensions of this aberration are well known but it is worth repeating a few of them here.

Farm producers in rich countries receive farm-gate prices that are almost one-third higher than world prices; moreover, half the value of their production at the farm gate—or roughly three-quarters of the value added—is still derived from transfers. Yet, Organisation for Economic Co-operation and Development (OECD) farmers get only a small portion of all the money poured into agriculture—only 25 to 30 cents of every dollar or euro of support go to OECD farmers' incomes. The remaining 70 to 75 cents end up in the pockets of land renters and suppliers of other farm inputs or is wasted through inappropriate (subsidy-based) choices of crops. Furthermore, the smallest 25 percent of European farms receive less than 4 percent of total European support (the same as in the United States), whereas the largest 25 percent of European farms receive 70 percent (80 percent in the United States) of the total. The fact that existing farm support disproportionately benefits large farmers should be communicated more clearly to the general public in rich countries who endorse farm policies out of a desire to assist small family farms. Moreover, current OECD farm policies have largely failed in practice to protect the rural environment because they result in intensive use of fertilizers and encourage production methods that pollute.

Because of OECD agricultural protection, resources are transferred from poorer OECD households to richer ones in the amount of US$250 billion per year. Consumers in those countries pay for that protection through higher taxes and higher food prices. It is their choice, but it must be stressed that by doing so they also impose a heavy burden on other agricultural producers, particularly in developing countries.

In addition to severely limiting access to their own markets, rich countries' farm policies generate large price volatility in world markets. While OECD farmers are sheltered from almost all possible risks because of price supports and other subsidies, developing country markets bear the burden of amplified price volatility, forcing farmers from developing countries to follow OECD subsidized prices for the products concerned. These same policies induce developing countries' farmers to over-invest in OECD least-subsidized products, such as coffee and cocoa, leading to excessive supply and depressed prices for these crops. Absent protection in developed countries, greater diversification in developing countries would be feasible.

Lastly, OECD policies provoke a perverse mimicking effect. Many governments of developing countries use OECD policies as a rationale for sheltering their own farmers from the depressed prices and amplified market volatility caused by trade-distorting OECD policies and in the process damage farm producers from other developing countries. These policies impose additional costs on poor countries. Contrary to widespread belief, closed OECD markets are not solely a problem for major agricultural exporting countries such as Argentina, Brazil, or Thailand; they also affect many of the poorest developing countries, which are often dependent on a very small set of commodities, many of them subsidized and protected by OECD countries, such as sugar, cotton, and rice.

Although not as severe as in farm products, trade barriers in nonagricultural products continue to be significant and particularly detrimental to developing countries. For example, developing countries' exports to developed countries face tariffs that are, on average, four times higher than those imposed on the exports of other developed countries. Developing countries' exports suffer from tariff peaks and tariff escalation imposed by rich countries on goods of great export potential.

Moreover, hard-won gains in market access in agricultural and nonagricultural products can be eroded when other policies recreate trade barriers or generate transaction costs and trigger uncertainty regarding the conditions of that access. Contingent protection, including antidumping, antisubsidies, and safeguards can all prevent developing countries from taking advantage of negotiated market access.

In the last decade, there has been an explosion in the total number of antidumping investigations initiated by WTO Member countries, both developed and developing; however, the targeted countries are predominantly developing countries, especially small ones, regardless of who is the initiator. In fact, per dollar of imports, developing countries are six times more likely to be targeted by industrial countries and three times more likely by other developing countries. The observed bias against developing countries underscores the importance and urgency of disciplining the use of antidumping as well as antisubsidy and safeguard actions, which are also becoming a very serious problem.

While trade in goods—particularly agriculture—commands most attention on the Doha Agenda, the potential gains from successful services liberalization may be much larger—by up to a factor of five by some estimates. Beyond the numbers, services are fundamental for development, both for efficiency and for the growth potential of the economy as a whole, as well as access to basic services to improve the lives of the poor.

Multilateral liberalization in services is attractive for three reasons. First, unilateral liberalization has not been spread equally across all services and modes of supply. Significant barriers remain, particularly in areas of great interest to developing countries, such as the movement of natural persons to supply services under mode 4 of the General Agreement on Trade in Services (GATS). Second, given that domestic politics and vested interests can make reforms difficult to sustain, GATS negotiations offer the scope to lock in policy reforms by offsetting pressures for protection with pressure from those who gain from increased exports. Third, in the mercantilist world of trade negotiations, preparedness by developing countries to lock in services reforms in GATS commitments can generate leverage to push for the necessary technical and financial assistance to implement regulatory reform or for commitments from trading partners across other parts of the WTO agenda. Done right, services negotiations offer developing countries an opportunity to act in their own economic interest and get paid for it.

The Doha Development Agenda was supposed to tackle these and other important issues with the aim of fixing the trading system's existing imbalance against the interests of developing countries. But this sense of purpose seems to have been short lived. For starters, some issues of questionable interest for developing countries were included in the Doha Agenda itself. And since its launch, the story of the Doha negotiations more frequently than not has been one of missed deadlines and mounting frustration.

The story is too well known to be repeated here in detail. Suffice to recall the failure at the Cancun WTO Ministerial, a misstep that took almost a year to fix, and then only partially, with the Work Programme framework agreed on August 1, 2004. Our report warned that the framework, while necessary to prevent the collapse of the round, was far from sufficient to sustain it and that the real work remained to be done. Unfortunately, progress in the negotiations following the August framework again became painfully slow. For example, it very nearly took a new crisis in the talks and then the muscle of an informal ministerial meeting (in Paris in early May) to solve a technical issue over which, in principle, there should not have been significant disagreement—that of conversion of non-ad valorem tariffs into ad valorem equivalents.

To be fair, all parties have contributed to the parsimony and disappointment of the negotiations.

Certainly, developing countries have not been ambitious reformers at the Doha Round. It would be very unfortunate if the defensive position exhibited by developing countries so far were to prevail through the end of the round, considering that in most cases the biggest gains from trade liberalization come from a country's own trade liberalization. Tariff reductions primarily benefit the country undertaking them. The costs of protection are paid for by the domestic economy—by its households, which pay more for the goods and services they consume, and by its firms, which pay more for the protected goods they use (consume) as inputs. Protection creates a bias against exports by raising the costs of inputs; that is, protection on imports reduces the competitiveness of exports. It distorts the allocation of resources in the domestic economy, encouraging investment in the most protected sectors—not the most potentially efficient ones. In sum, protection creates an unfriendly environment for implementing development and poverty reduction strategies.

Liberalization works in the converse direction, and while estimates of welfare gains vary according to the assumptions used, there is general consensus that these gains are significant and that developing countries could capture the largest gains relative to their GDP. Furthermore, tariff reductions promise real gains not only to the liberalizing countries themselves, but also to other developing countries. Nearly all analyses of the benefits of removing restraints to trade show that most of the gains to developing countries—some 60 to 80 percent—result from trade reforms in developing countries themselves. Trade among developing countries is growing faster than developed-developing country trade and now constitutes 25 percent of total trade. Liberalization by the more advanced developing countries is not only in their own interests, but would benefit the poorest developing countries as well.

Fears about preference erosion have become a powerful argument in some quarters against ambitious and Most Favored Nation (MFN) liberalization in the Doha Round. But is this correct? Have preferences conferred significant benefits, and what are the consequences of eroding them?

As we argued in our report, the truth is that rich countries have used preferences to divide developing countries and promote narrower regional, sectoral, and political objectives, often establishing complicated regulations effectively excluding exports from otherwise eligible countries. The poorest countries have seldom received more than limited benefits from preferences, partly due to the shortcomings of the schemes and partly because preferences are only an opportunity to achieve market access—they do not address the multiple supply-side constraints that limit the participation of the poorest countries in world trade. Any benefits are also often at the expense of other developing countries, and are smaller than would be the case with either direct transfers or multilateral liberalization. Ultimately, the price of defending preferences is continuing protection in rich countries. Given this fact, MFN liberalization—plus appropriate compensation for those countries that may suffer adjustment problems—is likely to be a better path.

The pursuit of so-called Special and Differential Treatment (SDT) has been another factor that has inhibited the liberalizing impetus of developing countries in this and previous rounds. Our report suggests that there is indeed a case for SDT, but hardly one to exempt countries from obligations in the trading system.

Having no obligations equals not only having no ability to prosecute negotiating interests effectively across the agenda, it also means having no ability to use the trading system to promote domestic reform and increase national welfare. The right balance entails an approach that requires developing countries to participate in liberalization in a way that is both commensurate with their current level of development and likely to serve their long-term development interests.

Developing countries are absolutely correct for being aggravated by rich countries' persistent protectionism, but are very wrong so ardently to stick to their own. It is downright self-inflicted pain. In developing countries, the idea that opening one's own markets is a concession leads to an almost perverse consequence. According to such a wrongheaded notion, the poorer a country is, the fewer, if any, *concessions* it should make. It so happens, however, that the less open a country is, the more likely it is to remain a poor country.

Recognizing that developing countries have displayed too much defensiveness during the Doha talks, I do believe, nonetheless, that the biggest responsibility for Doha's failure so far lies with the biggest developed players: the European Union, the United States, and Japan. These countries have failed to honor the core commitments established in the Doha Declaration. Developing countries were told that the only way to solve satisfactorily their pending issues was to launch the new round. And by far the pending issue that looms largest is agricultural protectionism in rich countries. As long as this problem is not addressed seriously by the multilateral trading system, it will be harder, if not impossible, to make progress on the other important questions that pertain to it. It is clear that the pertinent players have resisted serious agricultural reform to the utmost extent possible. I am aware that those countries' trade officials would claim otherwise, but any careful analysis of what they have brought to the negotiating table, and even this only after much wrangling, will show how little and how slowly they want real reform to occur. Rich countries cannot have it both ways: on the one hand, telling developing countries that this is the development round, and on the other hand being unwilling to change the way they deal with their agricultural sectors—to the detriment of the people not only in the developing countries, but also in their own.

Admittedly, a good part of the Doha Round's troubles stem from the very same mercantilist logic of reciprocal liberalization that for almost 60 years has driven the evolution of the multilateral trading system and the concurrent and impressive expansion of international trade. This logic has determined the lens through which politicians have become accustomed to view trade negotiations. They do not begin by acknowledging that unilateral liberalization is good in and of itself, rather, they generally assume that opening one's markets is a necessary evil in order to get access to others' markets, and therefore they will invariably expect their trade negotiators to minimize their country's concessions while maximizing others' concessions. No wonder, given the developed countries' reluctance to come forward with effective agricultural reform, that developing countries are being extremely cautious about their own liberalization proposals.

At this point, the question is whether the mercantilist approach to trade liberalization, so effective in the past, can continue driving the construction of the global public good of open markets.

The answer is barely, if one considers the large and diverse membership of the WTO, the veto power that for practical purposes every member holds, and the consequences of the single-undertaking procedure.

But in the absence of a strong supranational authority that would mandate trade liberalization for all, the mercantilist approach still seems to be the only game in town. To be successful, however, the mercantilist approach must be pulled from its own traps by those countries that have gained the most from trade and are bound to win even more if trade liberalization deepens further. The Quad countries (Canada, the European Union, Japan, and the United States) have a special responsibility, the greatest perhaps falling this time on Europe, which, on balance, is the biggest and most stubborn farm protectionist of all.

Without a special effort to tackle the agricultural question resolutely, the WTO will be drawn headfirst by its members into another failure at the Hong Kong (China) WTO meeting. And afterwards, who knows.

A real development round is still achievable but will require large amounts of enlightened, albeit self-interested, leadership on the part of the major players in both developed and developing countries. But frankly speaking, providing this kind of leadership is not within the realm of trade negotiators' capacities. Political leadership must be generated at a higher level, above even the ministerial level. It must be generated at the head-of-government level, as part of a coherent policy approach to meet the development challenge. The upcoming summits offer a last opportunity to seek a major political consensus on this crucial matter.

We believe that a successful conclusion to the Doha Round negotiations is unlikely unless the pertinent leaders agree on a grand vision of the multilateral trading system for the future. And we submit that such a grand vision ideally should contain the following elements:

- The most useful WTO would be one focused solely on trade and relieved of other global economic governance tasks, which could be better accomplished by other international instruments or entities.
- Duty-free and quota-free access for all exports from the poorest countries should be extended by all developed countries no later than January 1, 2006.
- In a conveniently distant long term (2025), the multilateral trading system must deliver the total removal of barriers to all merchandise trade, a substantial and extensive liberalization of trade in services, and universal enforcement of the principles of reciprocity and nondiscrimination in a way that supports attainment of the Millennium Development Goals. This target is ambitious but not impossible, with political will and appropriate support for adjustment.
- Developed countries should bind all tariffs on nonagricultural merchandise at zero by 2015. A mid-term target could be for no tariff higher than 5 percent by 2010. Ideally, developing countries should all be at zero tariffs by 2025. The poorest countries should also aim to bind all tariffs at a uniform and moderate rate.
- By 2015, no bound farm tariff should exceed 5 percent for OECD countries, 10 percent for developing countries, and 15 percent for the poorest countries. All nontariff barriers, including tariff-rate quotas, should be removed by 2010.
- As soon as possible and no later than 2010, all export subsidies should be abolished, with comparable disciplines on similar instruments.
- Domestic support must be made both less trade distorting and subject to an overall significantly lower limit. All countries should decouple all support payments to farmers by 2010. Also by 2010, all countries should cap all domestic support

measures at 10 percent of the value of agricultural production and at 5 percent by 2015. The WTO's Green Box of minimally trade-distorting subsidies should be maintained for the poorest countries—with marginal additions such as support for diversification, transportation subsidies for farm products, and public assistance for establishing farm cooperatives or institutions promoting marketing and quality control.

- The liberalization of mode 4 of the GATS (temporary movement of labor to provide services) should be adopted as a high-priority item on the international agenda, considering its potential benefits for both developing and developed countries as well as the need to manage the mounting migration pressures in the world in a more orderly fashion. Developing countries' liberalization to foreign direct investment must be gradually followed by developed country liberalization to foreign labor.
- The traditional approach to SDT must be revised away from the present counterproductive system of exemptions from obligations and complex webs of discriminatory preferences. A trading system limited to agreements that are in the trade and development interests of all WTO Members to implement under the framework of binding multilateral trade rules should be accompanied by SDT that affords appropriately long and flexible conditions to adjust to trade liberalization as well as real and substantial aid for trade. Poor countries must be supported in generating the sources of revenue needed to compensate for losses incurred as a result of lowering import duties, building the human and physical infrastructure they need to benefit from increased market opportunities, and adjusting to erosions of existing trade preferences that stem from multilateral negotiations.
- Greatly increased international technical and financial support for reform and adjustment by developing countries is needed to ensure achievement of the trade liberalization targets. A temporary "aid for trade fund" commensurate with the size of the task, or significantly ramped-up contributions through existing channels, is needed to support countries in addressing adjustment costs associated with the implementation of a Doha reform agenda.

Dear colleagues,

Some people might think that the economic and social benefits of increased trade are not worth the short-term political cost that usually is incurred when markets are further opened to foreign competition. The skeptics should then be invited to consider the benefits of trade for peace and security. They should be told of Immanuel Kant's assertion in his 1795 work, *Perpetual Peace,* that "The Spirit of Commerce sooner than later takes hold of every people, and it cannot exist side by side with war . . ."

Moreover, the skeptics should be reminded that Kant has been proven right by history. My Yale colleague Bruce Russett and his co-authors have used modern statistical techniques to analyze international experiences over a period of more than a century, up to the early 1990s, and have indeed confirmed that trade does increase the prospects for peace. They find that economic interdependence significantly reduces the likelihood that two states will be in conflict, and that it is not only bilateral trade that makes conflict less probable—openness in general has a substantial pacifying effect. They show that the more autarkic countries have usually been the ones to pose the biggest threats to peace, and that if economic interdependence declines the prospects for conflict rise. They also warn that a two-way causality might exist, conveying that conflict damages trade but also that trade helps to prevent conflict. Furthermore, they observe that trade between large states and small states tends to advance peace, meaning that countries that are trading partners do not need to be of comparable size to coexist without conflict.

Let us hope that these considerations, along with the value that trade holds for development, do come into play during the crucial deliberations and decisions of the months to come.

Thank you very much.

Macroeconomic Vulnerability

Macro Vulnerability in Low-Income Countries and Aid Responses

PATRICK GUILLAUMONT

The economic vulnerability of developing countries is not a new issue. In the development literature of 40 years ago, the issue of instability, especially for primary exports and international prices, was significant in the analysis of the problems faced by developing countries. The policy measures recommended were far from being convergent. But the fact is, during the first UNCTAD conferences, how to respond to world price instability was an important concern, with interest culminating in the mid-1970s (as evidenced by the Nairobi UNCTAD IV [1976] and its Integrated Program for Commodities—which proved overambitious and misdesigned.

Recently, the economic vulnerability of developing countries has appeared high again on the international agenda. Not only has the world economy remained unstable, but new aspects and consequences of that instability have become evident. Several trends and events contribute to this renewed interest in macro vulnerability.

First, small island developing states (SIDS) have repeatedly expressed concern about their level of vulnerability, as evidenced in 1994 at the Barbados Conference on Sustainable Development of Small Island Developing States. Following this conference, which asked for "the development of vulnerability indexes and other indicators that reflect the status of small island developing countries and integrate ecological fragility and economic vulnerability," (United Nations 1994) the United Nations General Assembly, in 1996, requested the Secretary General to prepare a report on the vulnerability index and the Committee for Development Planning (CDP) to examine this index. In 1998, the UN Commission on Sustainable Development urged CDP to present its conclusion and other UN bodies to accord priority to work on the vulnerability of SIDS. In 1999, the Committee for Development

Patrick Guillaumont is President, Centre d'Etudes et de Recherches sur le Développement International (CERDI) at Centre National de la Recherche Scientifique and Université d'Auvergne.

Annual World Bank Conference on Development Economics—Europe 2006

Policy (the new name of CDP), after considering several available indicators, proposed a new and relatively simple index (United Nations 1999). Ten years after the Barbados Conference, the Mauritius Conference (December 2004) reiterated the international community's concern about the vulnerability of small islands. A few days later, the Asian tsunami highlighted the relevance of this concern.

Second, in accordance with the suggestions of CDP, the General Assembly requested CDP to consider "the usefulness of the vulnerability index as a criterion for the designation of the Least Developed Countries" (LDCs) (United Nations 1997). In 1999, a new "economic vulnerability index" (EVI) was proposed by CDP as one of the criteria to be used for the identification of LDCs, in addition to the other two criteria (the level of GDP per capita and an index of human capital). CDP, in 2000 and again in 2003, in its review of the list of LDCs implemented the EVI as an identification criterion. This list—and the new vulnerability criterion—was endorsed by the UN Economic and Social Council (ECOSOC).

Third, and most important, the unsustainability of growth episodes in Africa has become a major intellectual and political challenge. Moreover, the problem of conflict, which is particularly acute in Africa, has drawn the attention of the international community to the risk of civil wars (and to the factors of their duration as well [Collier et al 2003]). It is mainly in reference to these situations and other possible sources of collapse that the World Bank has designed a special category of countries—low-income countries under stress (LICUS). The expression "fragile states" also reflects the vulnerability of these countries (Chauvet and Collier 2005).

Fourth, in answer to concerns about the instability of international commodity prices and their possibly higher impact on producers in a context of liberalized domestic agricultural markets, an International Task Force for Commodity Risk Management has been set up at the initiative of the World Bank to make proposals on the ways in which commodity-dependent economies can manage the risks of a market-based approach. Such proposals are specifically intended to cope with the vulnerability of these economies and to assess the extent of their vulnerability (World Bank 1999; Varangis et al 2004).

Fifth, in the second part of the 1990s, the "Asian crisis" made it clear that SIDS, LDCs, Africa, and commodity-dependent economies are not alone in their vulnerability. Many comments and analyses of the causes of the Asian crisis and other financial crises have underlined the vulnerability of some emerging countries, which before the crisis registered high level of capital inflows with weak financial structures. From that perspective, several authors have tried to assess the risk of a financial crisis (Berg and Patillo 1999), and others to estimate the factors behind GDP growth volatility (Easterly, Islam, and Stiglitz 2001; Combes et al 2000), which is another way to look at vulnerability.

Finally, the attention brought to vulnerability at the household level, which has emerged from the huge amount of work on poverty (and which is considered in Stephan Dercon's paper in this volume), has also reinforced the interest in vulnerability at the macro level. Vulnerability of households results to a large extent from macro vulnerability.

"Macro vulnerability" means the risk that poor countries will see their development hampered by the exogenous shocks they face, both natural and external. This paper considers two main kinds of exogenous shocks, then three main sources of vulnerability. The shocks include (a) environmental or "natural" shocks, such as earthquakes or volcanic eruptions, and the more frequent climatic shocks, such as typhoons and hurricanes, droughts, floods, and the like; and (b) external (trade and exchange related) shocks, such as slumps in external demand, instability of world commodity prices (and correlated instability of terms of trade), international fluctuations of interest rates, and so forth. Other domestic shocks may also be generated by political instability or, more generally, by unforeseen political changes. These shocks, however, are not included here as exogenous shocks.

Vulnerability can be seen as the result of three components:[1] (a) the size and frequency of the exogenous *shocks,* either observed (ex post vulnerability) or anticipated (ex ante vulnerability); (b) the *exposure* to the shocks; (c) the capacity to react to the shocks, or *resilience.*[2] Resilience is more dependent on current policy, more easily reversible, and less structural. But there may also be a structural element in the resilience component of vulnerability.[3]

A distinction thus can be made between *structural vulnerability,* which results from factors that are durably independent from the current political will of countries, and the *vulnerability deriving from policy,* which results from recent choices. For instance, the vulnerability of the Asian countries after the 1997 crisis is very different from the vulnerability of small economies that export raw materials, or of small islands, because it is less structural, more the result of policy, and more transient. This feature is clear when vulnerability is measured by the probability of a financial crisis, estimated mainly from financial and policy variables (see, for instance, Berg and Patillo 1999; Goldstein, Kaminski, and Reinhart 2000). If a vulnerability index is to be used for selecting certain countries and providing them with durable support from the international community, the vulnerability to be measured is naturally the structural type, which essentially results from the size of the shocks that can arise and the exposure to such shocks.

Without forgetting the various contexts in which the concept of macroeconomic vulnerability has appeared to be relevant, this paper examines two specific aspects of macro vulnerability: first, it focuses on the vulnerability of *low-income countries,* leaving aside the vulnerability of emerging economies and developed countries; second, it considers mainly *structural vulnerability,* which in the short term does not depend on policy, and is particularly high in many low-income countries.

The paper is organized as follows. The first section argues that vulnerability matters, particularly for low-income countries: drawing from the literature and some ongoing works, we examine how vulnerability lowers growth and slows down poverty reduction. The second part, devoted to concept and measurement issues, examines how to assess structural vulnerability and presents an index of economic vulnerability that could be used for development cooperation guidance, as is already the case for the identification of LDCs. The third section uses such an index to consider the implications for aid policy of the macro vulnerability of poor countries, with the view toward dampening the ex post consequences of the shocks, as well as toward lowering the uncertainty resulting from them.

Why Vulnerability Matters: The Impact of Structural Vulnerability

If vulnerability is the risk of being harmed by shocks, a first question is how to measure that harm. It could be the immediate loss of welfare resulting from a shock. When successive and opposite shocks of equal size occur, the welfare loss associated with the instability of income is due only to the decreasing marginal utility of income. Of main concern for low-income countries are the possible negative effects of the shocks on growth and development, which refer to a dynamic definition of vulnerability. Thus, the relevant vulnerability is the risk that economic growth will be markedly and durably reduced by shocks (or the risk that the long-term average rate of growth will be reduced by shocks).[4] Vulnerability is seen as a handicap to growth. Another dynamic definition, somewhat broader, is the likelihood of negative and durable effects of shocks on poverty reduction, either due to their effect on growth or to a direct effect on poverty, which is outlined below. Of course, while vulnerability is costly, it cannot be reduced without cost, and in any event cannot be totally cancelled.

This section examines the links between vulnerability and growth referring to the three main components of vulnerability identified above: shocks, exposure, and resilience. The section then underlines social effects of macro vulnerability, beyond those linked to growth.

Shocks: The Negative Impact of Instability on Growth

Focusing on instability

The negative impact of "one sided" natural shocks, such as earthquakes, typhoons, and floods, is indisputable. The damage caused by these events is often huge, first in the number of deaths, second in the destruction of physical capital. Rather, the debate surrounds the measurement of the size of these losses. However, when the shocks are "two sided" (characterized by peaks and valleys), as are many shocks, in particular external ones, their overall impact may seem less clear. Depending on the method used to measure the shocks, the respective sizes of positive and negative shocks (not their time profile) tend to equalize. It is the very nature of instability to be a succession of booms and slumps (for example, export prices, external demand, rainfall, and others). Therefore, what follows mainly considers the impact of instability or volatility rather than the impact of separate shocks. What is argued is that the impact of these successive "ups and downs" is not neutral. Their impact may result either from an asymmetry of ex post reactions to positive and negative shocks (even the time profile of these shocks may not be symmetrical), or from the uncertainty generated by the previous occurrence of shocks.[5] Thus, there are both ex post and ex ante effects of instability (as clearly underlined by Gunning 2004). Ex post effects may be easier to evidence than ex ante ones, which depend on a perception of the risk. Most measures used in cross-section literature rely on ex post concepts.

Because the observation of a succession of ups and downs (that is, the measurement of instability) needs a multiyear period, cross-sectional (or panel) regressions are often an appropriate tool for analyzing the effects of instability (on growth or other aggregates). Moreover, regressions can support the use of an internationally comparable index, considered in the next section. An important body of literature also examines the effects of trade shocks, both theoretically and through country case studies (for example, Collier and Gunning [1999] on mainly positive trade shocks), or compare time series (Deaton and Miller 1996), or model a typical economy (Koze and Reizman 2001).

Although some doubts exist about the static negative welfare effects of macroeconomic instability in a developed economy, as expressed by Lucas (2003), less doubt surrounds these effects in developing economies (Pallage and Robe 2003). It is argued here that there is little doubt, on the basis of cross-section studies including a large number of developing economies, that macroeconomic instability is unfavorable to growth. However, an issue rarely addressed is whether there is a threshold of instability above which such effects occur or, more generally, whether there are nonlinearities in the effects of instability.

Instability of growth and average growth

Three empirical studies offer a test of macro vulnerability, without considering specifically and separately the main sources of instability or vulnerability. A comprehensive test of macro vulnerability is given by Ramey and Ramey's well-known study (1995): it shows a significant link between the instability of the rate of economic growth and the average rate of growth itself. But this instability can be due to structural factors and to policy factors as well—providing one reason that the volatility of growth cannot be an approximate indicator of *structural* vulnerability, as argued below when we consider vulnerability indexes. Also without attempting to separate structural from policy sources of vulnerability, Rodrik (1999) found a significant negative influence on the change in the rate of growth between two 15-year periods from a multiplicative index of "conflict," which multiplies an index of "shocks" by an index of "latent social conflict" (the ethnolinguistic fragmentation index or a Gini coefficient of income inequality), then multiplies it again by an index of the quality of conflict-management institutions (namely, the lack of democracy or the quality of governmental institutions, as measured by Knack and Keefer [1995]). Each of these indexes, introduced alternately, appears highly significant. Rodrik also tests the respective effects of trade shocks and of either an exposure index or an index of the capacity to manage. A third, recent and systematic attempt to assess the link between output volatility and growth was made by Hnathovska and Loayza (2004), who demonstrate both a higher sensitivity of growth to volatility in low-income countries and an impact of volatility higher in the last two decades than during the previous ones. The authors also demonstrate that volatility is more detrimental when the quality of institutions is low (through a multiplicative variable). But they do not assess the impact of structural vulnerability, as such.

The effects of *export instability,* a main source of structural vulnerability in developing countries, have been discussed for many years in the literature using growth regressions. Two decades ago the results could appear mixed, due partly to methodological shortcomings and partly to an excess of concern about the effects on savings (see below). There now seems to be a consensus emerging from several studies to conclude that export instability (or in some studies, terms of trade instability) has a negative effect on growth.[6] More significant effects are found when the studies simultaneously test the positive effect of export growth and the negative effect of export instability, and when the export instability (size of the shocks) is either (a) weighted by the average exports-to-GDP ratio, a ratio which is, all other things equal, higher the lower the population size, during the period (Guillaumont 1994; Combes and Guillaumont 2002), or (b) is instability caused by the export-to-GDP ratio itself (Dawe 1996). The exposure to the shocks is thus taken into account.

The effects of export earnings instability are not the only ones to have been tested. We previously estimated the influence of several *primary instabilities,* mainly exogenous, on the rate of growth and argued that these instabilities, significantly higher in Sub-Saharan Africa than in other developing countries, may have been a major factor of the slow rate of growth in Sub-Saharan Africa during the 1970s and 1980s, because on average these instabilities appear to have been higher there than in other developing countries (Guillaumont, Guillaumont Jeanneney, and Brun 1999). These primary instabilities are the instability of the terms of trade, weighted by the average export-to-GDP ratio, or of the instability of the real value of exports, weighted in the same way; the instability of agricultural value-added (weighted by the average share of agricultural value-added in GDP); and political instability. The first and the third instabilities appeared to have a significant effect on growth, but instability of agricultural value-added did not. However, in another work, both the instabilities of real value of exports and of agricultural value-added, now unweighted, appear to be significant (Guillaumont and Chauvet 2001). Recently Miguel, Satyanath, and Sergenti (2004) evidenced the impact of rainfall variations on growth in African countries during 1981–99 and the following likelihood of civil conflict.[7]

What are the channels of transmission from shocks to growth? What are the intermediate variables that are rendered unstable, so that growth is negatively affected?

Factor productivity more affected than the rate of investment

As noted above, much of the literature on the effects of export instability is devoted to its effects on savings, which are ambiguous. On the one hand, instability has long been supposed to increase precautionary saving (Knudsen and Yotopoulos 1976), an assumption mainly relevant for private saving and dependent on the degree of risk aversion, as shown by Mendoza 1997. On the other hand, instability may also generate ratchet effects on consumption, mainly on public consumption. Instability can also restrain the private sector from investing, because of risk perception, as argued and tested by Aizenman and Marion 1999. The public sector, however, is often pushed to invest in the boom periods, possibly with the help of procyclical borrowing, with higher public indebtedness resulting. Not surprisingly, the net result on the overall rate of investment, if not on its composition, is ambiguous.

Effects of instability on productivity growth are, on the contrary, clearly negative and result in negative effects on GDP growth, as demonstrated by several studies.[8] In the previously cited cross-section growth regressions, the instabilities, either the so-called primary instabilities (Guillaumont, Guillaumont Jeanneney, and Brun 1999) or that of rate of growth (Ramey and Ramey 1995), essentially lessen the rate of growth of total factor productivity. Actually, the instability of the terms of trade appears to increase rather than lower the rate of investment (Guillaumont, Guillaumont Jeanneney, and Brun 1999) which makes the effect on the growth residual alone stronger than the total effect on growth.[9] Finally, no evidence is found in the literature on low-income countries of a possible cleansing effect of the recession periods: indeed, it was an expected effect of adjustment policy, but it does not seem to be associated with structural vulnerability. It may also work only below some threshold.

Instability channelled through investment, real exchange rates, and producer prices

Guillaumont, Guillaumont Jeanneney, and Brun (1999), tested the hypothesis that the primary instabilities (terms of trade, agricultural value-added, political) influence growth through two important *intermediate instabilities,* namely the instability of the rate of investment and that of relative prices. These two intermediate instabilities have negative effects on growth and are related to policy. This structural vulnerability weakens policy.

First, the instability of the rate of investment is a determinant, curiously neglected in the literature, of lower average capital productivity: as a result of the declining marginal productivity of investment, the gain in total output due to a high level of investment is less than the loss due to a low level of investment. This effect, illustrated during the boom periods by oversized, underprepared, and weakly productive projects, mainly concerns public investment.

The second intermediate instability, that of relative prices—proxied by the instability of the real effective exchange rate (REER)—also appears to have a strong negative effect on the rate of growth. It is assumed to blur market signals and induce a misallocation of investment. This negative effect of REER instability or volatility has also been evidenced in several papers (Aizenman and Marion 1999; Ghura and Grennes 1993; Serven 1997). It appears to not only have an effect on total factor productivity, but also a negative effect on the rate of investment (Guillaumont, Guillaumont Jeanneney, and Brun 1999).

Either due to the REER instability induced by macroeconomic policy or to the passing through to farmers of world agricultural price fluctuations, instability of real producer prices is generally considered a cause of lower average agricultural output (as well as a factor of lower welfare), noticeably through its effects on the adoption of new techniques, as is weather risk (Newbery and Stiglitz 1981; United Nations 2001b for a review of studies on the impact of risk on agricultural productivity).

Time series studies on producer price variability are most often related to some specific products and countries (for instance, Araujo 1995; Behrman 1968; Guillaumont and Bonjean 1991; Just 1974; Lin 1977). At a macro level, the effects of real producer price instability on the growth of agricultural production have also been found to be significantly negative from a sample pooling several products in many countries (Boussard and Gérard 1996; Guillaumont and Combes 1996) as well as the effects of real border price instability (Subervie 2006) on aggregate agricultural supply, effects conditioned by the macroeconomic environment.

Thus, it seems that external instability has negative effects through the instability of the rate of investment and of the real exchange rate, either by its impact on public finance when retained at the government level or by its impact at the producer level when passed through to producers.

Exposure: The Vulnerability of Small Countries

The main structural factor leading to greater exposure to exogenous shocks is the small size of a country. Among several ways to measure the size of a country, the most meaningful is the number of inhabitants. In some cases (possibly for natural shocks), small geographic area could be a more relevant measure of exposure, but to assess the main economic consequences of the size of a country, independent of its income per capita, the most usual measure is its population.

The vulnerability issue resurrects the old debate on the consequences of the size of nations (see recent works of Alesina and Spolaore 2004; Ocampo 2002; and Winters and Martins 2004). Country size has many consequences—none of them at first glance related to vulnerability—but in particular, scale economies in many sectors of both industrial and government activity (the unit costs of public administration are expected to be higher in smaller countries). However, when investigating the channels through which size matters for development, links with vulnerability more clearly appear. Small size influences the exposure components of vulnerability through at least three main channels (or intermediate variables): trade intensity, government size, and social cohesion.

Take first the *exposure to external shocks,* well reflected by the export-to-GDP ratio. The smaller the population size, the higher (all other things equal) the export-to-GDP ratio (and the more "dependent" on trade the economy). Country size is the main structural factor determining the export-to-GDP ratio, thus the main determinant of the "natural openness" (openness due to natural or structural factors) and the main factor to be neutralized if an index of "openness policy" is drawn from the observed ratios (Guillaumont 1989, 1994). It is clear that the impact of a given export shortfall is higher, the larger the share of export in GDP. For that reason, the impact of export instability (and of the instability of export growth, as well) is better estimated when the export instability variable (and export growth) is multiplied by the export-to-GDP ratio, that is, when it is a "weighted" instability. While natural openness, mainly determined by smallness, increases the exposure to trade shocks and consequently their negative effect on growth, openness policy has not only a positive influence on growth, but also is a factor leading to greater resilience (Guillaumont 1994, Combes and Guillaumont 2002).[10]

Moreover, diseconomies of scale associated with smallness result in more difficulty in diversifying at low cost. As a consequence, small, low-income countries face a higher risk than larger countries from implementing inefficient or costly policies when they adopt protectionist measures; for the same reason, a protectionist trend at the world level is likely to be more damaging for small countries. Alesina and Spolaore (2004) have tested such an effect in a cross-section growth regression through a multiplicative variable of the (log of) population and openness: the coefficient of this multiplicative variable is found significantly negative, while that of each of two variables added independently in the regression is significantly positive.

A second reason smallness is thought to be a factor of lower growth is its assumed impact on the *size of government.* The assumption of a negative relationship between population size and the relative size of government activities has been successfully tested by Alesina and Spolaore (2004). An interpretation can be found in a previous work by Rodrik (1998) who argued that a high export-to-GDP ratio (itself related to the population size) leads to an extension of the role of the state in providing more insurance to the citizens. Or this relationship can be linked to a stronger effect of public revenue instability on public consumption. If government activities are a source of higher costs, vulnerability due to smallness may be increased, likely lowering growth.

A third channel by which country size, as measured by population, may impact vulnerability and growth is through *social cohesion.* An advantage of smallness may be more social cohesion (less ethnic, linguistic, or religious fragmentation): if social fragmentation is a negative factor on growth *and* if fragmentation increases with population size, smallness is an advantage not a handicap. Fragmentation, as a handicap, is not unrelated to vulnerability: one reason fragmentation is assumed to negatively impact growth is that this structural factor influences the exposure or the resilience to shocks (Rodrik 1999). The reality may be more complex, and several works evidence nonlinear relationships where linear ones are assumed. In particular, social polarization rather than social fragmentation may be a handicap (and a factor of vulnerability) (Arcand, Guillaumont, and Guillaumont Jeanneney 2001). Polarization does not increase with population size: it (at least beyond a low threshold) decreases with it.[11] For that reason, smallness may appear to increase—not lower—vulnerability.[12]

Several cross-country regressions clearly show that when appropriate control variables are used the (log of) population size is a significant positive determinant of growth (Alesina and Spolaore 2004; Bosworth and Collins 2003; Guillaumont and Guillaumont 1988; Guillaumont and Chauvet 2001; Milner and Weyman-Jones 2003) and a negative determinant of export instability (Easterly and Kraay 2000). That small size lowers growth may be due either to higher vulnerability or to scale diseconomies or to their conjunction.

In addition to small population size, other factors of exposure to shocks must be considered. They are related to the structure of the economy and to the location of the country, primary economies and remote countries being more exposed to external and natural shocks. The extent to which this is true is examined in the next section, along with the indicators of exposure.

Resilience: The Ambiguous Role of Policy

As seen above, the instability of overall income transmitted to public revenue is a factor of public deficit and indebtedness, of instability, and thus of low productivity of public investment, of real exchange rate instability, and so forth. The hypothesis that structural vulnerability weakens policy is supported by the inclusion of a vulnerability indicator in a model in which the explained variable is a composite indicator of macro policy. Consider an indicator of macro policy similar to that used by Burnside and Dollar (2000), including as components the ratio of budget surplus to GDP, the rate of inflation, and the Sachs and Warner measure of openness, weighted by each component's impact on growth in a cross-section model with other common control variables (this model measures the impact on growth of these three identified factors, all other things equal). On a pooling of 10-year periods, this indicator of policy appears itself to be significantly and negatively influenced by the level of economic vulnerability, as measured by an index, and positively by the initial level of human capital (Guillaumont and Chauvet 2001). However, the long-run effect of the instability on the quality of institutions remains an open issue.

Structural vulnerability not only has an impact on the quality of economic policy; its direct effects (on growth) also depend on policy. Policy and institutions are the main determinants of resilience to shocks, that is, of the capacity of a country to effectively cope with exogenous shocks. This is why structural vulnerability has to be distinguished from overall vulnerability, which includes an autonomous policy component essentially through resilience. Indeed, institutions and policy are themselves influenced by other far-reaching factors, as argued by Acemoglu et al (2003), precisely to explain their impact on the volatility of growth and the occurrence of crises.

One important element of resilience, dependent on policy, is the capacity of a country to maintain an appropriate level of competitiveness. An outward-looking policy, even if it may increase the exposure of a country to external shocks, enhances its resilience. This means that in the growth regressions, the absolute value of the (negative) coefficient of the (weighted) export or terms-of-trade instability is smaller if policy is more outward looking (Combes and Guillaumont 2002; Guillaumont 1994). Thus, three effects of a more open trade policy can be identified: (a) the well-known positive effect of the growth of exports; (b) the negative effect of increased exposure to instability (the export-to-GDP ratio weighting the export instability); and (c) the positive effect of lessening the impact of a given export instability, which means greater resilience. As argued in the last part of this paper, foreign aid can be another important determinant of resilience.

Beyond Growth: Social Consequences of Vulnerability

Instability, by lowering growth, has deleterious consequences on the social variables that depend on economic growth, leading in particular to slower poverty reduction. Instability also has direct effects on these social variables, independent of its effects on growth. Two reasons make these direct effects likely. One is the feeling of frustration generated by a shortfall of income following a rapid expansion that creates new needs and exaggerated expectations. The second reason is a result of poverty traps, linked to the asymmetry of reactions of health, education, and employment to income fluctuations. These two possibilities are illustrated below by use of cross-section results.

Social frustration generated by instability

Recent studies have examined the economic factors influencing tragic social events, such as civil war and criminality, the results of which can be reinterpreted or modified when economic instability is taken into account. For instance, Collier and Hoeffler (2004) have demonstrated a higher risk of civil war in countries where primary commodities are a large share of exports. They explain this relationship mainly by the rent-seeking behavior of rebels and their easier access to finance. Another reasonable assumption is that export instability—which is even higher when exports are primary—exacerbates feelings of frustration. When the instability of exports, weighted by the openness rate, is introduced in a conflict-occurrence model such Collier and Hoeffler's, not only does the coefficient of determination significantly increase, but the share of primary commodities in exports becomes insignificant (Guillaumont et al 2005). Other exogenous shocks may have similar effects on the risk of conflict: Miguel, Satyanath, and Sergenti (2004), examining the impact of civil war on growth, link civil war to rainfall instability, which appears to be a significant determinant.

Several studies have examined the economic determinants of the rates of criminality (Fajnzylber, Lederman, and Loayza 2002; Neumayer 2003, 2005). Factors considered include average income per capita, the inequality of its distribution, and level of education—but not vulnerability factors. Using the database developed recently by Neumayer 2005, it has been found that the volatility of income growth is a significant determinant, both of rates of homicide and rates of robbery; for robbery, instability of exports and of agricultural value-added introduced as substitutes for growth volatility appear to be significant explanatory variables (Guillaumont and Puech 2006).

Anti-poor bias of unstable growth

The relationships presented above are related to specific events that reflect social resentment. Consider now the transmission of macroeconomic vulnerability to the overall social situation, independent of the effect expected from lower growth.

Perhaps the best single indicator of the evolution of the social situation in low-income countries is the under-five child mortality rate, as made available by the Demographic and Health Surveys and extended by the World Health Organization. Child mortality is a sensitive indicator, likely to reflect the strong asymmetric effect that can be expected from income instability: a rise in mortality resulting from an income shortfall will not be compensated for afterward by an equal income increase. Because child mortality has a lower limit, the best functional form to be tested is that where the dependent variable is expressed as a logit (log of the ratio of survival to mortality) (Grigoriou and Guillaumont 2003). Tested first with fixed effects, then in

TABLE 1.
Effects of Income Instability on Child Mortality

	Fixed effects		GMM system	
	Full sample	Low-income countries only	Full sample	Low-income countries only
	(1)	(2)	(3)	(4)
Income instability	0.004	0.024	0.025	0.054
	(0.64)	(2.59)**	(1.94)*	(3.77)***
Ln income per capita	–0.105	0.017	–0.840	–0.713
	(1.86)*	(0.21)	(8.03)***	(4.88)***
DPT immunization	–0.003	–0.006	–0.006	–0.004
	(3.67)***	(4.00)***	(2.84)***	(1.79)*
Constant	–1.499	–1.609	4.430	3.324
	(3.40)***	(2.85)***	(6.26)***	(3.10)***
Number of observations	401	126	401	126
Countries	96	33	96	33
R-squared	0.61	0.50		
p(Sargan)[a]			0.199	0.995
AR(1)[b]			0.000	0.182
AR(2)[c]			0.494	0.754

Source: Author, with C. Korachais.

Note: Dependent variable: logit transformation of under-five mortality. Periods: 1980, 1985, 1990, 1995, and 2000. DPT = diphtheria, pertussis, tetanus. Absolute value of t-statistics in parentheses for fixed effects estimations; robust value of t-statistics for GMM system estimations.

* significant at 10 percent level

** significant at 5 percent level

*** significant at 1 percent level

a. Sargan test is a test of overidentification restrictions.

b. AR(1) p value refers to Arellano Bond test for autoregressive correlations (order 1).

c. AR(2) p value refers to Arellano Bond test for autoregressive correlations (order 2).

Generalized Method of Moments (GMM), with observations every five years from 1980 to 2000, the effect of previous income instability on child mortality appears to be significantly positive for a subsample of low-income countries, but to a lesser extent on a larger sample and only in GMM (the control variables being the level of income per capita and DPT [diphtheria, pertussis, tetanus] immunization) (table 1). Income instability is measured on the five previous years (from a 10-year mixed trend, both determinist and stochastic, see next section).[13]

Finally, we introduce the macro vulnerability concern in the burgeoning cross-country research on the determinants of the level and evolution of poverty, made feasible by the extension of comparable data sets at the World Bank. The main concern until now has been to assess the growth and inequality elasticities of poverty (Adams 2004), but without similar concerns for the effects of income instability on poverty reduction. (Guillaumont Jeanneney and Kpodar [2005], however, examined the

TABLE 2.
Effect of Income Instability on Poverty Change

	Full sample		Low-income countries only
	(1)	**(2)**	**(3)**
Income instability	0.052	0.081	0.020
	(0.037)	(0.039)**	(0.027)
Income growth	–3.171	–2.708	–2.301
	(0.655)***	(0.617)***	(0.757)***
Income instability × income growth	0.369	0.341	0.332
	(0.098)***	(0.105)***	(0.181)*
Gini coefficient growth	3.966		2.174
	(1.060)***		(0.609)***
Initial poverty	–0.189	–0.205	–0.309
	(0.074)**	(0.083)**	(0.109)***
Constant	–0.405	–0.478	–0.095
	(0.160)**	(0.171)***	(0.103)
Number of observations	135	135	60
R-squared	0.35	0.26	0.52

Source: Author, with C. Korachais.

Note: Dependent variable: variation of the poverty headcount index (%). Periods: 1981–90 and 1990–9. Method: Ordinary Least Squares. Robust standard errors in parentheses.

* significant at 10 percent level

** significant at 5 percent level

*** significant at 1 percent level

effects of financial instability on poverty.) Starting from the standard model (as used by Adams 2004), where the change in the level of poverty depends on growth in income per capita and on change in inequality, we have estimated an augmented model including as an additional variable the instability of income per capita. The assumption is that income instability pushes people into poverty traps (poor people develop health handicaps, children leave school, workers stay out of the labor market, and so forth), so that the poverty reaction to a rise of average income is less than its reaction to a fall (see, for instance, de Janvry and Sadoulet 2000 in the context of Latin America). This effect is expected to lower the absolute level of the average growth elasticity of poverty, or to increase poverty independently of income growth and inequality change, or both: the instability of income must thus be introduced both additively and multiplicatively with income growth. Poverty change is the change in the log of the headcount index of poverty. As for the child mortality model, income instability is the standard deviation of the level of income per capita from its trend value estimated by a "mixed" (determinist and stochastic) trend (Guillaumont and Korachais 2006).

The model is tested (in ordinary least squares, as by Adams [2004]) on a sample of 10-year spells of change in poverty (generated from POVCAL data of the World Bank). Moreover the initial level of poverty is controlled for. The results are significant (see table 2). The direct impact of 3 percent income instability in developing countries is to lower by approximately one-third the income elasticity of poverty, and by one-half in only low-income countries. Income instability is also correlated with the increase of inequality: a higher coefficient is obtained without this last variable, which is consistent with the idea that instability increases inequality, as found by Breen and Garcìa-Peñalosa (2005).[14] In addition to its direct impact on poverty, income instability, as seen above, lowers the average rate of growth. Briefly, not only is "growth good for the poor," and stability is good for growth, but stability makes growth better for the poor. Stable growth is pro-poor growth.

How to Measure Structural Vulnerability: Designing an Economic Vulnerability Index

Because structural vulnerability matters for growth and poverty reduction, it is reasonable to take it into account in the formulation of international cooperation policies, which involves the development of a synthetic measurement of vulnerability that is comparable across countries. To design an economic vulnerability index (EVI) to be used for the full set of low-income countries requires that appropriate components reflecting the main structural sources of vulnerability of these countries be chosen, and then, as for any composite index, that an adequate way to aggregate them be found. Because the primary formal attempt to design such an index was done for the purpose of identifying Least Developed Countries (LDCs), this paper also refers to this purpose.

This paper considers a composite index rather than a single one such as *growth volatility*, which has been used in many econometric works. The volatility or instability of the rate of growth of income per capita reflects ex post macroeconomic instability that does depend on exogenous shocks and structural factors of exposure, but also on policy factors, either as a reaction to the shocks or as independently of the shocks. Clear empirical evidence enlightens the influence of policy factors on growth volatility (Combes et al 2000; Easterly, Islam, and Stiglitz 2001).[15] For that reason, growth rate volatility cannot be considered a good synthetic indicator of structural vulnerability. Moreover, the negative impact of shocks on growth does not necessarily involve growth instability, if costly insurance or compensatory mechanisms are at work. In any event, growth volatility is high in developing countries (see table 3), even if it has been declining in the 1990s: it declined significantly from the 1970s to the 1990s in the middle-income developing countries, but was rather stable in the low-income ones, where it is now higher than in the middle-income ones. It is also higher in the LDCs than in the non-LDC low-income countries.

Choosing the Components of a Structural Vulnerability Index

Indicators of structural economic vulnerability must be drawn from the analysis of the shocks likely to affect low-income countries and of their exposure to these

TABLE 3.
Growth Volatility among Developing Countries

Economy type (number)	1970–80	1980–90	1990–2001	1980–2001
Developing (131)				
average	6.22	5.43	4.50	5.40
median	4.50	4.66	3.51	4.67
Low- and middle-income (121)				
average	5.91	5.50	4.57	5.48
median	4.49	4.67	3.51	4.68
Low-income (57)				
average	5.36	5.25	5.43	5.96
median	4.50	4.43	3.99	4.90
Middle-income (64)				
average	6.40	5.72	3.80	5.05
Median	4.38	4.83	3.18	4.59
EIT		(16)	(27)	(16)
average	—	4.59	10.10	7.84
median	—	4.59	8.91	7.79
LDCs (49)				
average	5.98	5.87	5.73	6.39
median	4.50	5.20	3.99	4.98
Low-income non-LDCs (15)				
average	5.46	4.22	3.68	4.54
median	6.17	4.12	3.35	4.66
Oil exporters (25)				
average	8.29	6.12	4.40	5.66
median	8.17	5.92	3.48	5.15

Source: United Nations (calculations made at the UN Department of Economic and Social Affairs for the author). The figures are the standard deviations of the annual rate of growth of GDP per capita.

Note: EIT = Economies in transition. LDCs = Least developed countries.

— Not available.

shocks. The indicators also need to be largely available and reliable. As noted earlier, in 2000 and again in 2003, CDP used an Economic Vulnerability Index (EVI) in its review of the list of LDCs.[16] In March 2005, CDP revised the definition and measurement of EVI, corresponding to a large extent to the principles presented below (and in Guillaumont 2004a, 2004b, forthcoming).

Shock indicators and instability measurement

Climatic and other natural shocks are a main source of vulnerability in many developing countries and cover a large variety of events: earthquakes, typhoons or hurricanes, floods, droughts, insect invasions, and so forth. An indicator of the risk of natural catastrophes might be the frequency of such events, measured over a long period. However, as demonstrated by the December 2004 Asian tsunami, the most severe and exceptional events do not correspond to any measurable probability. The potential negative impact of these very different events differs from one to the next, and even within one kind of event. Measuring the economic losses resulting from these events in all the developing countries concerned seems to be an impossible task. Taking the number of people affected, if it is known, seems to be a better approach, but people may be more or less severely affected. Indicators of the average proportion of the population affected by these events can be used, specific to the way in which the population is affected (killed, displaced) (Atkins, Mazzi, and Ramlogan 1998).[17] The percentage of population displaced due to natural disasters (homeless index) has been retained as a component of EVI only since 2003, when comparable data became available.

Because of this data problem and of the fact that not all natural shocks (as, for instance, recurrent droughts in Sahelian countries) were registered as "disasters," another proxy had to be found—the instability of agricultural production measured with regard to its trend value. Whereas the trend, if significantly measurable, of agricultural production may be supposed to depend mainly on the economic policy pursued and on permanent factors, the fluctuations around the trend may be supposed to reflect the occurrence and severity of natural shocks, because they are likely to affect agricultural production.[18] For these reasons this indicator was retained as a component of the EVI.

The previous two measures of natural shocks, which are not correlated, are only complementary proxies of the size of the natural shocks likely to affect growth prospects (that is, likely to be aggregated in a single average level of natural economic shocks). They give a picture of the average size of past shocks, which is only a proxy of the risk of similar future shocks. The risk of the most severe or exceptional natural shocks, such as the December 2004 Asian tsunami, cannot be captured ex ante by any index of the likelihood of the shock. It can only be reflected ex post in the measures here presented, and more as a durable damage, that is, a structural handicap, than as a risk. This difficulty leads to focusing more on exposure indexes.

An indicator of trade shocks is given by the instability of real export proceeds around its trend. This indicator has to be applied to the total exports of goods and services: shocks affect service exports as well goods exports, and often service exports are a large part of total export receipts in small developing countries. Some private transfers, such as migrant remittances, could also be included. It is assumed that for small countries this instability is structural, resulting from exogenous events (namely, fluctuations in world prices and in external demand), and from domestic events (for instance, climatic shocks) not related to policy. Of course, some fluctuations of export volume around its trend may be due to the instability of policy itself, but it can be supposed that policy influences more the trend than the fluctuations of export volume.

The use of instability indexes as components of a vulnerability indicator raises measurement problems. Instability is always relative to a reference or trend value.

It is measured, for instance, by the average absolute deviation from the reference or the trend value, or more often, by the variance of this deviation. Thus, a critical issue is the choice of this reference value, in particular the estimation of the trend. A deterministic trend has long been assumed (for instance, in the literature on export instability), but was often inappropriate due to the possibility of non-stationarity of the series. However, the series may also not be purely stochastic; thus, the reference value can be conveniently estimated from a "mixed" function, combining a deterministic element and a stochastic element. This is how instabilities of exports and of agricultural production have been estimated in the EVI used by CDP and the method retained in this paper for the next simulations. Several other measures are used in this in the empirical literature on these matters. For instance, measurements of growth volatility generally use the standard deviation of the rate of growth (which may not be appropriate, when the rate of growth is not stationary). Other works on volatility (in particular on aid volatility, considered in the next section) use empirical filters such as the Hodrick-Prescott filter, from which a series is split into "cycle" and "trend" components. In most cases these measures, intended to be internationally comparable, only reflect ex post instabilities—the deviations from a trend observed in the past—not a risk variable perceived by economic agents, which would involve specification of a model of anticipations, possibly differing among countries.

Exposure indicators: population size, output structure, and location

Among the three components of EVI considered to reflect exposure to shocks, the first and least debatable is population size (expressed in logarithm), corresponding to the idea that, other things equal, countries are more vulnerable the smaller they are and, more generally, that small size is a negative determinant of growth. In particular, small population size is considered the main structural factor explaining a high export-to-GDP ratio, and thus, the exposure to trade shocks, and a better indicator of structural exposure than the exports-to-GDP ratio itself, because the latter depends not only on structural but also on policy factors.[19] Small size is also associated with a greater exposure to natural shocks.

A second indicator of exposure included in EVI is the Hirschman export concentration coefficient, as calculated for many years by UNCTAD in its regular *Handbook of Statistics*. Export concentration is indeed supposed to increase the risk of export instability. However, the variable could be given up without loss of useful information. It does not include services, which are a large part of total exports in many countries of interest: no classification of services corresponding to the Standard Industrial Trade Classification (SITC) has been devised. Moreover, the export concentration index is sometimes misleading, such as when it involves breaking down exports of the same kind of product between several SITC categories (without a corresponding decrease in dependence on one kind of product and instability).

A third indicator of exposure to shocks should be related to the structure of production. Until recently, CDP used the share of manufacturing and modern services in GDP (actually 100 minus this share). This indicator, itself inherited from the past, has been usefully replaced by the share of agriculture (including forestry and fisheries) in GDP, for at least three reasons. First, among modern services, tourism increases rather than decreases the exposure to shocks. Second, an increasing international concern surrounds the special exposure to shocks due to agricultural policies in developed countries. Third, because the index is intended to be used for granting preferential treatment, it must not give an advantage to countries benefiting from mineral resources.

Another indicator of exposure, remoteness from the main world markets, can be added, as now used by CDP among the components of EVI. Remoteness involves high transport costs and relative isolation. It is a structural obstacle to trade and growth and a possible source of vulnerability when shocks occur. It reflects a specific handicap of numerous SIDS. It may also be adjusted upward for landlocked countries. Even in the present wave of globalization, distance remains a critical impediment to trade. Several recent papers have demonstrated its persistent influence on trade, an influence even now increasing for low-income countries (see Brun, Guillaumont, and de Melo 1999; Brun et al 2005; Carrère and Schiff 2004). Remoteness or related notions have been considered a possible component in several attempts to build an index of vulnerability.[20] For the purpose of this paper, remoteness is designed as an index of a weighted average of the distance to the main world markets. Relevant weights are the relative shares in world trade of the main world importers, which means identical weights for all countries. So designed, remoteness is the potential average distance to the world market. This weighting is preferable to the relative shares of the different importers (exporters) in each country's exports (imports), which would give for each country an actual average trade distance, because the latter is endogenous: a distant and isolated country may trade relatively little with the largest markets precisely because they are far away.[21] However, because using the (identical) relative share of world markets does not allow differentiating between a country that neighbors one of the largest markets but is far from other large markets (for instance, Mexico) and a country midway between two or more large markets (for instance, Togo), the relevant distance to markets should be better specified as the minimum average distance to reach a minimum size of the world markets (Guillaumont forthcoming). This would be an exogenous measure, but with different weights for each country.

Landlocked countries face higher impediments to trade, with higher transportation costs for a given distance (Limao and Venables 2001; see also Faye et al 2004). This justifies an upward adjustment of the remoteness measure for landlocked countries, but to what extent? An adjustment coefficient can be obtained by estimating the relative marginal impact on the export-to-GDP ratio of the unadjusted remoteness index and a dummy variable for being landlocked. Using this method, it was found that a 10 percent adjustment for being landlocked was an acceptable minimum. Faye et al (2004), when measuring the ratio of freight and insurance to value of exports (but not controlling for distance), evidenced on a regional basis an even higher difference between the average ratios of landlocked and maritime countries. Another way is to compare the coefficients obtained in gravity models of bilateral trade for the log value of the distance and for the dummy variable equal to one for landlocked countries: here the ratio appears to be higher, around 30 percent.

It could be argued that even if remoteness is a structural handicap to growth, it is not necessarily a factor of vulnerability, nor a relevant component of an EVI. However, remoteness may delay the arrival of basic goods when needed, which does increase vulnerability (Encontre 1999). Moreover, because resilience to shocks depends on competitiveness, these higher transportation costs may be seen as a negative structural factor of resilience, limiting the adaptive capacity of the economy when shocks occur. As for landlocked countries, the specific vulnerability due to their location is not only linked to higher transportation costs, but is also associated with several forms of dependence on neighbors (Faye et al 2004).[22] In any event, it has to be recognized that exposure indicators all refer to structural handicaps that influence growth beyond a narrow definition of vulnerability.

Resulting components of a revised EVI

The new EVI then relies on the following components. Three indexes would reflect exogenous shocks: (a) for external shocks, the instability of exports of goods and services; (b) for natural shocks, an average of the instability of agricultural production; and (c) the "homeless" component of the natural disaster index. Three indexes would reflect the structural exposure to shocks: (a) an index of smallness of the (log of the) population size; (b) remoteness from world markets (adjusted for being landlocked); and (c) the relative share of agricultural value-added in GDP (possibly averaged with an export concentration coefficient in an index of structural weakness).

Aggregating the Components: Weighting and Averaging Issues

The weighting and averaging of the component indicators in a composite vulnerability index must be examined to ensure they reflect the meaning of vulnerability.

Arbitrary or revealed weights: vulnerability measured as an expected loss of growth

The simplest and most transparent way to aggregate is, after measuring each component on the same scale depending on maximum and minimum values so they fall between zero and 100, to calculate an unweighted average of these components (as is commonly done for some popular indexes such as the Human Development Index). This weighting is indeed arbitrary, because the actual weight is given by the number of components, which results from the choice of the components themselves. But it may seem reasonable to give equal weight to shock components and to exposure components so that the vulnerability index is an average of a shock index and an exposure index. It is also reasonable to give equal weight to trade shocks and natural shocks. For the exposure index, because the main factor of exposure is the (small) size of the population, it could be given a half weight, the other half being shared between the other components (location and structure). This is the solution used by CDP in March 2005 (with the export concentration coefficient included within the second half of the exposure index).

To avoid the arbitrariness of equal weighting, some measures of vulnerability weight the components by their estimated impact on the rate of growth or on the instability of the rate of growth. For instance, Guillaumont and Chauvet (2001) and Chauvet and Guillaumont (2004) used a set of component indicators to build a composite indicator of vulnerability, with the weights not chosen in advance, but drawn from an econometric regression so they reflect the estimated impact on economic growth of the different component indicators (which is consistent with the definition of vulnerability as a handicap to growth). The resulting vulnerability indicator is the impact on economic growth of the exogenous shocks and exposure variables, all else being equal. It is the estimated loss of growth due to structural vulnerability.[23] It must be recognized that this method of measurement of structural vulnerability, which is dependent on the quality of the regressions, seems more appropriate for academic use than for international policy. Moreover, specific problems arise when aggregating vulnerability indicators, which are now addressed.

Reflecting the interaction between shocks and exposure

Assume the index of economic vulnerability relies on the four following elements: a shock index composed of (a) a trade shock index and (b) a natural shock index; and an exposure index composed of (c) a (low) size index and a (d) "location and structure index." Several averaging methods may be used to combine shocks and exposure indexes. The traditional arithmetic averaging of the four indexes does not distinguish between the two categories of indexes, each index being considered independently of the others. To take into account the fact that structural vulnerability depends on the interaction of shocks and exposure, two other methods of averaging may be considered.

The more illustrative method here is "semi-geometric" averaging. It combines a geometric averaging of the two composite shock and exposure indexes and an arithmetic averaging of the respective components of these shock and exposure indexes: the exogenous shock indexes, because these shocks have independent effects and can be considered substitutes, are arithmetically averaged in an index of the shocks, and an index of the exposure to the shocks is similarly measured as an arithmetic average of the corresponding components—but the two respective indexes of shocks and of exposure to the shocks are geometrically averaged, because shocks and exposure have multiplicative effects. Shocks make a country all the more vulnerable if it is more exposed. Exposure makes a country all the more vulnerable if the shocks are stronger.

Reflecting the increasing marginal impact of vulnerability components

The geometric average of the shock and exposure indexes (EXP and SK, respectively) can be calculated in two ways. One is to calculate

$$EVI = \sqrt{EXP \times SK}$$

The second way would be to assign a higher impact to whichever of the two shock and exposure indexes is the higher, reflecting a possibly increasing marginal impact of these two components, and to calculate

$$EVI = 1 - \sqrt{(1 - EXP)(1 - SK)}$$

The EVI is then calculated from a multiplicative index of low vulnerability. The relevance of this measurement can be illustrated by the 2004 tsunami: because the likelihood of shocks is not easy to assess, it is all the more important to consider very exposed countries as vulnerable, even if the past frequency of the shocks has been low.[24]

Another kind of averaging, which is an intermediate, but also convenient, solution, is to take an arithmetic average of the indexes of the log values of both the shock and exposure components. It allows the various interactions between these elements in the determination of vulnerability to be captured (each component being first measured as a low vulnerability indicator, transformed in log, then taken as one less the index of this log value, so as to reflect a likely increasing marginal impact of factors of vulnerability). The resulting EVI is fully decomposable into each of the four indexes (and their subgrouping in shocks and exposure indexes) (Guillaumont forthcoming). With the semi-geometric average as calculated by the first of the two previous formulas, and as can be seen in figure 1, a decomposition is obtained that does not reflect the possibly higher marginal impact of the higher component; the second formula only leads to a decomposition between low vulnerability components.

Relevance of the Economic Vulnerability Index

A vulnerability index was initially designed and used in 2000 and 2003 for the purpose of LDC identification. A revision, similar to the EVI proposed above, was recommended by CDP in March 2005, accepted by ECOSOC, and retained for the 2006 review of the list of least developed countries.[25] We now examine the relevance of such an index, both with regard to its initial purpose and with the view that a relevant macroeconomic vulnerability indicator may be used in designing aid policies.

Higher average vulnerability of LDCs, regardless of the measure

As seen above, LDCs have a more unstable growth pattern than other low-income countries and than middle-income ones. They are also, according to EVI, regardless of its definition, more vulnerable than other developing countries and in particular than other low-income countries (of course, at the country level the measurements are sensitive to the choice of components and averaging). The average EVI of the 49 LDCs is always significantly higher than that of the 15 other low-income countries (using 2003 data). For instance, with the revised EVI of this paper (and semi-geometric averaging), over the 64 LDCs and other low-income countries, the median rank is 40 for the LDCs and 11 for the other low-income countries. The difference between LDCs and other low-income countries is significant, both for the composite index and

FIGURE 1.
Schematic of Revised EVI

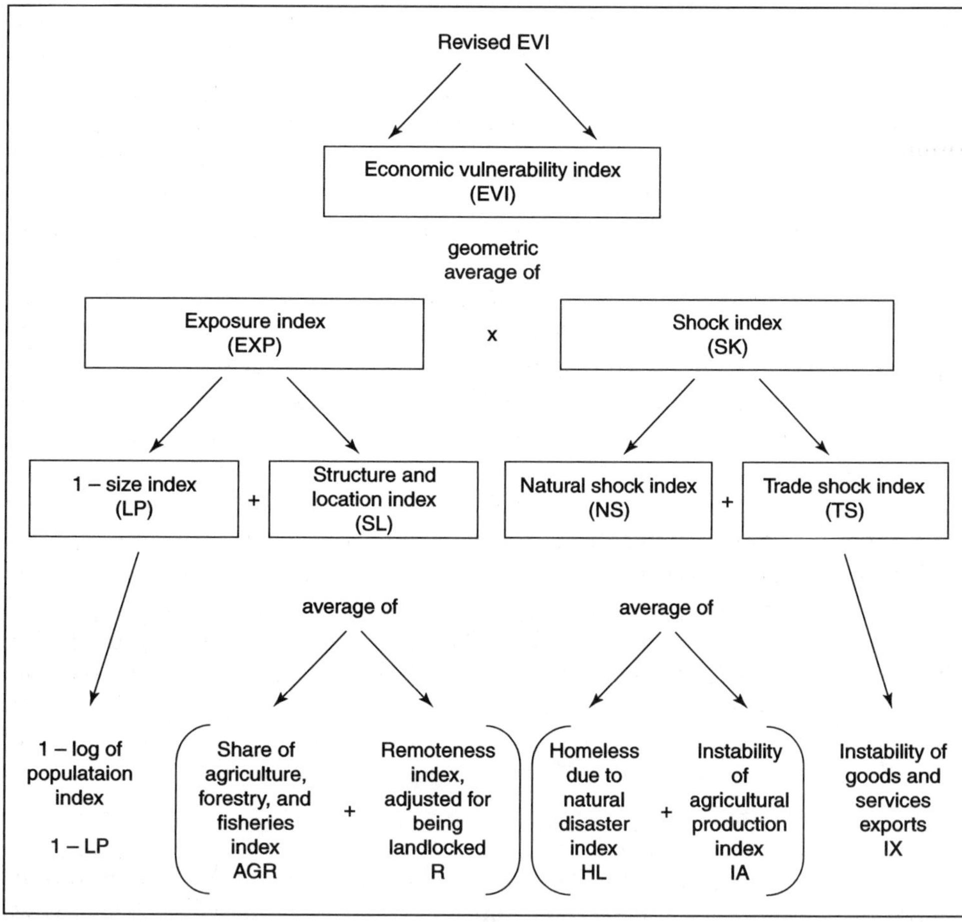

Source: Author.

Note: This figure of a revised EVI has been initially presented in the draft chapter of Guillaumont (forthcoming) and used in a form close to this to present the new EVI agreed upon by CDP in its 2005 report, with slight differences (see note 25 to this paper).

for each of its components: the LDCs have on average a smaller population; a higher remoteness index; a higher share of agriculture, forestry, and fisheries in GDP; a higher export concentration coefficient; a stronger instability of export proceeds, and of agricultural production as well; and a higher "homeless" index. The differences are significant not only with regard to the other low-income countries, but also with regard to the full set of other developing countries.[26]

Sensitivity of indexes to the choice of components and averaging

A rather low correlation between the various components leads to an expectation of significant consequences for the choice of the components and averaging. The impact on EVI of the different choices of components appears when the initial EVI with five components (used by CDP in 2000 and 2003) is compared to the augmented EVI of this paper, but still with arithmetic averaging of the components. The average of absolute country rank difference is rather high, close to 10. The impact of alternative averaging has been measured with the components of the revised EVI of this paper: compared to the arithmetic average, we note a moderate impact of the semi-geometric average, slightly lower than that of the arithmetic average of the log indexes (average absolute rank difference of 4.0 versus 6.1). Both indexes increase the EVI of small countries. Although on the whole the impact of averaging appears rather lower than the impact of the choice of the components, it is not true for all countries, in particular for small islands, as demonstrated by the extreme case of Maldives, the country for which the rank differences between various measures is the highest. In December 2004, Maldives was devastated by the Asian tsunami. The occurrence of the tsunami could hardly have been taken into account ex ante in the shock index components; it will only increase ex post the level of these components and consequently the vulnerability index of Maldives. If a higher impact had been given to the high exposure index of this country, as with semi-geometric averaging of low exposure and low shock indexes, Maldives' level of vulnerability would have been increased ex ante.

EVI as a relevant index to explain lagging growth

The first section surveyed several studies showing the impact of instability on growth under various conditions. A test of the relevance of EVI as an indicator of structural handicap to growth would be to examine whether it is a good predictor of the lack of growth and simultaneously an adequate indicator for the identification of LDCs. An econometric test supports this view: when estimating over 30 years a cross-country GDP per capita growth regression, previous EVI (with the five components recalculated on average for the whole period) was found to be a significant negative factor, in addition to the initial GDP per capita (convergence factor) and the composite human assets index, the low level of which is the other criterion of structural handicap used for LDC identification (Guillaumont forthcoming). The empirical relevance of the revised index was also tested with a smaller sample, due to the lack of data needed to measure the revised EVI over past decades. The result not only is as significant as that obtained with the initial EVI, but, when added, the LDC dummy variable, which remained significant using the initial EVI (and human assets index) was no longer so. This means that the new EVI, more logically grounded, better reflects the vulnerability of the present set of LDCs.

In conclusion, it appears feasible to build an indicator of structural macroeconomic vulnerability relevant for low-income countries. As designed in 2000, recently refined, and possibly to be improved, the EVI used at the UN can be used, in conjunction with an index of human capital, to identify the low-income countries suffering the most from structural handicaps to growth, which may be of interest in the formulation of aid policy.[27]

How Aid Interacts With Vulnerability: Implications for Aid Allocation and Design

If structural economic vulnerability is an obstacle to growth and poverty reduction, it follows that it is a key variable to be considered in the formulation of aid policies, after considering the way in which aid actually contributes to dampening or to enhancing the effects of vulnerability.

Aid Effectiveness and Vulnerability

Aid effectiveness higher in vulnerable countries

The debate initiated by the influential paper by Burnside and Dollar (2000) and the book *Assessing Aid* (World Bank 1998) made clear that aid effectiveness depends on specific features of the recipient country. The focus of Burnside and Dollar (then of Collier and Dollar 2001, 2002) was on the quality of economic policy and of institutions. The resulting message, that priority should be given in aid allocation to countries with "good" policies and institutions, supported a moral sentiment not always grounded on an assessment of aid effectiveness. The debate on the Burnside-Dollar thesis has been mainly related to the robustness of their econometric results, secondarily to the relevance of the underlying hypotheses (see Hansen and Tarp 2001). Two previous papers (Chauvet and Guillaumont 2004; Guillaumont and Chauvet 2001) argued that a major factor conditioning aid effectiveness in recipient countries was the economic vulnerability of those countries. In vulnerable countries, foreign support is highly productive in preventing collapses when shocks occur or in staving off longstanding recessions afterward; support is expected to smooth public expenditure and lower the risk of fiscal deficit. Consequently, the marginal contribution of aid to the growth of recipient countries is expected to be higher the more vulnerable those countries are.

This effect of vulnerability on aid effectiveness was captured in a growth regression by a multiplicative explanatory variable (aid-to-GDP ratio × vulnerability indicator), similar to the variable used by Burnside and Dollar (2000) (aid-to-GDP ratio × policy indicator), and found significantly positive.[28] The measure of the vulnerability variable was not the same in Guillaumont and Chauvet (2001) and Chauvet and Guillaumont (2004). Only Guillaumont and Chauvet (2001) used a concept of vulnerability close to that used for LDC identification, including small population size, export instability, and agricultural production instability. Chauvet and Guillaumont (2004) used a narrower concept, limited to export instability and negative terms of trade trend, but extended the analysis to the impact on aid effectiveness of political instability (a negative effect), of present economic policy (a positive effect), and of previous economic policy (a negative effect, due to the possible effect of aid on policy improvement from a "bad" initial situation, an effect neglected in the standard Burnside-Dollar model). Collier and Dehn (2001) also evidenced the role of aid as a factor dampening export price shocks considered on a year-by-year basis, defined from a forecasting model, and retained only if these shocks were on the tail of the distribution. Although the Collier and Dehn model did not allow measurement of the long-term effect of instability on growth, it made a useful distinction between the effect of a change of aid (found to lower the negative effect of a negative shock), and the effect of the aid level itself (found to increase the positive effect of a positive shock). Finally, Collier and Hoeffler (2004) tested the higher effectiveness of aid in post-conflict situations (which also can be regarded as an expression of vulnerability).[29]

Aid volatility, procyclicality, and destabilizing impact: a misplaced concern?

Recently several papers, followed by political declarations, have underlined the problem raised by aid volatility (Bulíř and Hamann 2003, 2005; Lensink and Morrissey 2000; Pallage and Robe 2001; Rand and Tarp 2002): if aid is unstable, it may contribute to macroeconomic instability, thus becoming another factor of vulnerability. This concern has been reinforced by the prospect of an acceleration of disbursements that cannot be sustained in the future. Indeed, aid is volatile at the recipient level, although not at the donor level. Measured by a cycle component with regard to a trend drawn from a Hodrick-Prescott filter, the volatility of aid, measured over 1970–99 on six five-year subperiods, is equal on average to 8.8 percent. This volatility is often compared (at the country level) to that of domestic aggregates, most often tax revenue (curiously through a ratio of the two instabilities rather than a difference, which may lead to enormous ratios when the reference aggregate is fairly stable). Beyond the nonnegligible measurement problems, criticism of aid volatility may be misplaced if aid has a compensatory profile, which could be be consistent with the finding that aid is more effective in more vulnerable countries. In that case, aid volatility would be a solution rather than a problem.

Therefore, the volatility of aid is not so much to be criticized as is its unpredictability and its procyclicality. Unpredictability of aid is certainly harmful, but is difficult to assess. An assessment of the unpredictability of aid would require a forecasting model of aid at the recipient level, where the predicted level depends, among other factors, on the kind of aid delivered and on the shocks precipitating its disbursal. Procyclicality is easier to assess. It appears not to be the rule, not even in the majority of cases, as is sometimes asserted. The procyclical character of aid can be measured by the correlation between the "cycle" of aid (that is, its deviation from its trend) and the "cycle" of the aggregate to which aid is compared. A usual comparison is with tax revenue, to examine the effect of aid instability on public budget stability. In this paper, the preference is to compare the aid cycle to that of exports. Because the concern is with macroeconomic vulnerability, it is more relevant to compare aid with the aggregate most likely to be affected by exogenous shocks: tax revenue is influenced by the overall impact of exports, as well as by aid. Moreover, all aid flows are not channelled through the public budget. We here consider as a reference flow exports of goods and services, but not international capital flows, the volatility of which may exacerbate the consequences of trade shocks in middle-income countries, as in the case of Chile (Caballero 2002): extending the reference flow to capital movements seems less relevant for low-income countries. In emerging economies, the issue is less the procyclicality of aid than of capital flows (underlined by Kaminsky, Reinhart, and Végh 2004).

Using the Hodrick-Prescott filter and considering more than 100 developing countries for the period 1960–99 (465 observations on five-year averages), the country correlation between the cycle of net aid disbursements and the cycle of exports of goods and services appears to be nearly as often negative as positive (222 cases versus 243, Chauvet and Guillaumont 2006): this means that aid is not clearly procyclical. The evolution (on a varying sample, because data do not cover all countries over the whole period) demonstrates that only in the 1980s was aid on average clearly more often procyclical. Furthermore, in the majority of cases the correlation coefficients on which the comparison relies are not significant: for a large set of 115 countries the correlation during the 1990s has been found significant in only 13 positive cases and 13 negative cases[30] (Chauvet and Guillaumont 2006).

Counter- or procyclicality is indeed an important parameter. But it is not the only relevant one in determining whether aid inflow is stabilizing or destabilizing. Procyclical aid can still be stabilizing (on the total aid plus export flow) if its volatility, expressed in relative terms, is lower than the volatility of exports. There may also be cases where aid is countercyclical and destabilizing, when its volatility is significantly higher than that of exports, in a proportion depending on the relative level of aid and exports.[31] What is the real picture? To assess the stabilizing character of aid, an index was constructed that is the difference between the instability (volatility) of exports and that of the aid plus exports flow: if the difference is positive, aid is stabilizing; if it is negative, aid is destabilizing. On average, it has been stabilizing and more clearly so during the 1990s than during the previous periods: the average of the indicator (the difference between the value of the two volatilities) may seem low (0.016 over 1970–99), but it represents 18 percent of the average value of the volatility of exports (28 percent for a subsample of African countries). In the majority of cases in which aid was procyclical, it was, however, stabilizing (214 cases among 243, and it was destabilizing in only 29 cases). When aid was countercyclical, it was, as expected, generally stabilizing (218 cases out of 222, and destabilizing in 4 exceptional other ones). On the whole, aid was destabilizing in less than one-tenth of cases.

To summarize, aid volatility is high, but is a matter of concern only if it is destabilizing, which occurs in a minority of cases, more likely when it is procyclical rather than countercyclical. The stabilizing impact of aid also depends on the relative volatility and on the relative level of aid and the other flows to which aid is compared.

Aid stabilizing impact and aid effectiveness: an augmented model

Does the fact that on average aid has been more stabilizing than destabilizing explain why aid is more effective in more vulnerable economies? This issue can be addressed by relying on a model similar to those already used in the papers where vulnerability appears as a determinant of higher aid effectiveness (Guillaumont and Chauvet 2001; Chauvet and Guillaumont 2004). Again, an index of aid "stabilizing impact" is used, built with reference to exports, considering only the instability of exports as the main source of instability. In this case, the instability and the stabilizing impact are measured with regard to trends drawn from an econometric adjustment (mixed,

TABLE 4.
Aid, Export Instability, and Per Capita Income Growth

	GMM-SYSTEM		
Ln income per capita, time	**(1)**	**(2)**	**(3)**
Ln income per capita, t-5	0.968***	0.969***	0.961***
	(0.000)	(0.000)	(0.000)
ICRG rating (100 = low risk; 0 = high risk)	0.007**	0.007**	0.008***
	(0.025)	(0.019)	(0.008)
Instability of exports	–0.011**	–0.008**	–0.007
	(0.037)	(0.028)	(0.139)
ODA/GNI	–0.389	–0.228	–0.373
	(0.189)	(0.231)	(0.136)
ODA/GNI × Instability of exports	0.045**		0.026
	(0.049)		(0.407)
Instability of exports – Instability of exports + aid		0.016°	0.005
		(0.109)	(0.790)
Dummy 1980–4	–0.110***	–0.104***	–0.104***
	(0.000)	(0.000)	(0.000)
Dummy 1985–9	–0.110***	–0.100***	–0.094***
	(0.000)	(0.000)	(0.000)
Dummy 1990–4	–0.171***	–0.162***	–0.153***
	(0.000)	(0.000)	(0.000)
Dummy 1995–9	–0.186***	–0.177***	–0.183***
	(0.000)	(0.001)	(0.000)
Constant	0.144	0.067	0.088
	(0.553)	(0.767)	(0.650)
Observations	304	304	304
Countries	79	79	79
F-test	0.000	0.000	0.000
AR(1) (*p*-value)[a]	0.000	0.000	0.000
AR(2) (*p*-value)[b]	0.883	0.522	0.546
Sargan (*p*-value)[c]	0.471	0.517	0.453
Number of instruments	63	66	77

Source: Chauvet and Guillaumont 2006.

Note: Second-step GMM-SYSTEM estimations, corrected for small-sample bias (Windmeijer 2000). *p*-values in parentheses. ICRG = International Country Risk Guide. GNI = gross national income. ODA = official development assistance.

° significant at 15 percent level

* significant at 10 percent level

** significant at 5 percent level

*** significant at 1 percent level

a. AR(1) p value refers to Arellano Bond test for autoregressive correlations (order 1).

b. AR(2) p value refers to Arellano Bond test for autoregressive correlations (order 2).

c. Sargan test is a test of overidentification restrictions.

that is, with both a deterministic and a stochastic component), as is generally done in the tests of the negative effects of export instability referred to previously. First, a baseline model was tested (table 4) where the rate of growth depends on, in addition to traditional control variables (log of initial income per capita, quality of institutions measured by the International Country Risk Guide), the following variables of interest (the expected sign of coefficient is in parentheses): the aid-to-GNI ratio (+), the instability of exports (–), and a variable multiplicative of the two previous ones (+). The model is estimated using the GMM system over 1975–99 with five four-year periods related to 89 recipient countries (and checked in GMM difference). All the coefficients have the expected sign (column 1 in table 4), and all are significant, except the aid-to-GNI ratio. The results support the hypothesis that aid lowers the negative impact of instability and is more effective in more vulnerable countries. Then (in column 2 of table 4) we replace in an alternative model the multiplicative variable (aid ratio × export instability) with the stabilizing impact of aid (that is, the difference instability of exports minus instability of exports plus aid"), which also appears to be significant (but at only the 11 percent level). Because these two alternative variables are highly correlated, they are not simultaneously significant (column 3 of table 4). (See more details in Chauvet and Guillaumont 2006.)

Recall that the previous effects are effects on average growth. The stabilizing or destabilizing impact of aid has other effects, both static and dynamic. Without any impact on growth, as argued by Pallage, Robe, and Bérubé (2004), foreign aid has the potential to increase welfare by a simple reallocation of flows across time. Moreover, because, as argued above, instability makes growth less "good for the poor," aid may contribute to the reduction of poverty beyond its effect on average growth, when it has a stabilizing impact. These results have implications for aid policy.

Aid Policy in the Face of Vulnerability

Three main lessons for aid policies, perhaps of decreasing importance, can be drawn from the previous analysis. First, vulnerability must be taken into account in the design of aid selectivity. Second, aid needs to be examined for potential use as insurance. Third, how aid can be targeted with a view toward lowering the structural vulnerability of low-income countries needs to be considered. In all three lessons, special attention must be focused on LDCs, which are more vulnerable than other low-income countries (a recent review of responses to terms-of-trade shocks can be found in Varangis et al 2004).

Vulnerability as a Criterion of Aid Selectivity: A Case for LDCs

An important debate recently emerged on the guiding principles of selectivity in aid allocation. In line with the Burnside and Dollar (2000) and Collier and Dollar (2001, 2002) approaches, it has been argued that selectivity must essentially rely on the extent of poverty and the quality of governance of the recipient countries. The supposed rationale is that the aim of aid is to minimize the number of poor in the world, that poverty reduction essentially depends on growth, and that the growth effectiveness of aid essentially depends on the quality of policy, institutions, and governance. A clear illustration of this position is given in the 2004 and 2005 IMF/World Bank *Global Monitoring Reports* (World Bank 2004, 2005) in material relying on a paper by Dollar and Levin (2004): an index of selectivity is built for each donor, which is the average of its aid elasticity to policy (measured by the Country Policy and Institutional Assessment [CPIA]) and the negative of its aid elasticity to income per capita. Vulnerability does not appear in this quantitative analysis of selectivity (nor in other more refined analyses such as that of Roodman [2004b]), which raises two problems.

The first is that structural economic vulnerability, as discussed above, is just as important a determinant of aid effectiveness as policy, institutions, or governance, as reflected by CPIA ratings. Thus, to make aid on the whole more effective, aid selectivity has to include among its criteria the structural economic vulnerability of developing countries. From this perspective, the availability of the revised EVI, transparent and agreed upon at the UN, may appear useful.

The second problem raised by the omission of vulnerability from the design of selectivity is related to the aim of aid. Aid may reasonably aim at promoting equality of chance, corresponding to the view of Rawls justice (Cogneau and Naudet 2004; Llavador and Roemer 2001). If we look for the equality of chance among nations to reduce poverty (through growth), structural handicaps to growth must be compensated for, at least partly, and be included in selectivity criteria. This is an additional reason to retain vulnerability as a criterion, not only in addition to other factors of aid effectiveness, as argued above, but also in addition to other structural handicaps, the main one being a low level of human capital. From that perspective, the preference officially given in aid allocation to LDCs—identified as the low-income countries suffering the most from structural handicaps, in particular from vulnerability—seems legitimate.

To illustrate the change brought to the assessment of selectivity when vulnerability is taken into account, it is enlightening to compare the index of selectivity as calculated by Dollar and Levin (2004) and used in *Global Monitoring Report 2004* (World Bank 2004) and *Global Monitoring Report 2005* (World Bank 2005) with a similar index relying on other sets of criteria, including vulnerability, measured by the EVI as defined and recently revised at the UN (Amprou, Guillaumont, and Guillaumont Jeanneney 2005). The aid elasticities are estimated for each donor from an allocation function (of gross 2003 official development assistance) between developing countries using as explanatory variables the indicators retained as selectivity criteria. Three variants are estimated including, in addition to GNI per capita, either a governance index[32] or EVI or both of these two last indexes as well as the human assets index used for LDC identification. The ranking of the 22 Organisation for Economic Co-operation and Development donors according to their "aid selectivity" changes radically when different criteria are used. Compared with the rankings established by Dollar and Levin (2004), we observe a large average absolute value of rank differences, reaching 7.6, when using EVI as a criterion instead of CPIA (table 5).

TABLE 5.
Aid Elasticities Measured Using Two Models of Geographical Aid Allocation

	(1) Income per capita	(2) EVI	(3) Average [(2)-(1)]/2	(4) Rank	(5) Rank Dollar and Levin, 2002	(6) Différence between ranks
Australia	0.425	3.025	1.300	6	16	–10
Austria	–0.118	1.019	0.569	18	6	12
Belgium	–0.605	2.033	1.319	5	8	–3
Canada	0.263	1.603	0.670	15	14	1
Denmark	–0.609	1.772	1.191	7	1	6
Finland	–0.106	1.187	0.647	16	7	9
France	–0.077	1.331	0.704	13	20	–7
Germany	–0.528	–0.760	–0.116	21	11	10
Greece	0.549	2.595	1.023	8	21	–13
Ireland	–0.470	3.457	1.964	2	10	–8
Italy	–0.318	1.139	0.729	12	17	–5
Japan	0.780	0.793	0.007	20	13	7
Luxembourg	0.019	3.852	1.917	3	9	–6
Netherlands	–1.085	0.443	0.764	11	4	7
New Zealand	0.720	4.525	1.903	4	18	–14
Norway	–0.976	0.945	0.961	9	5	4
Portugal	0.467	6.150	2.842	1	19	–18
Spain	0.179	–0.286	–0.233	22	22	0
Sweden	–0.869	1.020	0.945	10	3	7
Switzerland	–0.627	0.729	0.678	14	12	2
United Kingdom	–0.736	0.468	0.602	17	2	15
United States	–0.718	0.357	0.538	19	15	4

Source: Amprou, Guillaumont, and Guillaumont Jeanneney 2005.

Note: Average of absolute value of rank differences: 7.6.

Aid as Insurance: How to Make Compensatory Finance Effective

Because aid is more effective (as well as welfare enhancing) when it is stabilizing, there is some advantage to making it more stabilizing. This role for aid is all the more important if there is little room to reduce the size of shocks, including international commodity price shocks. As the experiment of the international commodity price agreements has shown, it is difficult to smooth efficiently the evolution of world prices. A need for insurance thus appears at two levels. As seen above, at the macroeconomic level, shocks affect macroeconomic variables; in particular, they are deleterious for public budget management and, because they are increasingly passed through to producers, have strong microeconomic consequences. Low-income countries, to some extent differing from middle-income countries, are not in a position to manage their external trade shocks through the insurance instruments available on the market. Moreover, their public external debt is mainly toward public bilateral donors or international institutions. Hence, this paper does not consider how international institutions can offer insurance to emerging countries facing financial crisis and capital outflows, as proposed by Caballero (2002). But we confront two issues common to any macro insurance scheme: how to deliver resources on time, and how to ensure that insurance promotes rather than halts needed reforms (see Cordella and Levy Yeyati 2004).

The idea of offering aid to developing countries to compensate for the negative shocks they face is not new. The Compensatory Finance Facility was established over 40 years ago, in 1963.[33] The Stabex was created 30 years ago with the Lomé Convention (1975), and replaced in the Cotonou Agreement (2000) by a new facility, the Fluctuations of Export scheme, or Flex. This long but only partially successful experiment precisely enlightens the conditions necessary to implement effective insurance schemes supported by official development assistance (ODA). The emphasis here is on Stabex, more thoroughly examined elsewhere (Collier et al 1999). Stabex (a European scheme of compensation for shortfalls in specific agricultural exports due to international prices or to export volume) was set up with two innovative but somewhat contradictory principles: it was both intended to be automatic and to be targeted toward compensation of agricultural sectors affected by export shortfall. For this reason from one Convention to another under the pressure of European countries, control of the European Commission over the use of Stabex funds was strengthened at the cost of greater and greater delays in disbursements; this turn of events eliminated any countercyclical use of funds, without guaranteeing that the farmers affected by the shortfall would be genuinely compensated. This loss of Stabex automaticity was reinforced by the fact that the resources allocated to the mechanism repeatedly fell short of the mark—an outcome of a poor understanding of the cyclical and long-term components of export shortfalls: the calculation of the shortfalls, which used an arithmetic mean of past values, led to an underestimation of the shortfalls whenever the shortfalls occurred following an upward trend (the most frequent situation in the 1970s) and an overestimation following a downward trend (as was the case for many products in the 1980s and even in the 1990s). The new Flex of the Cotonou Agreement has not really addressed the issues raised by Stabex, but is designed such that it could do so.

An insurance scheme should be credible, which first means having adequate resources; allow quick disbursements to be truly compensatory; and induce right incentives to avoid moral hazard. Thus, an insurance scheme needs to take into account positive as well as negative shocks, and to address the issue of instability rather than only the issue of shortfall. Such a scheme could be designed along the following lines.

First, insurance should be considered a contract: it offers a guarantee conditioned by rules. The international community cannot content itself with stressing the importance of sound domestic macroeconomic management over the entire cycle for purposes of dampening shocks, because instability makes the conduct of economic policy more difficult. The role of the international community in response to shocks could be to act to provide insurance and to promote sound management simultaneously.

The general idea is that the international community could help to introduce automatic stabilization mechanisms by financing the costs of these mechanisms subject to the prior adoption of agreed on and controllable management rules. In short, the international community would offer a guarantee in exchange for a commitment to rules. This principle can be applied on a macroeconomic scale and on a microeconomic or sectoral scale.

Second, debt service can be adjusted in response to shocks, so that aid can be quickly delivered and so that smoothing might cover ups as well as downs.[34] A now-frequent proposal is to tie the way debt is treated to developments in commodity export prices. Easing debt service when prices are low and raising it when prices are high exerts a countercyclical effect on public finances: the easing of external debt service makes it possible to maintain other domestic expenditures despite the decline in tax receipts induced by the drop in export earnings, while increasing debt service in a period of spiking prices prevents a destabilizing increase in public expenditure that would be difficult to reverse. Such a system could be put in place for any country that wanted it and would undertake to increase debt service in the event of commodity price increases. A problem to be resolved is the introduction of a financial mechanism making it possible to scale back debt service automatically while ensuring that creditors share the cost equitably. Conceivably, a multilateral rescheduling fund could be introduced to this end, which would be funded by the surplus debt service received from debtor countries benefiting from high prices as well as from an initial endowment from bilateral and multilateral donors and lenders. One important question, not possible to examine here, concerns the modalities for modulating debt cost—should the mechanism be interest payments or amortization payments? Note that the proposal may also apply to the occurrence of natural disasters.

Countries eligible for the Highly Indebted Poor Countries (HIPC) Initiative, which are particularly dependent on commodity exports, could find this new mechanism interesting even though they are benefiting from debt cancellation. The objective of the HIPC Initiative is to reduce the ratio of debt-to-exports to 150 percent when the completion point has been reached. However, the analysis of the sustainability of that debt level assumes that exports will expand at a given rate, without any explicit provision being made to adjust the debt and debt service levels in light of export price developments.

Third, low-income countries not qualified for HIPC relief should be offered a similar scheme. This type of proposal should not mask the reality that other countries, while not heavily indebted, remain extremely dependent on their commodity exports and subject to significant price shocks (and natural shocks as well). It would be paradoxical for a new international initiative intended to address such shocks not to take such countries into account or to exclude them for the simple reason that they are not heavily indebted. The logical response would then be for automatic assistance in loan form to be extended to them in the event of price drops, indexed on commodity prices, or in grant form beyond a certain threshold of price declines, subject to the sole condition that the country undertake to limit the growth of its public expenditure during periods of high prices. The country would thus be prompted to set aside a portion of the gains registered when prices are high to maintain its spending levels when prices decline, to the extent such drops are not offset by the international community. This would thus play the role of insurance and constitute an incentive for self-insurance. It should be possible to mobilize the resources necessary for a new mechanism for automatic assistance insofar as it would be limited to LDCs.

Fourth, macroeconomic and sectoral supports must be interconnected. Because instability has unfavorable effects at both the macroeconomic and sectoral levels, it is logical for the mechanisms to be designed to remedy the effects of instability at each of these levels. That is, if aid is to be used as insurance at the macro level in low-income countries, it would be useful to link this support with the promotion of insurance schemes, possibly private, at the sectoral or micro level. This holds both for natural disaster insurance, as examined by Dayton-Johnson (2004), and for price shocks. The focus here is on mechanisms aimed at attenuating the effects of price instability in the agricultural sector. The intensity with which international price instability is transmitted to exporters and agricultural producers depends on the tax and parafiscal policies of the government for agricultural exports. In the absence of such levies, price changes are transmitted in their entirety, which does not preclude an influence on general tax receipts owing to the impact of price changes on national income. In the case of levies that are proportional to the value of exports and constant, the direct income gain or loss is shared by the government and the sector, which may result in greater producer price instability than international price instability if marketing costs are rigid. Naturally, by modifying its tax rates, the government changes the conditions under which gains or losses are divided between itself and the stakeholders in the sector. For this reason, external support for a policy aimed at using insurance mechanisms to reduce the risks incurred by producers owing to price variability must ensure that it does not constitute a pretext for a greater transfer of risk from the government to producers. In other words, it must be accompanied by fiscal conditionality.

The international community could assist with establishing insurance mechanisms for agricultural producers in low-income countries who currently find them out of reach owing to their cost. The external support should both cover a portion of the costs of managing the options and guarantee the financing of the possible gap between the option exercise price and the producer price corresponding to the international price at the time the export product is sold. Details are given in Collier et al 1999 (see also Sarris 2003). The advantage of this solution is that the sale of options could be managed by private operators. Moreover, it could be associated with insurance on the volume of harvests.

This highlights the objective of reducing the variability of the prices paid to producers, notwithstanding the flaws in the operation of former stabilization funds. Conceivably, the international community could provide its support to guarantee funds whose operations would meet two key conditions, not met in the past, that pertain to the flexibility of the reference price and the placement of the monetary assets involved. The price guaranteed to the producer should be calculated on the basis of an international price that is gradually adjusted toward the international market trend. The cash assets of the guarantee fund, built up both by contributions from producers during periods of high prices and by international assistance, should be managed by a body that is independent of the government and preferably has an international status or is the property of producers. These funds would thus be beyond the government's reach, which is necessary to ensure the credibility of the system and would make it possible to use the funds countercyclically.

Fifth, long-term signals must not be blurred. The compensatory purpose is related to short- or medium-term fluctuations around long-term trends against which no automatic insurance can be offered. This holds, of course, for the reference export or import price to be used in debt indexation, as well as for the producer price. The past trend, whatever its kind, must be used both to avoid shortage of finance and wrong incentives at the macro and micro level. This same caveat applies to the possible calculation of a volume reference.

Structural Vulnerability Reduction as Aid Target

Implementing aid as insurance is supposed to enhance the resilience of low-income countries to shocks. As has been presented here, insurance is closely linked to the management of shocks. Is there a role for aid to help a country lower its exposure to exogenous shocks? Or even the likelihood of such shocks? Many answers are possible, but they may be more or less effective. Project or sector support confronts the problem of fungibility. Moreover, if the objective is to diversify, support is a long-term answer, and diversification is to a large extent endogenous (diversification results from development, rather than causes it [Imbs and Wacziarg 2003]); otherwise diversification is costly and its cost has to be compared to the expected benefits of lower vulnerability. Other aid responses, at a regional or global level, may be effective. One response might be to support regional integration, an underestimated tool for reducing structural vulnerability. Another is to finance research on the prevention (or the assessment of risks) of natural disaster and climatic shocks (including research on resistant agricultural varieties). Finally, developed countries have a major responsibility in lowering the sources of instabilities both through macroeconomic management and agricultural policies. In the present global economy, adequate responses to shocks occurring in emerging economies, not considered in this paper, may also contribute to lowering the vulnerability of low-income countries.

Conclusion

This paper attempts to underline the importance of structural vulnerability for low-income countries, in particular for LDCs, where structural vulnerability is significantly higher than in other developing countries. Structural vulnerability weakens policy. It lowers growth. It discriminates against the poor.

At the macroeconomic level, several analytical issues remain unsolved, the main ones following: The difference between ex ante and ex post effects of vulnerability is not well documented. Threshold effects have not been thoroughly investigated (vulnerability might only matter above some threshold). Pass-through mechanisms are crucial and may have changed over time. Finally, the macroeconomic links between macro vulnerability and poverty, suggested above, must be explored with the help of micro and macro country case studies.

The implications for aid policy can be briefly summarized: First, aid selectivity principles have to be revisited so that vulnerability becomes one of the main criteria, both because it increases aid effectiveness and because it is a structural handicap to growth; thus it legitimately should be compensated for, at least partly, by the international community. This is a good reason to make more use of the LDC category, which precisely identifies those among the low-income countries suffering the most from structural handicaps, in particular from vulnerability. Second, aid can be used as insurance in a new conditionality framework, where a guarantee is offered under the condition that some rules of shock management are ex ante agreed on. Finally, and more difficult, decreasing the size of shocks and the exposure of low-income countries remains in multiple policy areas a matter to consider, with regard to costs and benefits: actions at the regional level may be among the most promising.

Notes

1. A similar decomposition has been used to study the transmission of cycles from one area to another one (Guillaumont 1985), the three components being sensitivity, dependence, and receptivity.
2. The concept of resilience is mainly used in works more specifically oriented toward the environmental or natural sources of vulnerability (Kaly et al 1999), and in some cases about macroeconomic vulnerability (Briguglio and Kisanga 2004). A distinction close to the previous one can be found in Rodrik (1999) who, looking for the risk of social conflict in countries facing external shocks, considered separately the severity of the shocks, the depth of latent social conflict (likely to increase the impact of the shocks), and the quality of conflict management institutions.
3. Consider, for instance, a small country that is a primary commodity exporter. Its vulnerability to trade shocks results first from world price fluctuations, reflected by the instability of its terms of trade, second from the exposure to the shocks expressed by the ratio of commodities export to GDP, and third from the capacity of the country to efficiently manage such shocks. The size of the shocks (its export price instability) for a price-taker small country is clearly an exogenous determinant of instability. The resilience, or the capacity to manage instability, clearly depends on the policy pursued. The exposure to the shocks is more ambiguous: it is mainly a structural factor, but to some extent it is also dependent on policy and all the more so if the period considered is longer.
4. At first glance *vulnerability* (with regard to growth) may appear simply as the opposite of the *sustainability* of growth, a concept even more extensively used: the more vulnerable a country, the less sustainable its growth, all other things equal. But the sustainability of growth not only negatively depends on the vulnerability to shocks, but also results from other and permanent factors, such as the rate of human and physical capital accumulation, and natural resources preservation.

5. We have distinguished risk and ratchet effects of export instability in previous papers (Guillaumont 1987, 1994).
6. See, for instance, Bleaney and Greenaway 2001; Combes and Guillaumont 2002; Dawe 1996; Fosu 1992, 2002; Glezakos 1984; Guillaumont 1994; Guillaumont et al 1999; Gyimah-Brempong 1991; Lutz 1994; Mendoza 1997; and the review of the literature by Araujo Bonjean, Combes, and Combes Motel 1999.
7. Actually the aim of Miguel, Satyanath, and Sergenti (2004) was to test the impact of negative growth shocks on the likelihood of civil conflict, and only use rainfall variations as an instrumental variable for economic growth.
8. Growth regressions on instability or vulnerability indicators either include or exclude the rate of investment in addition to other control variables. When the rate of investment (investment-to-GDP ratio) is included, the coefficient of the instability or vulnerability indices only express their impact on the growth residual, whereas when it is excluded, the coefficient is assumed to assess their total effect, both through the rate of investment and the growth of factor productivity.
9. Similar results about the effects of export instabilities were found by Guillaumont (1994) and Dawe (1996), who underline the effects through the growth residual rather than through the rate of investment. These instabilities are "weighted" by the export-to-GDP ratio.
10. Because natural shocks or disasters generally concern some specific groups of the population, the larger the population, the smaller the aggregate exposure: in a large country, climatic shocks are likely to affect only a small part of the population.
11. Even the assumption of a negative correlation between population size and linguistic fragmentation is debatable: when fragmentation is explained both by the population size and the geographic area, the coefficient of population size is significantly negative, while that of area is (significantly) positive. Because the absolute value of the coefficients are similar, it means that fragmentation decreases with population density (internal work in process at CERDI).
12. The greater social cohesion of small islands is also debated by Helleiner (1996).
13. The specific impact of structural vulnerability is demonstrated when export instability and agricultural production instability are used instead of income volatility as explanatory variables.
14. We have also estimated another model in a panel form, with a slightly different assumption—that the level of previous instability (as an additive variable) influences the level of rather than the change in poverty. Alternative specifications are presented in Guillaumont and Korachais (2006).
15. For instance, Easterly et al (2001) have stressed the negative effect (up to a point) of financial depth and the positive effect of openness on volatility. More specifically, concerning the effects of openness, Combes et al (2000) find first that structural vulnerability (depending on structural factors, including population size) makes growth more unstable, whereas outward-looking policy makes it more stable. Bleaney and Fielding (2002) also examine the impact of the exchange rate regime on output volatility, in addition to the impact of exogenous factors such as the instability of the terms of trade.
16. The EVI was measured from five components, with a sixth one used in 2003 for a supplementary measure: (1) small population size (in log); (2) small share of manufacturing and modern services in GDP; (3) merchandise export concentration coefficient; (4) instability of exports of goods and services; (5) instability of agricultural production; and optionally (6) "homeless"—share of population displaced by natural disasters.
17. The main source of the data was the Emergency Events Database, compiled by the Center for Research on Epidemiology of Disaster (CRED) at the School of Public Health,

Université Catholique de Louvain; data is also given and supplemented in the International Red Cross annual *World Disasters Report.* Relying on these data, a picture of natural disasters in each LDC can be found in UNDP (2001).

18. This indicator was used in several previous works (for instance, Guillaumont and Guillaumont 1988; Guillaumont, Guillaumont Jeanneney, and Brun 1999).

19. The exports-to-GDP ratio has, however, been used in several attempts to measure economic vulnerability (for instance, Atkins, Mazzi, and Ramlogan 1998; Briguglio 1995; Crowards 1999; Easter 1998).

20. For instance, Briguglio (1995) retains "remoteness" or "peripherality" proxied by the ratio of the cost of insurance and freight to the import value as a component of his vulnerability index. Easter (1998), following Atkins, Mazzi, and Ramlogan (1998) considered this measurement without retaining it in the final calculation. Limao and Venables (2001) also use this measure, but as a proxy of transport costs, so not specifically for remoteness. The reliability and coverage of this proxy of remoteness is actually under debate.

21. For the same reason, independently of its low reliability and frequent inconsistency, the average ratio of the gap between the f.o.b. value of export and the c.i.f. value of the corresponding imports is not an appropriate measure of "remoteness."

22. Other geographical features can influence economic vulnerability, in particular to natural disasters. One of them, tragically demonstrated by the Asian tsunami, appears to be the location of population in areas at very low altitude, close to sea level. Populations living close to volcanoes as well as those living in areas prone to earthquakes also appear exceptionally vulnerable. A vulnerability index cannot really capture the risk of exceptional shocks, but only the risk of shocks likely to have some frequency (thus some probability) and hence likely to be considered a structural handicap to growth.

23. Another example of an econometric weighting is given by the Commonwealth Secretariat index of vulnerability (Atkins, Mazzi, and Ramlogan 1998; Easter 1998). This index is an estimated value of instability of the rate of growth, with three explanatory variables empirically chosen from among many (more than fifty), which reflect policy factors as well as structural factors. One main problem with this indicator is that it measures vulnerability with regard to growth volatility, which, as noted previously, is not a good synthetic indicator of structural vulnerability because it depends on policy factors as well as structural ones. An alternative method would be to consider a "natural growth volatility" estimated from a regression including only structural factors, not depending on policy, as the components of EVI are supposed to be. But such a measure would not be preferable to the estimation of the impact on growth of the structural vulnerability components: structural vulnerability has been designed with reference to growth, and would be better measured by a loss of growth than by excess volatility.

24. It would indeed be conceivable to weight the respective shock indicators by corresponding exposure indicators. In other words, each indicator of the size of the shocks could be weighted by an indicator of the exposure assumed to correspond to the shocks, and the aggregate index of vulnerability could be decomposed in vulnerability sub-indices related to each kind of shock. But there is no simple correspondence between shock and exposure indicators, for instance, small size economies appear to be more exposed to natural shocks, not only to trade shocks (Maldives, for example). Thus, it seems easier and more relevant to weight the average shock index by the average exposure index.

25. See United Nations (2005). There are two differences between the CDP's EVI and that proposed in this paper: first, the CDP EVI still includes the export concentration index as a component; second, the CDP EVI does not indicate any kind of averaging, and is actually measured by an arithmetic average.

26. All information in this paragraph is based on Guillaumont (forthcoming).

27. The estimated model was specified as follows: Growth = f [log initial income per capita, log(100–human assets index), log EVI, Dummy LDC]. This log specification, suggesting a mutual reinforcement of the two kinds of structural handicaps retained as criteria of LDC identification, gave by far the best result: it thus supported to some extent the principle according to which these criteria are treated as complementary.
28. This was not the case, however, in Guillaumont and Chauvet (2001) for the aid times policy variable.
29. Moreover, Roodman (2004b) presents a thorough assessment of the econometric robustness of various papers, confirming the relative robustness of the results of Guillaumont and Chauvet (2001) (Chauvet and Guillaumont [2004] was not analyzed). The Guillaumont and Chauvet results are found to be more robust than those by Collier and Dehn, themselves more robust (for the effect of aid change) than those of Burnside and Dollar, but less robust than the results of Hansen and Tarp, who do not address the vulnerability issue.
30. At a 15 percent threshold.
31. The arithmetic condition is that in one year the absolute value of the ratio of the relative cycles must exceed one by twice the ratio of exports to aid.
32. This exercise used the Kaufmann, Kraay, and Mastruzzi (2003) governance index instead of the CPIA used by Dollar and Levin (2004), which was not available outside World Bank.
33. Since the presentation of this lecture, the Compensatory Finance Facility has been supplemented, as of late November 2005, by the new Exogeneous Shocks Facility offered by the IMF at concessional terms to countries eligible for the Poverty Reduction and Growth Facility or for the Policy Support Initiative.
34. This part of the section is adapted from Guillaumont and Guillaumont (2003) and Guillaumont et al (2005). Proposals to link debt service to terms of trade are also examined in Gilbert and Tabova (2005).

References

Acemoglu, D., S. Johnson, J. Robinson, and Y. Thaicharoen. 2003. “Institutional Causes, Macroeconomic Symptoms: Volatility, Crises and Growth.” *Journal of Monetary Economics* 50 (1): 49–123.

Adams Jr., R. H. 2004. “Economic Growth, Inequality and Poverty: Estimating the Growth Elasticity of Poverty.” *World Development* 32 (12): 1989–2014.

Aizenman, J., and N. Marion. 1999. “Volatility and Investment: Interpreting Evidence from Developing Countries.” *Economica* 68 (26): 157–80.

Alesina, A., and E. Spolaore. 2004. *The Size of Nations*. Cambridge, MA: MIT Press.

Amprou, J., P. Guillaumont, and S. Guillaumont Jeanneney. 2005. “Aid Selectivity According to Augmented Criteria.” Working Paper, Agence Française de Développement, Paris.

Araujo, C. 1995. “Les producteurs brésiliens et l’instabilité des prix: différences de comportement entre le Nord et le Sud.” *Canadian Journal of Agricultural Economics* 43 (3): 443–61.

Araujo Bonjean, C., J.-L. Combes, and P. Combes Motel. 1999. “The Economic Consequences of Export Instability in Developing Countries: A Survey.” CERDI, Etudes et Documents, University of Auvergne, France.

Arcand, J-L., P. Guillaumont, and S. Guillaumont Jeanneney. 2001. “Are Policy Reform and Growth in Africa Sustainable?” *CERDI Etudes et Documents, E 2001.05,* Clermont-Ferrand, France. Originally presented at the second ABCDE Europe, Paris, June 2000.

Atkins, J., S. Mazzi, and C. Ramlogan. 1998. *A Study of the Vulnerability of Developing and Island States: A Composite Index*. London: Commonwealth Secretariat.

Behrman, J. R. 1968. *Supply Response in Underdeveloped Agriculture.* Amsterdam: North-Holland Publishing Company.

Berg, A., and C. Patillo. 1999. "Are Currency Crises Predictable: A Test." *IMF Staff Papers* 46 (2): 107–13.

Bleaney, M., and D. Fielding. 2002. "Exchange Rate Regimes, Inflation and Output Volatility in Developing Countries." *Journal of Development Economics* 68 (1): 233–45.

Bleaney, M., and D. Greenaway. 2001. "The Impact of Terms of Trade and Real Exchange Rate Volatility on Investment and Growth in Sub-Saharan Africa." *Journal of Development Economics* 65 (2): 491–500.

Bosworth, Barry P., and Susan M. Collins. 2003. "The Empirics of Growth: An Update." *Brookings Papers on Economic Activity* 2: 113–207.

Boussard, J. M., and F. Gérard. 1996. "Price Stabilization and Agricultural Supply." In *Economics of Agricultural Policies in Developing Countries,* Vol. 2, ed. M. Benoit-Cattin, M. Griffon, and P. Guillaumont, 269–86. Paris: Edition Revue Française d'Economie.

Breen, R., and C. Garcìa-Peñalosa. 1999. "Income Inequality and Macroeconomic Volatility: An Empirical Investigation." *Review of Development Economics* 9 (3): 380–98.

Briguglio, L. 1995. "Small Island States and their Economic Vulnerabilities." *World Development* 23 (9): 1615–32.

Briguglio, L., and E. J. Kisanga, eds. 2004. *Vulnerability and Resilience of Small States.* Malta: Commonwealth Secretariat and Islands and Small States Institute of the University of Malta.

Brun, J-F., P. Guillaumont, and J. de Melo. 1999. "La distance abolie? Critères et mesures de la mondialisation du commerce extérieur." In *Globalisation et politiques économiques: les marges de manœuvre,* ed. A. Bouet and J. Le Cacheux. Paris: Economica.

Brun, J-F., C. Carrere, P. Guillaumont, and J. de Melo. 2005. "Has Distance Died? Evidence from a Panel Gravity Model." *World Bank Economic Review* 19 (1): 99–101.

Bulíř, Aleš, and A. Javier Hamann. 2003. "Aid Volatility: An Empirical Assessment." *IMF Staff Papers* 50 (1): 64–89.

———. 2005. "Volatility of Development Aid: From the Frying Pan into the Fire?" IMF draft working paper.

Burnside, C., and D. Dollar. 2000. "Aid, Policies and Growth." *American Economic Review* 90 (4): 847–68.

Caballero, R. J. 2002. "Coping with Chile's External Vulnerability: A Financial Problem." In *Central Banking Analysis and Economic Policies,* Vol. 6, ed. N. Loayza and R. Soto, 377–416. Santiago: Banco Central de Chile.

Carrère, C., and M. Schiff. 2004. "On the Geography of Trade," Policy Research Working Paper 3206, World Bank, Washington, DC.

Chauvet, L., and P. Guillaumont. 2004. "Aid and Growth Revisited: Policy, Economic Vulnerability and Political Instability." In *Toward Pro-Poor Policies—Aid, Institutions and Globalization,* ed. B. Tungodden, N. Stern, and I. Kolstad. Washington, DC: World Bank/Oxford University Press.

———. 2006. "Aid, Volatility and Growth." Unpublished, CERDI, Clermont-Ferrand, France.

Chauvet, L., and P. Collier. 2005. "Policy Turnarounds in Failing States." Centre for the Study of African Economies, Department of Economics, Oxford University and IRD-DIAL, Paris.

Cogneau, D. and J.-D. Naudet. 2004. "Who Deserves Aid? Equality of Opportunity, International Aid and Poverty Reduction." DIAL DT/2004/10, DIAL, Paris.

Collier, P., and J. Dehn. 2001. "Aid, Shocks, and Growth." World Bank Working Paper No. 2688, Washington, DC.

Collier, P., and D. Dollar. 2001. "Can the World Cut Poverty in Half? How Policy Reform and Effective Aid Can Meet International Development Goals." *World Development* 29 (11): 1787–802.

———. 2002. "Aid, Allocation and Poverty Reduction." *European Economic Review* 46 (8): 1475–500.

Collier, P., P. Guillaumont, S. Guillaumont Jeanneney, and J. Gunning. 1999. "Reforming Stabex." *The World Economy* 22 (5): 669–82.

Collier, P., and J. Gunning, eds. 1999. *Trade Shocks in Developing Countries: Theory and Evidence.* Oxford: Oxford University Press (Clarendon).

Collier, P., and A. Hoeffler. 2004. "Aid, Policy and Growth in Post-Conflict Societies." *European Economic Review* 48 (5): 1125–45.

Collier, P., L. Elliott, H. Hegre, A. Hoeffler, M. Reynal-Querol, and N. Sambanis. 2003. *Breaking the Conflict Trap. Civil War and Development Policy.* Washington, DC: World Bank.

Combes, J.-L., and P. Guillaumont. 2002. "Commodity Price Volatility, Vulnerability and Development." *Development Policy Review* 20 (1): 25–39.

Combes, J.-L., P. Guillaumont, S. Guillaumont Jeanneney, and M. Combes. 2000. "Ouverture sur l'extérieur et instabilité des taux de croissance." *Revue Française d'Economie* 15 (1): 3–33.

Cordella, T., and E. Levy Yeyati. 2004. "Country Insurance," IMF Working Paper WP/04/148, Washington, DC.

Crowards, T. 1999. "An Economic Vulnerability Index for Developing Countries, with Special Reference to the Caribbean: Alternative Methodologies and Provisional Results." Barbados: Caribbean Development Bank.

Dawe, D. 1996. "A New Look at the Effects of Export Instability on Investment and Growth." *World Development* 24 (12): 1905–14.

Dayton-Johnson, J. 2004. "Natural Disasters and Adaptive Capacity." OECD Development Centre, Working Paper No. 237, Paris.

Deaton, A., and R. Miller. 1996. "International Commodity Prices, Macroeconomic Performance and Politics in Sub-Saharan Africa." *Journal of African Economies* 5 (3): 99–191.

de Janvry, A., and E. Sadoulet. 2000. "Growth, Poverty and Inequality in Latin America: A Causal Analysis." *Review of Income and Wealth* 46(3): 267–87.

Dollar, D., and V. Levin. 2004. "The Increasing Selectivity of Foreign Aid, 1984–2002." Policy Research Working Paper No.3299, World Bank, Washington, DC.

Easter, C. 1998. "Small States and Development: A Composite Index of Vulnerability." In *Small States: Economic Review and Basic Statistics.* Annual series: Fourth Volume, December 1998, pp. 24–46. London: Commonwealth Secretariat.

Easterly, W., and A. Kraay. 2000. "Small States, Small Problems? Income, Growth, and Volatility in Small States." *World Development* 28 (11): 2013–27.

Easterly, W., R. Islam, and J. Stiglitz. 2001. "Shaken and Stirred: Explaining Growth Volatility." In *Annual Bank Conference on Development Economics,* eds. B. Pleskovic and N. Stern, 191–213. Washington, DC: World Bank.

Encontre, P. 1999. "The Vulnerability and Resilience of Small Island Developing States in the Context of Globalization." *Natural Resources Forum* 23: 261–70.

Fajnzylber P., D. Lederman, and N. Loayza. 2002. "What Causes Violent Crime?" *European Economic Review* 46 (7): 1323–57.

Faye, Michael L., J. W. McArthur, J. D. Sachs, and T. Snow. 2004. "The Challenges Facing Landlocked Developing Countries." *Journal of Human Development* 5 (1): 31–68.

Fosu, A. K. 1992. "Effect of Export Instability on Economic Growth in Africa." *The Journal of Developing Areas* 26 (3): 323–32.

———. 2002. "Economic Fluctuations and Growth in Sub-Saharan Africa: The Importance of Import Instability." *The Journal of Development Studies* 37 (3): 71–84.

Ghura, D., and T. J. Grennes. 1993. "The Real Exchange Rate and Macroeconomic Performance in Sub-Saharan Africa." *Journal of Development Economics* 42 (1): 155–74.

Gilbert, C. L., and A. Tabova. 2005. "Can We Link Concessional Debt Service to Commodity Prices?" Discussion Paper 8, Group of Research and Analysis on Development, University of Trento, Italy. Background paper for the report: "Managing the Debt Risk of Exogenous Shocks in Low-Income Countries," World Bank, May 2005.

Glezakos, C. 1984. "Export Instability and Economic Growth: Reply." *Economic Development and Cultural Change* 32 (3): 615–23.

Goldstein, M., G. L. Kaminski, and C. M. Reinhart. 2000. *Assessing Financial Vulnerability. An Early Warning System for Emerging Markets.* Washington, DC: Institute for International Economics.

Grigoriou, C., and P. Guillaumont. 2003. "A Dynamic Child Survival Function: Natural Convergence and Economic Policy." *Etudes et documents,* CERDI, Clermont-Ferrand, France.

Guillaumont, P. 1985. *Economie du développement.* Volume III: Dynamique internationale du développement. Paris: PUF.

———. 1987. "From Export Instability Effects to International Stabilization Policies." *World Development* 15 (5): 633–47.

———. 1989. "Stratégie de développement et ouverture sur l'extérieur." *African Development Review* 1 (1): 40–57.

———. 1994. "Politique d'ouverture, exportation et croissance économique: les effets de la croissance et de l'instabilité des exportations." *Revue d'Économie du Développement* 1: 91–114.

———. 2004a. "A Revised EVI." CDP/2004/PLEN/16, 31/03/2004. United Nations.

———. 2004b. "On the Economic Vulnerability of Low Income Countries." In *Economic Vulnerability and Resilience of Small States,* ed. L. Briguglio and E. J. Kisanga, 54–71. Malta: Formatek Malta.

———. Forthcoming. *Moving out of the Trap: The Least Developed Countries.* Economica.

Guillaumont, P., and C. Bonjean. 1991. "Effects on Agricultural Supply of Producer Price Level and Stability with and without Scarcity: The Case of Coffee Supply in Madagascar." *Journal of International Development* 3 (2): 115–33.

Guillaumont, P., and L. Chauvet. 2001. "Aid and Performance: A Reassessment." *Journal of Development Studies* 37 (6): 66–92.

Guillaumont, P., and J.-L. Combes. 1996. "The Effects of Producer Price Trends and Instability on the Growth of Agricultural Exports: A Cross-section Analysis." In *Economics of Agricultural Policies in Developing Countries,* ed. M. Benoit-Cattin, M. Griffon, and P. Guillaumont, 287–300. Paris: Revue Française d'Economie.

Guillaumont, P., and S. Guillaumont, eds. 1988. *Stratégies de développement comparées zone franc et hors zone franc.* Paris: Economica.

———. 2003. "Dampening Price Shocks." In *Natural Resources and Violent Conflict,* ed. I. Bannon and P. Collier, 353–67. Washington, DC: World Bank.

Guillaumont, P., and C. Korachais. 2006. "Growth Instability against Pro-Poor Growth." Unpublished, CERDI, Clermont-Ferrand, France.

Guillaumont, P., and F. Puech. 2006. "Macroeconomic Instability and Crime." *Etudes et documents 2006/2,* CERDI, Clermont-Ferrand, France.

Guillaumont, P., S. Guillaumont Jeanneney, and J. F. Brun. 1999. "How Instability Lowers African Growth." *Journal of African Economies* 8 (1): 87–107.

Guillaumont, P., S. Guillaumont Jeanneney, P. Jacquet, L. Chauvet, and B. Savoye. 2005. "Attenuating through Aid the Vulnerability to Price Shocks." In *Economic Integration and Social Responsibility,* ed. F. Bourguignon and P. Jacquet. Washington, DC: World Bank.

Guillaumont Jeanneney, S. and K. Kpodar. 2005. "Financial Development, Financial Instability and Poverty." WPS/2005–08, Centre for the Study of African Economies, University of Oxford.

Gunning, J. W. 2004. "Why Give Aid?" Second AFD-EUDN Conference "Development Aid: Why and How?" Paris, November 25.

Gyimah-Brempong, K. 1991. "Export Instability and Economic Growth in Sub-Saharan Africa." *Economic Development and Cultural Change* 39 (4): 815–28.

Hansen, H., and F. Tarp. 2001. "Aid and Growth Regressions." *Journal of Development Economics* 64 (2): 547–70.

Helleiner, G. K. 1996. "Why Small Countries Worry: Neglected Issues in Current Analyses of the Benefits and Costs for Small Countries of Integrating with Large Ones." *The World Economy* 19 (16): 759–65.

Hnathovska, V., and N. Loayza. 2004. "Volatility and Growth." World Bank Policy Research Working Paper No. 3184, Washington, DC.

Imbs, J., and R. Wacziarg. 2003. "Stages of Diversification." *American Economic Review* 93 (1): 63–86.

Just, R. E. 1974. "An Investigation of the Importance of Risk in Farmers' Decisions." *American Journal of Agricultural Economics* 2 (February): 14–25.

Kaly, U., L. Briguglio, H. McLeod, S. Schmall, C. Pratt, and R. Pal. 1999. "Environmental Vulnerability Index (EVI) to Summarize National Environmental Vulnerability Profiles," SOPAC Technical Report No. 275, South Pacific Applied Geosciences Commission, Fiji.

Kaminsky, Graciela L., Carmen M. Reinhart, and Carlos A. Végh. 2004. "When It Rains, It Pours: Procyclical Capital Flows and Macroeconomic Policies." NBER Working Paper No. 10780, National Bureau of Economic Research, Cambridge, MA.

Kaufmann, D., A. Kraay, and M. Mastruzzi. 2003. "Governance Matters III: Governance Indicators for 1996–2002." Policy Research Working Paper No.310, World Bank, Washington, DC.

Knack, S., and P. Keefer. 1995. "Institutions and Economic Performance: Cross-Country Test Using Alternative Institutional Measures." *Economics and Politics* 7 (3): 207–27.

Knudsen, O., and P. Yotopoulos. 1976. "A Transitory Approach to Export Instability." *Food Research Institute Studies* 15: 91–108.

Koze, M. A., and R. Reizman. 2001. "Trade Shocks and Macroeconomic Fluctuations in Africa." *Journal of Development Economics* 65 (1): 55–80.

Llavador, H. G., and J. E. Roemer. 2001. "An Equal-Opportunity Approach to the Allocation of International Aid." *Journal of Development Economics* 64 (1): 147–71.

Lensink, Robert, and Oliver Morrissey. 2000. "Aid Instability as a Measure of Uncertainty and the Positive Impact of Aid On Growth." *Journal of Development Studies* 36 (3): 30–48.

Limao, N., and A. J. Venables. 2001. "Infrastructure, Geographical Disadvantage, Transport Costs, and Trade." *World Bank Economic Review* 15 (3): 451–80.

Lim, D. 1980. "Income Distribution, Export Instability and Savings Behavior." *Economic Development and Cultural Change* 28 (2): 359–64.

Lin, W. 1977. "Measuring Aggregate Supply Response under Instability." *American Journal of Agricultural Economics* 5 (December): 903–7.

Lucas, R. E. 2003. "Macroeconomics Priorities." *American Economic Review* 93 (1): 1–93.

Lutz, M. 1994. "The Effects of Volatility in the Terms of Trade on Output Growth: New Evidence." *World Development* 22 (12): 1959–75.

Mendoza, E. G. 1997. "Terms-of-Trade Uncertainty and Economic Growth." *Journal of Development Economics* 54 (2): 323–56.

Miguel, E., S. Satyanath, and E. Sergenti. 2004. "Economic Shocks and Civil Conflict: An Instrumental Variables Approach." *Journal of Political Economy* 112 (4): 725–53.

Milner, C., and T. Weyman-Jones. 2003. "Relative National Efficiency and Country Size: Evidence for Developing Countries." *Review of Development Economics* 7 (1): 1–14.

Neumayer, E. 2003. "Good Policy Can Lower Violent Crime: Evidence from a Cross-National Panel of Homicide Rates 1980–97." *Journal of Peace Research* 40 (6): 619–40.

Neumayer, E. 2005. "Inequality and Violent Crime." *Journal of Peace Research* 42 (1): 101–12.

Newbery, D., and J. Stiglitz. 1981. *Theory of Commodity Price Stabilization: A Study in the Economics of Risk*. Oxford: Clarendon Press.

Ocampo, J. A. 2002. "Small Economies in the Face of Globalisation." Third William G. Demas Memorial Lecture at the Caribbean Development Bank. Cayman Islands, May 14.

Pallage, Stéphane, and M. A. Robe. 2001. "Foreign Aid and the Business Cycle." *Review of International Economics* 9 (4): 641–72.

———. 2003. "On the Welfare Cost of Economic Fluctuations in Developing Countries." *International Economic Review* 44 (2): 677–98.

Pallage S., M. A. Robe, and C. Bérubé. 2004. "On the Potential of Foreign Aid as Insurance." Working Paper 04-04, Centre interuniversitaire sur la risque, les politique économique et l'émploi, Canada.

Ramey, G., and V. Ramey. 1995. "Cross Country Evidence on the Link Between Volatility and Growth." *The American Economic Review* 85 (5): 1138–51.

Rand, John, and F. Tarp. 2002. "Business Cycles in Developing Countries: Are They Different?" *World Development* 30 (12): 2071–88.

Rodrik, D. 1998. "Why Do More Open Economies Have Bigger Governments?" *Journal of Political Economy* 106 (5): 997–1032.

———. 1999. "Where Did All the Growth Go? External Shocks, Social Conflict and Growth Collapses." *Journal of Economic Growth* 4 (4): 385–412.

Roodman, David. 2004a. "The Anarchy of Numbers: Aid, Development, and Cross-Country Empirics." Working Paper 32, Center for Global Development, Washington, DC.

———. 2004b. "An Index of Donor Performance." Working Paper 42, Center for Global Development, Washington, DC.

Sarris, A. 2003. "Une assurance du prix des matières premières fondée sur le marché pour les pays en développement: vers une nouvelle approche." *Revue d'économie du développement* 2003 (1): 5–41.

Serven, L. 1997. "Irreversibility, Uncertainty and Private Investment: Analytical Issues and Some Lessons for Africa." *Journal of African Economies* 6 (3): 229–68 (supplement to issue).

Subervie, J. 2006. "The Impact of World Price Instability on Agricultural Supply According to Macroeconomic Environment." Etudes et documents, CERDI, Clermont-Ferrand, France.

UNDP (United Nations Development Programme). 2001. "Disaster Profiles of the Least Developed Countries." Third UN Conference on Least Developed Countries, Brussels, May 14–20.

United Nations. 1994. "Report of the Global Conference on the Sustainable Development of Small Island Developing States." Report A/Conf.167/9, United Nations Department of Economic and Social Affairs.

———. 1997. "Report of the Committee on Development Planning." Report A/56/625. New York.

———. 1999. *Vulnerability and Poverty in a Global Economy—Report of the Committee for Development Policy on the First Session.* New York.

———. 2000. *Poverty Amidst Riches: The Need for Change—Report of the Committee for Development Policy on the Second Session.* New York.

———. 2001a. *World Economic and Social Survey 2000. Vulnerability in a Globalizing World.* Department of Economic and Social Affairs, New York.

———. 2001b. *The Costs of Poverty and Vulnerability.* Department of Economic and Social Affairs, New York.

———. 2005. *Development Challenges in Sub-Saharan Africa and Post-Conflict Countries—Report of the Committee for Development Policy on the Seventh Session.* New York.

Varangis, P., S. Varma, A. dePlaa, and V. Nehru. 2004. "Exogenous Shocks in Low-Income Countries: Economic Policy Issues and the Role of the International Community." Paper presented at Inwent International Policy Workshop, "Debt Sustainability, External Shocks and Financing Instruments in LICs," Berlin, November 22.

Windmeijer, F. 2000. "A Finite Sample Correction for the Variance of Linear Two-Step GMM Estimations." Working Paper 00/19, Institute for Fiscal Studies, London.

Winters, L. A., and P. M. G. Martins. 2004. "When Comparative Advantage is Not Enough: Business Costs in Small Remote Economies." *World Trade Review* 3 (3): 347–83.

World Bank. 1998. *Assessing Aid: What Works, What Doesn't and Why.* Oxford: Oxford University Press.

———. 1999. *Dealing with Commodity Price Volatility in Developing Countries: A Proposal for a Market-Based Approach.* International Task Force on Commodity Risk Management in Developing Countries. Washington, DC.

———. 2004. *Global Monitoring Report 2004—Millennium Development Goals: From Consensus to Momentum.* Washington, DC.

———. 2005. *Global Monitoring Report 2005—Policies and Actions for Achieving the Millennium Development Goals and Related Outcomes.* Washington, DC.

Comment on "Macro Vulnerability in Low-Income Countries and Aid Responses," by Patrick Guillaumont

DUNCAN GREEN

First, let me thank the organizers for inviting me to speak on this important issue. Oxfam GB is a member of Oxfam International, a confederation of 12 organizations working together with over 3,000 partners in more than 100 countries to find lasting solutions to poverty, suffering, and injustice. (See http://www.oxfam.org/eng/about.htm for details.) Although most of our work remains operational, we pay increasing attention through our research, advocacy, and campaigning work to issues such as aid, trade, and debt, where we greatly value the opportunity to engage in constructive dialogue with the donors, whether multilateral or bilateral.

Overall, I found Professor Guillaumont's paper extremely interesting. He has impassively marshaled a massive body of econometric evidence on a large number of determinants and impacts of vulnerability in low-income countries. For that he should be congratulated.

In general, he sets out in a compelling manner the special problems faced by small developing states. He finds that they are particularly vulnerable to various forms of volatility due to their greater openness to events beyond their borders (expressed in high trade-to-GDP ratios) and are usually less economically diversified, increasing the risks of shocks should one or another of their export products vary sharply in price. He argues that this vulnerability needs to be recognized and built into the allocation of aid, where the debate is currently dominated by poverty and governance issues, rather than vulnerability. All this is a sharp contrast to the views of Easterly and Kraay (2000), who concluded that small states are no different from large states and should receive the same policy advice that large states do.

The paper also addresses some of the weaknesses in past discussions of vulnerability, for example, by acknowledging that the growing reliance of small developing states on services such as tourism and remittances can introduce new forms of volatility that are lost if the discussion confines itself only to trade in goods.

Duncan Green is Head of Research, Oxfam GB.

Annual World Bank Conference on Development Economics—Europe 2006

Overall, the paper is strong in setting out the problem, but then becomes somewhat bogged down in a lengthy discussion on building an index. This begs the question of whether the search for a completely robust and single number to describe vulnerability should really be such a central focus of the endeavor, because it comes at the expense of what is for me the most important section of the paper—the "so what?" discussion on policy implications. Below, I set out a few ideas for cutting through the Gordian knot of multiplying and ever more complex vulnerability indexes and getting to what matters—reducing vulnerability and making aid as effective as possible.

Unforeseen or Unforeseeable?

Professor Guillaumont argues that vulnerability means the risk of being harmed or wounded (negatively affected) by unforeseen events, but he does not discuss whether the events are inherently unforeseeable, or have merely escaped the notice of forecasters. A recent evaluation by the IMF (2004) concluded that "Over longer horizons [IMF] programs systematically over-estimate growth, especially in low-income countries." Interestingly, Martin and Bargawi (2004) point to what could be a more reliable source of forecasting—developing country governments.

If Highly Indebted Poor Countries (HIPC) Debt Sustainability Analyses (DSAs) forecasts are compared with those forecast by African HIPCs in their own national Debt Strategy Reports (DSRs), compiled with assistance from the HIPC Debt Strategy and Analysis Capacity-Building Programme (see www.dri.org.uk),

- the negative shocks assumed in national DSRs are generally larger than those in DSAs. This is because countries analyze in detail the past effects of shocks on the economy. In contrast, shocks assumed in DSAs are frequently small, limited in many cases to export growth rates that are 2 percent lower (and well above historical trends). Almost all African HIPCs feel that the scale of downside risk assessed in the DSAs is not large enough.
- the shocks calculated in the DSRs are generally fed through and analyzed for all of their primary (and in some cases, secondary) impacts on the balance of payments and budget, therefore producing additional financing gaps that will also increase debt. In contrast, many DSAs adjust one line item of the balance of payments or budget and recalculate financing gaps accordingly, without looking at the potential effects of a shock on GDP and other elements of the balance of payments or budget. African HIPC ministers have often expressed the view that the effects of shocks should be analyzed more comprehensively.
- DSRs take much more frequent account of climate shocks. DSAs included them only for Mali and Mozambique, although 28 African HIPCs have had recent climate shocks.

Clearly, it can be argued that African HIPCs could have an interest in exaggerating the threats to win more generous debt relief, but equally, it can be argued that officials at international financial institutions are under pressure to be optimistic in their predictions. In the end, only a test against actual outcomes can determine whether pessimism or optimism is more likely to be right.

This discussion highlights a wider issue in the paper: the reliance on cross-country regressions as the sole source of useful evidence. When a problem presents itself, the paper opts for ever more complex regressions, when good country case studies or simply conducting a well-designed survey of aid recipients might be both easier and more useful.

Are Capital Market Shocks Irrelevant to Low-Income Countries?

While Professor Guillaumont sees capital crises as largely an emerging market issue, and therefore of little relevance to a discussion on low-income countries, increasing evidence points to the contrary. Actual capital flows are two to three times the internationally published figures (see Bhinda et al 2001; Martin 1999). These large flows have caused currency crises and macroeconomic instability in low-income countries. These are comparable in magnitude to the major crises in emerging market economies (Argentina, Brazil, the Russian Federation, Turkey, and East Asia), but have remained largely unnoticed by the international community. According to Martin and Bargawi (2004), at least 13 countries—as well as the whole CFA (African Financial Community) franc zone before the devaluation in 1994—have suffered major crises related to surges and slumps of foreign private capital in the last 10 years, with particularly severe examples in Ghana, Zambia, and Zimbabwe.

The Politics of the Exogenous

From the point of view of a campaigning nongovernmental organization, there is political risk attached to categorizing some risks as "exogenous" as opposed to "structural," if this boils down to accepting the status quo, merely adding better safety nets. Issues such as low prices for developing country sugar or maize farmers are highly influenced by the distorting effect of developed country trade and agriculture policies, while added risk of floods and droughts due to climate change clearly require action in the North, as well as adaptation in the South.

Exogenous or Endogenous

Professor Guillaumont goes to great lengths to distinguish between "structural" factors that are beyond developing countries' control, and policy factors that are not. At first, this seems sensible—policy factors can change more easily, and any attempt to increase aid flows based on vulnerability faces the moral hazard issues raised by "rewarding" poorly managed countries with a higher vulnerability index.

However, while this emphasis on structural vulnerability may make it easier to "sell" the idea to donors, in practice it is often hard to make a clear distinction between such "deserving" and "undeserving" cases. Are high levels of inequality structural or policy-based, given that they stem from centuries of history, and are remarkably resilient to policy interventions? Crowards (2004) identifies a more sophisticated spectrum of five groups of drivers: factors determining vulnerability may be truly inherent (such as a country being landlocked), exogenous (such as commodity prices determined by world markets), endogenous (such as policies affecting resources available as a buffer against shocks), historical (perhaps determining institutional structures), or social (such as ethnic cohesion).

The paper's insistence on trying to disentangle exogenous and endogenous factors leads it into some fairly painful intellectual contortions. At one point, it is reduced to arguing that "small population size is considered the main structural factor explaining a high trade-to-GDP ratio, and thus, the exposure to trade shocks, and a better indicator of structural exposure than the exports-to-GDP ratio itself, because the latter depends not only on structural but also on policy factors," that is, population is a better proxy for exposure to trade than trade itself, because trade is somehow contaminated by policy issues!

Moreover, while moral hazard is a plausible risk, I would question the level of priority implied in the effort to separate structural from policy factors. At an extreme level, is it really likely that a government would deliberately mismanage the economy to gain a couple of points on its vulnerability rating? More subtly, moral hazard can lead to the blunting of incentives for reform, but there are various ways to overcome this, such as a "sunset clause" that places time limits on a country's eligibility; or determining country vulnerability in groups rather than on an individual basis (see below). More generally, if aid is allocated as a function of vulnerability, poverty, and governance, it can be argued that taking the quality of policy into account in the calculations of both vulnerability and governance amounts to double counting.

It would be unfortunate if an overzealous concern with the second order issue of moral hazard became a serious obstacle to making progress on the first order issue of allocating aid according to vulnerability. In practice, I feel it may well be simpler to accept that the factors determining vulnerability are likely to remain a messy mix of exogenous and endogenous factors.

Do We Need an Economic Vulnerability Index?

A large part of the paper is devoted to a discussion of how to devise a single robust index of economic vulnerability. Such an index would make it easy for policy makers to weight aid allocations according to vulnerability. However, while a laudable aim, the search for such an index has thrown up a large number of competing and contradictory methodologies. Gonzales (2000) notes, "A comparison of the various vulnerability classifications reveals a large amount of inconsistency." Crowards (2004) concludes that the exercise may not be worth it, arguing that "[t]here are a number of difficulties associated with drawing these variables into a single index, and there seems to be limited scope for employing such an overall index beyond proving that small developing states are generally more vulnerable. Instead, the focus should be on individual characteristics that define a country's vulnerability to particular types of shock."

The paper comes up with its own proposal for an economic vulnerability index (EVI), but here, too, I had a number of questions on the methodology employed. Above all, the EVI seems to introduce a small-state bias when it takes smallness, measured by population size, as "the main structural factor" of exposure to vulnerability. It is clearly *a* factor, but is it the main one? The result is doubtless congenial to the small island states that first promoted the discussion on vulnerability as a counterweight to their increasing marginalization in a debate dominated by poverty headcounts, but it seems somewhat unconvincing.

A Different Approach

To avoid getting bogged down, an alternative approach to getting a "good enough" vulnerability index could take the following steps:

- Use historical fluctuations in consumption or GDP as a reasonable guide to likely future vulnerability.
- Reduce the risk of moral hazard by grouping developing countries into clusters, according to income, population, or structure of production (for example, commodity dependence). Then a badly managed country will fail to "profit" from its poor performance, because it would merely drag down the average index by a small amount, while a well-managed economy would receive a bonus in the form of a better vulnerability rating (and so more aid) than would be justified by its performance alone.
- Aid could then be allocated as a function of indicators on vulnerability, poverty, and governance.

Implications for Aid Policy: Volatility

When it comes to aid itself, the paper is relatively sanguine, concluding that, despite its well-known volatility, "on average aid has been more stabilizing than destabilizing." Other authors disagree, finding that aspects of the current aid system are part of the problem as well as part of the solution. In a recent paper for the IMF, Bulíř and Hamann (2005) find that aid remains "volatile, procyclical, and unpredictable" and that "the consequences of aid volatility for aggregate growth and consumption were found to be very high, approximately equivalent to the impact of the Great Depression."

Bulíř and Hamann also argue that conditionality exacerbates volatility by encouraging donors to cut aid when developing countries go off track after a shock. One hopes this will be addressed in this year's review of conditionality by the Bank.

Conclusions

Professor Guillaumont concludes with some excellent recommendations for the kinds of aid policy required to deal with vulnerability:

- Compensatory finance schemes such as FLEX need to be much better funded and quicker to disburse funds.
- Debt service obligations need to be modulated to rise and fall with key factors such as commodity prices. The author makes some valuable suggestions about how this can be done.
- Non-heavily indebted low-income countries also need such a scheme because many are equally dependent on commodity prices, for example, triggering automatic assistance in the event of price drops.
- National stabilization funds, if well designed to avoid the pitfalls of some of their predecessors, can play a valuable role in cushioning the impact of volatility on poor farmers.

To the author's list could usefully be added some of the issues raised in this paper, notably greater attention to capital market instability and improved forecasting. While a single vulnerability index that filters out structural from policy factors would greatly simplify the business of gaining political support and resources to aid vulnerable economies, it may pose so many methodological difficulties that its pursuit imposes unnecessary and unacceptable delays on the process. Instead, donors may have to accept a second-best means of assessing vulnerability, finding other ways to curb any perceived risk of moral hazard.

References

Bhinda, N., S. Griffith-Jones, J. Leape, and M. Martin. 1999. *Private Capital Flows to Africa: Perception and Reality.* FONDAD. The Hague.

Bulíř , Aleš, and A. Javier Hamann. 2005. *Volatility of Development Aid: From the Frying Pan into the Fire?* International Monetary Fund. Washington, DC.

Crowards, Thomas. 2004. *Macroeconomic Vulnerability of Small Developing States: Will It Squeeze into a Single Index?* University of Malta and Commonwealth Secretariat. London.

Easterly, W., and A. Kraay. 2000. "Small States, Small Problems? Income, Growth, and Volatility in Small States." *World Development* 28 (11): 2013–27.

Gonzales, Anthony Peter. 2000. "Policy Implications of Smallness as a Factor in the Lome, FTAA and WTO Negotiations." Caribbean Regional Negotiating Machinery Technical Paper.

IMF (International Monetary Fund). 2004. "Policy Formulation, Analytical Frameworks, and Program Design," Policy Development and Review Department, Washington, DC.

Martin, Matthew. 1999. "Financing Africa's Development in the 21st Century." The Gilman Rutihinda Memorial Lecture, Bank of Tanzania.

Martin, Matthew, and Hannah Bargawi. 2004. "Protecting Africa Against 'Shocks.'" Background Paper for UK Commission for Africa, Development Finance International, London.

Vulnerability: A Micro Perspective

Vulnerability: A Micro Perspective

STEFAN DERCON

High downside risk to income and livelihoods is part of life in developing countries. Climatic risks, economic fluctuations, and a large number of individual-specific shocks leave these households vulnerable to severe hardship. The paper explores the links between risk, vulnerability, and poverty, taking a micro-level perspective. Risk does not just result in variability in living standards. Increasing evidence shows that the lack of means to cope with risk and vulnerability is in itself a cause of persistent poverty and poverty traps. Risk results in strategies that avoid taking advantage of profitable but risky opportunities. Shocks destroy human, physical, and social capital, limiting opportunities further. The result is that risk is an important constraint on broadly based growth in living standards in many developing countries. It is a relatively ignored facet when designing anti-poverty policies and efforts to attain the Millennium Development Goals (MDGs). The paper discusses conceptual issues, the evidence, and the policy implications.

This paper discusses risk and vulnerability, and their links with poverty. It introduces recent work that has highlighted the crucial role played by risk and vulnerability in determining people's living conditions and opportunities to escape poverty. Many development practitioners and researchers have long recognized that individuals, households, and communities face a large number of risks, related to, for example, climate, health, or economic shocks. Different disciplines including economics, geography, and nutritional studies have analyzed the consequences of life in this risky environment. Specific policies such as preventive health care, safety nets, or famine

---

Stefan Dercon is Professor of Development Economics at the University of Oxford. *stefan.dercon@economics.ox.ac.uk*.
The opinions in this paper are those of the author. However, many of the insights in this paper are based on joint work, including with Cesar Calvo, John Hoddinott, and Pramila Krishnan, as well as on collaborative efforts with Emil Tesliuc, Hans Hoogeveen, and Renos Vakis, and chapter authors in *Insurance against Poverty* (Dercon 2004). Cesar Calvo and an anonymous referee provided detailed and helpful comments on an earlier draft.

Annual World Bank Conference on Development Economics—Europe 2006

early warning systems form a well-established part of the aid and policy efforts in developing countries.

It would therefore be wrong to suggest that risk has been largely ignored. However, in much analysis on development and in the design of anti-poverty policies, risk has remained on the periphery, an add-on in a more general analysis. This paper presents evidence that should encourage policy makers to give risk and uncertainty a more central place in their thinking about poverty and destitution. The central argument is that risk is not just another expression or dimension of poverty, but is also an important cause of persistent poverty and poverty traps.

The term "vulnerability" has been used in a variety of related but different meanings. In one of its most well-known definitions, Chambers (1989) stated that vulnerability "refers to exposure to contingencies and stress, . . . which is defencelessness, meaning a lack of means to cope without damaging loss" (p. 1). The *World Development Report 2000/2001* (World Bank 2001) made security a central part of the framework underlying its analysis. It provided a number of related definitions, of which "vulnerability measures . . . the likelihood that a shock will result in a decline in well-being" (p. 139) is most relevant for our purposes. Alwang, Siegel, and Jorgenson (2001) present a number of different definitions found in the literature. A common thread appears to be that vulnerability relates to a sense of insecurity, of potential harm people must feel wary of—something bad may happen and spell ruin. This paper uses vulnerability as the existence and the extent of a *threat* of poverty and destitution—the danger that a socially unacceptable level of well-being may materialize.

This analysis will focus on *risk-related* vulnerability: the exposure to risk and uncertainty, the responses to these, the welfare consequences, and the implications for policy. The downside risk people face is a central ingredient in this analysis. It is also useful to make clear what this paper is *not* intending to do. The term "vulnerability" is used in some research and policy analysis in another sense, referring to particular "vulnerable groups," such as the elderly, orphans, widows, or even more generally, the landless or low-paid workers. In these cases, vulnerability is used as referring to some more general weakness or defenselessness. Such groups may face risk-related vulnerability as well; however, their defining characteristic is not related to risk, but to their general inability to take advantage of profitable opportunities, so that without substantial support they may end up in severe and persistent poverty. A focus on these groups is obviously justified, but it is not the subject of this paper, which is narrower. This narrow concentration is practical from a policy point of view, even if some of the instruments that would help for risk-related vulnerability would also assist "vulnerable groups." The final section will develop this policy focus further, building on the earlier findings in the paper.

The next section first briefly introduces some of the typical findings and implications of risk on household welfare, but also focuses on the strategies people use to cope with risk and shocks. This will lead to the core part of the analysis in the subsequent section, where risk and shocks as a cause of poverty are discussed. In particular, the exposure to risk and the responses and actions taken by households to cope with risk conspire to result in poverty persistence or even poverty traps, whereby households are stuck permanently in poverty, unable to take advantage of sufficiently profitable, yet risky, activities. One of the key consequences is that the possibility for broadly based growth is undermined.

In the third section, "Vulnerability as a Normative Welfare Concept," the paper examines whether vulnerability has any bearing on the current debate on developing better ways to measure poverty. Not only concepts such as income or consumption poverty, but also attempts to operationalize capabilities and the inherent multidimensionality of poverty are effectively derived in a world of certainty, in which little room is afforded to risk and vulnerability. In this section, some efforts to measure vulnerability are discussed. The paper measures vulnerability by assessing the extent of the *threat* of poverty, evaluated ex ante, before the veil of uncertainty has been lifted. This can be compared to poverty, which is an expression of the extent of low welfare outcomes, but as observed without uncertainty and low welfare results from outcome levels below some accepted poverty line. The final section concludes by highlighting the policy implications of the analysis in the paper. Throughout the analysis, the paper highlights recent examples from the literature, and reports on more recent findings of the author's work with collaborators on Ethiopia.

It is worth briefly defining what "risk" means in this analysis. Risk is used as potential states of the world, exogenous to the person. Which state of the world will occur is not known to this person. In economic analysis, it is usually assumed that the person has formed a subjective distribution of the likelihood of particular states occurring, and much of the analysis underlying some of the papers quoted below makes this assumption. The fact that risk is exogenous does not mean that it affects all people in the same way. Some risks may be irrelevant, for example, frost is irrelevant for a farmer growing only crops that do not suffer from occasional frost. A crucial ingredient of the analysis below is also that households try to shape the impact of risk using a variety of risk strategies.

A common distinction is between risk and uncertainty; uncertainty includes those states of the world that the person could not have foreseen even possibly occurring, and in any case does not take specifically into account in any strategies.[1] It is hard to ignore the fact that uncertainty so defined exists, as the 2004 Asian tsunami highlighted. For much of the analysis, the distinction is not crucial and not emphasized, but it will be picked up again in the discussion of the policy response to risk and vulnerability.

Risk and Vulnerability: A Central Part of Poor People's Lives

One of the more striking findings in qualitative work using both short and longer lifetime histories and other methods is that an essential part of the lives of the poor is trying to cope and survive in the face of recurring misfortune—such as illness, loss of employment, and harvest failure (for examples, see the background papers for the *Voices of the Poor* work [Narayan, Chambers, et al 2000; Narayan, Patel, et al 2000; Narayan and Petech 2002], as part of the preparations for the *World Development Report 2000/2001*).

TABLE 1.
The Incidence of Serious Shocks in Rural Ethiopia, 1999–2004

Shock	Percentage
Drought	46.8
Death of head of household, spouse, or another person	42.7
Illness of head of household, spouse, or another person	28.1
Inability to sell outputs or decreases in output prices	14.5
Pests or diseases that affected crops	13.8
Crime	12.7
Difficulty in obtaining inputs or increases in input prices	11.3
Policy or political shocks (land redistribution, state confiscation of assets, resettlement, forced contributions, or arbitrary taxation)	7.4
Pests or diseases that affected livestock	7.0

Source: Dercon, Hoddinott, and Woldehanna 2005.

Note: Based on recorded three worst shocks per household (of those affected by a shock), leading to serious loss of income, consumption, or assets. At least one serious shock was reported by 95 percent of households.

These shocks take on a variety of forms and many lead to substantial loss of income, wealth, or consumption. A simple household questionnaire–based investigation in rural Ethiopia yielded that over a five-year period (1999–2004), virtually all households, 95 percent, reported experiencing a shock that caused substantial loss of income, assets, or consumption. Table 1 reports the breakdown. Of those households hit by a shock, 47 percent reported that a drought had affected them, 43 percent that a death, and 28 percent that an illness in the household had seriously affected them. Other instances, such as marketing, pests, crime, or policy or political issues were investigated as well, and while important for specific people, in general they were less important.[2]

This evidence is, of course, suggestive at best. One of the most thriving parts of the analysis of risk and shocks in developing countries has been the study of the mechanisms people use to cope with these shocks. Indeed, these coping mechanisms have been widely acknowledged as a central part of people's livelihoods. To begin with, households have strategies to cope ex post with shocks, to smooth consumption and nutrition when shocks happen even if formal credit markets and insurance are not available. They may use savings, often in the form of live animals, built up as part of a precautionary strategy against risk; or engage in informal mutual support networks, for example, clan- or neighborhood-based associations, or even more formal groups such as funeral societies.[3]

However, group-based systems cannot work effectively in the face of covariate shocks, affecting the whole group, while the lack of efficient stores of wealth, with limited risks, also means that building these buffer stocks is highly costly and not as effective as hoped for. An example of the latter occurred when households in Northern Wollo in Ethiopia tried to use their standard smoothing device—selling livestock—to cope with drought and famine in the mid-1980s. Livestock prices collapsed due

TABLE 2.
Impact of Shocks on (log) Consumption Per Capita, 2004

Variable	Estimated coefficient	t-statistic (absolute value)
Drought, 2002–4	–0.163	2.46*
Drought, 1999–2001	–0.137	2.72*
Pests or diseases that affected crops, 2002–4	–0.006	0.07
Pests or diseases that affected crops, 1999–2001	–0.052	1.05
Pests or diseases that affected livestock, 2002–4	–0.002	0.18
Pests or diseases that affected livestock, 1999–2001	0.022	0.24
Difficulty in obtaining inputs or increases in input prices, 2002–4	0.055	0.63
Difficulty in obtaining inputs or increases in input prices, 1999–2001	0.001	0.02
Inability to sell outputs or decreases in output prices, 2002–4	–0.187	2.23*
Inability to sell outputs or decreases in output prices, 1999–2001	–0.026	0.36
Lack of demand for nonagricultural products, 2002–4	–0.037	0.19
Lack of demand for nonagricultural products, 1999–2001	–0.195	2.28*
Crime shocks, 2002–4	–0.018	0.36
Crime shocks, 1999–2001	0.083	0.99
Death of head, spouse, or another person, 2002–4	0.043	0.69
Death of head, spouse, or another person, 1999–2001	–0.001	0.02
Illness of head, spouse, or another person, 2002–4	–0.019	0.32
Illness of head, spouse, or another person, 1999–2001	–0.151	2.33*
R^2	0.34	
Sample size	1,290	

Source: Dercon, Hoddinott, and Woldehanna 2005.

Note: Specification includes controls for female headship, age of head, schooling, household size, dependency ratio, land holdings (quintiles), livestock, ethnic minority, religious minority, holding official position in the Peasant Association or important place in social life, all in 1999. Peasant Association dummies, month of interview dummies, and perceptions of rainfall in previous harvest year are also included but not reported. Standard errors are robust to locality cluster effects.

* significant at the 5 percent level.

to oversupply and lack of demand in the face of high grain prices, providing a classic case of entitlement failures, as in Sen 1981.

Overall, it tends to be found that households manage to keep consumption and nutrition smooth to some extent, but by no means entirely (Dercon 2002; Townsend 1995). Large covariate shocks are typically not insured and for some or in some settings, idiosyncratic (household-specific) shocks also affect outcomes. For example, table 2, based on the Ethiopian rural survey used in table 1, gives regression results using a simple specification linking consumption per adult in 2004 (almost 80 percent of which is basic food consumption) to initial conditions in 1999 defined by household demographics, land, livestock, and other household characteristics, as well as community fixed effects. As can be seen, reporting a serious drought shock in the last two years is correlated with 16 percent lower consumption, while a shock in the preceding two years is still reducing consumption by 14 percent (suggesting slow recovery). A problem in local markets linked to declining crop prices or lack of demand in recent years reduced consumption by 19 percent. Note that all these shocks are typically covariate—affecting many people in the same community, and by nature hard to insure. At the same time, however, many of the reported shocks, typically idiosyncratic ones, appear to have had relatively limited impact on consumption, and not a systematically significant impact on those reporting the event. The only significant idiosyncratic shock relates to illness between three and five years ago, but not recent ones. One possible explanation is that some of the immediate effects of illness can be handled by mutual support or savings, but illness can have debilitating effects on productivity in the medium term.

This inability to smooth consumption has implications for poverty in a direct way: households may occasionally drift below some socially acceptable level, possibly bounce back up, and drift back under. Uninsured shocks result then in poverty fluctuations, and this is indeed what has been found in data sets. A concept that allows some assessment of this is *transient poverty* as distinct from *chronic poverty,* as formalized by Ravallion (1988). The chronically poor are defined as those with average consumption below the poverty line. Chronic poverty for an individual can then be measured using average consumption as the welfare indicator. Transient poverty for an individual is average poverty over time minus chronic poverty. Aggregation using procedures as in standard poverty measures provides an overall measure of transient poverty. The definition involved is not restricted to poverty headcount, so the overall poverty measure may contain elements of chronic and transient poverty for each individual. Using these definitions, Ravallion (1988) finds that about half of total poverty is transient in the International Crops Research Institute for the Semi-Arid Tropics (ICRISAT) sample; Jalan and Ravallion (2000) find high transient poverty in panel data from four provinces in rural China: about half of the mean squared poverty gap is transient. In Ethiopia, using earlier data from the Ethiopian Rural Household Survey (ERHS) (1994–5), it was found that about 36 percent of the poverty gap was transient poverty.

While useful, the use of transient poverty as defined above poses an important problem. Transient poverty is measured as a residual, thus it contains all the measurement error that may bedevil the concept and measurement of consumption. The regression in table 2 can provide an alternative means of assessing the relevance of "transient" poverty, defined in the same spirit but *not* calculated as a residual, using direct shock measures instead. Simple simulations can provide an estimate of the contribution of particular shocks to poverty. In particular, consumption can be predicted for the case in which the shocks would not have occurred, to allow some estimate of "chronic" poverty, while "transient" is the poverty added due to the shocks.[4] It is also straightforward to calculate the contribution of each significant shock to overall poverty. Table 3 reports these contributions for the significant shocks, grouped as drought, market, and illness shocks, using the headcount index of poverty, based on an absolute poverty line defined as the consumption level needed to reach some minimal basket of basic needs.

TABLE 3.
The Impact of Shocks in 1999–2004 on Poverty in Ethiopia in 2004
(percentage of households below the poverty line)

Indicator	Head count index
Actual poverty	47.3
Predicted poverty (based on table 2)	43.8
Predicted poverty without drought shocks	33.1
Predicted poverty without illness shocks	40.4
Predicted poverty without input or output market shocks	41.2
Predicted poverty without shocks	29.4
Transient as share of total (predicted) poverty	32.8

Source: Ethiopian Rural Household Survey 2004.

Note: The poverty line is a revalued poverty line based on the 1994 round of the same survey, valued at 61.48 Ethiopian birr in 2004 prices per month (approximately US$8 per month). Based on 1,370 complete observations. Note that the transient poverty share is calculated relative to the predicted poverty level. As an estimate of "national" poverty, it is deficient in terms of offering a comparison with national and other figures, because methods differ.

Drought shocks have had the most serious impact, contributing the largest share of transient poverty in this period. Overall, poverty would appear to have been only about 29 percent, but is about 50 percent higher due to the occurrence of shocks (that is, shock-related transient poverty accounts for about a third of total poverty). In other words, if these shocks had been insured and smoothed, either via household strategies or via interventions, poverty would have been lower in rural Ethiopia in 2004 by a third. Doing the same calculations but based on a distribution-sensitive poverty measure (such as the squared poverty gap), the share of transient in total poverty is predicted to be even larger, at about 47 percent. These estimates are high, but also cover a difficult period in Ethiopia's recent history, with development efforts, aid, and reforms first stalled by the Ethio-Eritrean conflict (1998–2000), and subsequently by a serious drought affecting large parts of the country in 2002.

These figures can be viewed as a first-order approximation of the poverty reduction that could be gained by removing transient poverty and the inability of current policies and interventions to deal with shocks. Indeed, it is this type of concern that is behind much of the safety net thinking, whereby the presence of a real risk that individuals and families may experience poverty episodes due to shocks justifies more intervention to avoid them. At the same time, however, it can be inferred from this analysis that there is another group, arguably more deserving of attention: those that rarely if ever manage to achieve outcomes above the socially accepted poverty line, the destitute or "chronic" poor. These are the poor who even without shocks would have been predicted to be poor in 2004, based on their characteristics in 1999. In that view, safety nets or, more generally, policies that focus on managing the risks faced by people in developing countries, are more of a luxury that threaten to distract from the core activities of stimulating growth or reducing poverty of the chronically poor.[5]

The foregoing is a powerful argument against a focus on risk and shocks, but incorrect or at least incomplete. Risk and shocks have further implications for poverty: they are a cause of poverty. The actions people take to reduce the impact of risk have poverty implications as well. First, households organize their livelihoods taking risk into account before any shocks materialize. A standard example is income diversification, whereby activities and assets are diversified so that risks are spread, or alternatively the formation of low-risk activity and asset portfolios, with activities skewed to more certainty at the expense of mean returns. Indeed, rural and urban households in developing countries usually engage in a variety of crops, some with low risks but low mean returns; keep different small and larger livestock; and are involved in a multitude of petty business activities, temporary migration, and so on (Dercon 2002; Morduch 1995). A key issue is that these diversified or low-risk portfolios, while offering lower overall risks, may come at the expense of larger mean returns, if compared to more profitable but more risky activities and asset portfolios. Thus, households may have to *choose* to be relatively poor to avoid even more serious hardship and destitution induced by shocks. This is one mechanism through which risk may be a *cause* of poverty.

A second mechanism through which poverty may be caused by risk is related to assets lost or destroyed due to shocks. Despite the fact that households actively try to manage risk, shocks affect them, and at best, the evidence suggests only partial smoothing of welfare and nutrition. Assets and, more generally, households' livelihoods and their ability to generate future income are affected, in part due to the necessity to cope with shocks requiring that assets be sold off. Sometimes the asset base may be, and often is, directly affected by the shocks—such as death of livestock or loss of human capital due to illness or temporary poor nutrition.

Both mechanisms imply that risk can be a cause of poverty and that the concept of transient as opposed to chronic poverty is misleading: if anything, poverty related to risk is underestimated when using transient poverty, and the true poverty cost of risk is substantially higher. How substantial is an empirical issue, and the next section turns to some of the emerging evidence.

Risk and Vulnerability as a Cause of Poverty

At least three bodies of literature on development issues have long recognized that risk is an important factor explaining levels of poverty and deprivation. It is helpful to briefly discuss them and explain how they fit in with the more general issue of risk as a cause of poverty, as argued in this paper. The first is the literature on fertility, where it is commonly argued that high infant and child mortality, that is, the risk that children will not survive beyond a certain age, increases the fertility rate. This increase often puts pressure on women's health and well-being and can cause some of the well-documented externalities on the environment, land pressure, and the well-being of others (for a balanced discussion of these issues, see Dasgupta [1993]). Alongside this view are more general arguments of the family-level benefits of more labor or old age security, especially in circumstances in which limited entitlement to alternative social protection measures is available. Note that this is an example in which the risk inherent in living conditions induces ex ante behavioral responses by households (effectively an overinvestment in children) that may well divert resources from more profitable assets.

A second body of literature is largely based on evidence from agricultural economics, although it makes a broader point, well-established in basic textbook economics. It focuses on preferences toward risk, and more specifically risk aversion (a preference trait whereby people are willing to pay to avoid being faced with a risky choice, in favor of a less risky choice). Risk aversion will lead to profitable opportunities not being taken up in favor of less risky choices with lower expected returns. Wide evidence supports behavior consistent with risk aversion, and more importantly, demonstrates that risk aversion is higher when expected incomes are lower, in particular in developing countries (Binswanger 1981; Newbery and Stiglitz 1981). It leads to a well-established view that the poor are more risk averse, which will contribute to persistence in poverty, because they will not take the entrepreneurial risk required to enter into particular profitable activities.[6]

While acknowledging that risk aversion matters, this paper will argue that the risk-aversion theory's emphasis on preferences is essentially misleading, both as a complete theory of how risk causes poverty and as a guide to policy.

A third body of literature is that regarding nutrition, which argues that poor nutrition in certain periods in a child's early life may contribute to poorer long-term nutrition circumstances, in the form of stunting (height-for-age levels below some level observed in healthy populations). Short-term shocks to nutrition may then lead to lower nutritional outcomes in the long run as well, that is, a persistent health effect. While there is evidence for this process, it is not borne out by all studies: some have suggested that "catch-up" remains possible: that is, that over time children may recover the lost nutrition and return to their personal growth curve. Again, this is an empirical issue, and most evidence would suggest that stunting is a serious, permanent problem, especially in early years, because evidence suggests a strong correlation between child height at age three and adult height (Martorell 1999).[7]

These nutritional effects may have far-reaching consequences. Children with slow height growth are found to perform less well in school, score poorly on tests of cognitive functions, and develop more slowly. Short adult height is correlated with low earnings and productivity, poorer cognitive outcomes, and premature mortality due to increased risk of cardiovascular and obstructive lung disease. Taller women experience lower risks of child and maternal mortality. For adults, an increasing body of evidence links adult weight or BMI[8] (Body Mass Index, also known as the Quetelet Index) to agricultural productivity and wages (Dasgupta 1993; Dercon and Krishnan 2000a; Pitt, Rosenzweig, and Hassan 1990; Strauss and Thomas 1998). Low BMI is correlated with a large number of health-related indicators, including early onset of chronic conditions and increased risk of premature mortality (Fogel 1999).

For the purposes of this paper, it is interesting to trace these effects from direct evidence on shocks beyond the nutritional impact to broader outcomes. To take one example, Alderman, Hoddinott, and Kinsey (2003) trace the impact of the 1982, 1983, and 1984 droughts in Zimbabwe, as well as exposure to the civil war preceding independence, on longer term measures of child health and education in the 1990s in a rich panel data set in particular resettlement areas. They focus on shocks on children in the critical 12–24 month age category—generally recognized as the most critical time for child growth. These children were interviewed again 13 to 16 years later. Using an instrumental variables estimator, with maternal fixed effects, they show that lowered stature as a preschooler leads to lowered stature in late adolescence as well as delays in school enrollment and reductions in grade completion. The magnitudes of these impacts are meaningful. Using careful estimation methods, they found that the drought shock resulted in a loss of stature of 2.3 centimeters, 0.4 grades of schooling, and a delay in starting school of 3.7 months for this particular age group. Using the values for the returns to education and age-job experience in the Zimbabwean manufacturing sector provided by Bigsten et al (2000), the impact of the shock translates into a 7 percent loss in lifetime earnings.

These *permanent* effects from effectively *transitory* events are not restricted to nutrition or health. Lack of insurance and access to credit markets indicates that recovery of assets used to cope with a crisis or destroyed by it will not be straightforward and immediate. For example, Rosenzweig and Wolpin (1993) show that bullocks are one of the mechanisms used to cope with shocks in rural South India, resulting in suboptimal levels of capital goods. These effects are also not restricted to physical capital: for example, studies in India have found that negative income shocks caused households to withdraw children from school. Even if children later return to school, the hiatus causes lower educational levels, affecting the children's ability to build up a better life for themselves (Jacoby and Skoufias 1997). Recent work in Zambia has shown that teacher absenteeism, closely linked to illness shocks in the context of the HIV/AIDS epidemic, reduces cognitive achievement by children, again affecting long-term outcomes (Das et al 2004).

This evidence suggests processes in which incomes and levels of well-being are permanently affected by transitory shocks. It is possible to conceptualize these as poverty traps,[9] equilibrium levels of poverty from which there is no possible recovery without outside intervention. One mechanism could be the classic nutrition-productivity poverty trap (Dasgupta and Ray 1986). It is well established that below some critical nutritional level, no productive activity of any sort is possible. If during a crisis, all assets are wiped out except a person's labor, and if the crisis also pushes the person's nutritional status below this threshold, that person has no hope of ever recovering using his or her own productive means. Only a serious windfall, such as aid, could induce the person to climb out of poverty, provided the assistance is sufficient to pass the threshold value of nutritional status. While the evidence for this to be a direct description of actual poverty traps is limited, it provides a useful narrative for more general poverty traps: there may be thresholds for some productive assets that if pushed below these asset thresholds, the person finds no possible recovery, but rather an equilibrium level of very low asset holdings and poverty. Barrett and Carter (2004) use evidence from Kenya to suggest that such thresholds can be observed at least among pastoralists, given that minimum herd sizes are required for possible accumulation and escape from a potential "asset poverty trap."

The existence of poverty traps has been tested more directly by Lokshin and Ravallion (2002) and Jalan and Ravallion (2004) for Bulgaria and China. Most interestingly, they find no evidence of poverty traps, but they do find relatively long persistence of the effects of shocks: it takes many years to recover, and the recovery period is longer for the poor. Their method exploited the insight that transition paths of incomes or consumption, when poverty traps exist, are nonlinear, allowing for multiple equilibria. Another way of looking at whether there is evidence of long-lasting effects from shocks was used by Dercon (2004a), using a subset of the same panel data households reported in tables 1 to 3.[10]

In that paper on the long-term impact of shocks, detailed data were exploited on the experience during the 1984–5 famine, more specifically the extent to which households had to resort to famine-coping strategies, such as cutting meals and portions, selling valuables, relying on wild foods, and moving to feeding camps. An index of these experiences in the mid-1980s was then introduced in a model of consumption growth based on data from 1989 to 1997, regressing changes in food consumption on initial levels of food consumption at the household and community levels and on a number of common and idiosyncratic shocks. Note that if shocks only have transitory effects, lagged shocks should have no effect. However, in table 4 it is reported that rainfall shocks several years before the period in which growth was measured still affect growth. Most strikingly, the extent of the famine impact, as measured by the index of severity of coping strategies, strongly affected growth in the 1990s. This growth impact was substantial: depending on the estimation

TABLE 4.
Testing for Persistent Effects of Shocks on Food Consumption Growth
Dependent variable: change in ln food consumption per adult between survey waves (1989–94 and 1994–7).

	Δln food cons (1)		Δln food cons (2)	
Variable	**Coeff**	**p-value**	**Coeff**	**p-value**
Ln food consumption$_{t-1}$	–0.318	0.000	–0.204	0.000
Village mean ln food cons$_{t-1}$	0.211	0.000	0.135	0.004
Rainfall shocks$_t$	0.622	0.000	0.614	0.002
Rainfall shocks$_{t-1}$	0.069	0.016	0.195	0.013
Adult serious illness	–0.043	0.076	–0.053	0.064
Crop shock (–1 is worst)	–0.014	0.757	–0.217	0.041
Livestock shock (–1 is worst)	–0.018	0.704	–0.009	0.910
Severity of famine impact	–0.116	0.079	–0.397	0.068
Constant	0.519	0.000	0.920	0.071
Number of observations	636		319	

Source: Dercon 2004a, table 6.

Note: Regression (1) uses the Hausman-Taylor model, and assumes rainfall shocks, livestock shocks, and crop shocks as time-varying, exogenous variables, and demographic changes, illness shocks, and lagged consumption at household and village levels as time-varying endogenous variables. The index of the severity of the crisis experienced (coping index) was treated as time-invariant exogenous, as was (if applicable) whether there was a road available. As time-invariant exogenous variables and instruments, the presence of harvest failure during the famine period, the estimated percentage of households suffering in each village, and the logarithm of livestock before the famine were used. Regression (2) uses the Jalan-Ravallion estimator. Details on the econometric techniques used can be found in Dercon (2004a).

method, comparing the 25th and 75th percentiles of households in terms of the severity of suffering, the latter had about 4 to 16 percentage points lower growth in the 1990s, a period of on average substantial recovery of food consumption and nutrition levels after crisis and war in the 1980s. Furthermore, it took on average 10 years for livestock holdings, a key form of savings and asset accumulation in rural Ethiopia, to recover to the levels seen before the 1984–5 famine.

In general, only limited evidence exists on the persistent effects of shocks, due largely to the lack of data available for this purpose. Still, careful analysis of available evidence can typically uncover some of these effects. An example is recent work on the longer term impact of the Indonesian crisis in 1998. Suryahadi and Sumarto (2003) estimated that the poverty rate more than doubled between the onset of the crisis and its peak, effectively one year. The results in Thomas et al (2004) suggest that there was some disinvestment in schooling, particularly among the poorest households. Subsequently, GDP recovered quickly, and positive growth was restored by 2000; poverty may even have fallen between 1997 and 2000 (Thomas et al 2004). Lokshin and Ravallion (2005) argue nevertheless that this hides a geographically diverse picture. Using a series of extensive cross-section data sets, they find that living standards in many districts were still affected by the shock, even five years after it began, and three years after the sharp recovery. They suggest that a majority of those living below the poverty line in 2002 would not have done so except for the 1998 crisis: in other words, they experienced persistent poverty effects from the 1998 shock.

All the previous evidence is related to a persistent or permanent effect from a shock, thus, uninsured risk is a cause of poverty. Evidence also shows that the mere presence of uninsured risk changes household behavior regarding investment and activity portfolios. The fertility example at the beginning of this section can be so viewed. In addition to the fertility example, further evidence indicates that such behavior may be directly linked to risk and be a cause of perpetuating poverty. Morduch (1990), using the ICRISAT sample, shows that asset-poor households devote a larger share of land to safer traditional varieties of rice and castor than to riskier but higher return varieties. Dercon (1996) finds that Tanzanian households with limited liquid assets (livestock) grow proportionately more sweet potatoes, a low-return, low-risk crop. A household with average livestock holdings allocates 20 percent less of its land to sweet potatoes than a household with no liquid assets. The crop portfolio of the wealthiest quintile yields 25 percent more per adult than that of the poorest quintile. Choosing a less risky crop portfolio thus has substantial negative consequences for incomes.

Rosenzweig and Binswanger (1993) suggest that the portfolio of activities (and investments) in the ICRISAT villages is affected by high risk. Increasing the coefficient of variation of rainfall timing by one standard deviation reduces farm profits of the poorest quartile by 35 percent; for the richest quartile the effect is negligible. Efficiency is affected, and the average incomes of the poor decline. Wealthier farmers are not affected and are therefore able to earn higher incomes. This phenomenon affects wealth distribution: 54 percent of wealth is held by the top 20 percent of households. Jalan and Ravallion (2001) cite other examples, focusing on both asset and activity portfolios, although their evidence is mixed.

Elbers, Gunning, and Kinsey (2003) use simulation-based econometric methods to calibrate a growth model that explicitly accounts for risk and risk responses, applied to panel data from rural Zimbabwe. They found that risk substantially reduces growth, reducing the capital stock (in the steady state) by more than 40 percent. Two-thirds of this loss is due to ex ante strategies by which households try to minimize the impact of risk, that is, they build up livestock holdings to cope with consumption risk. Dercon and Christiaensen (2005), using the same Ethiopian data set discussed above, find a significant increase in fertilizer use if insurance is offered against downside consumption risk, because when rains fail, financial returns to fertilizer use are typically negative. They reach this conclusion from finding significant sensitivity of fertilizer use to the predicted levels of consumption were rains to fail. Because they also control for actual current levels of assets, it is clear that the problem is not just a matter of seasonal credit.

These results on the impact of uninsured risk on assets, activities, and technology choices do not follow simply from differences in risk preferences: controlling for preferences, those with less access to insurance possibilities select a low-risk, low-return portfolio while others take on a riskier set of activities. These results reflect the constraints on the options available to specific households, and *not* simply the risk preferences of households, as some of the earlier agricultural economics literature mentioned earlier often would let us believe: regarding these choices as only governed by preferences devalues the problems faced by households in their efforts to cope with uninsured risk. As Kochar (1995) notes, "the set of options faced by farmers offers little role for preferences" (p. 159). The behavior of the poor with few insurance possibilities may *look* as if they have more (innate) risk-averse preferences, but it is the lack of insurance and credit, and the set of options available to them that forces them to take less risk and therefore forgo income (see Eswaran and Kotwal, 1989, for a careful theoretical discussion).[11]

In sum, increasing evidence demonstrates that uninsured risk increases poverty through ex ante behavioral responses affecting activities, assets, and technology choices, as well as through persistent and possibly permanent effects from transitory shocks via the loss of different types of assets. This clearly has important implications for the design of policies, putting strategies to reduce risk and resulting vulnerability at the core of poverty reduction efforts. Given that poverty concepts rarely incorporate risk, however, the next section discusses the emerging literature on the possible use of a concept of vulnerability to poverty as a guide to policy making.

Vulnerability as a Normative Welfare Concept

The preceding analysis emphasized that uninsured risk has potentially serious consequences for poverty, as measured in observable outcomes in income, consumption, health, education, and other dimensions. If, however, risk and uncertainty are an essential part of a person's livelihood and well-being, the next question is whether vulnerability as a concept or dimension of welfare deserves more attention as well.

Development in recent years has evolved such that multidimensionality is part of mainstream thinking about poverty. Some have viewed it as a progression in keeping with a basic needs approach, emphasizing the attainment of "human development" outcomes, such as education and life expectancy (as in the UNDP Human Development Reports [UNDP 2005]). Others have brought in a more eclectic view, for example, as reflected in the *World Development Report 2000/2001* (World Bank 2001), which emphasized poverty as a lack of opportunities, vulnerability and insecurity, and lack of power. All appear to have embraced the broad thinking on well-being entailed in Sen's capabilities approach, emphasizing that poverty is the lack of freedom to achieve particular outcomes, broadly defined (Sen 2000). Some of these achieved outcomes or functionings could be measured and are essentially multidimensional, while the means to achieve them—such as incomes or endowments—are only instrumental to well-being.

On the basis of much of the preceding analysis, it would be appropriate to emphasize the instrumental role of risk as a cause of poverty and deprivation. Viewed as such, risk has a role in the analysis of poverty but it does not ask for further consideration in any discussion of appropriate concepts of well-being. However, it could be argued that the risk of being poor and the uncertainty about one's ability to secure decent living conditions in the future are essential parts of the experience of well-being. Concepts of "capabilities" and "achieved outcomes" without recognizing risks to translating capabilities into outcomes may miss an important element or dimension of well-being. More specifically, measuring achieved outcomes in health, nutrition, consumption, longevity, or education would miss the point that ex ante they could potentially have been better or worse. Furthermore, given that risk is intrinsically linked to all other dimensions of well-being, it can hardly be seen as a separate dimension.

Poverty measurement, made operational via the measurement of achieved outcomes, tends to involve three steps: the choice of a welfare indicator; the identification of the poor via some norm, the poverty line; and an aggregation procedure. However, the entire analysis tends to take place in a world of certainty: poverty measures are defined after all uncertainty surrounding the individual welfare indicator has been resolved. In many instances this is not a serious problem. For example, when assessing the impact of a new transfer scheme after it has been introduced, data on its actual impact and the resulting poverty outcomes are obviously relevant. However, when deciding to commit resources to competing schemes in advance, evaluating which one will be more effective to reduce poverty will have to take into account potential outcomes in different states of the world. Furthermore, the possibility of serious hardship contains information relevant for assessing low well-being. For example, consider two families, both with the same expected consumption, above some accepted norm, but one with a positive probability of hardship, and the other one facing no uncertainty. Neither is expected to be poor, and after the fact we may observe them to have the same consumption, but surely the possibility of downside risk for the former has some bearing on the ex ante analysis of welfare.

It is surprising that the calculus of risk has not systematically entered into the welfare-economic or quantitative analysis of poverty until fairly recently. Even Sen's (1981) seminal contribution on famines is, in its welfare analysis, concerned with the ex post consequences of the crisis on poverty and destitution. Policy analysis is done with the benefit of hindsight, even though the sequence of events unfolding during the Bangladesh famine in 1974 and the realized outcomes were just one set among a number of possible scenarios ex ante.

The rest of this section introduces recent work on vulnerability concepts and measurement. The concern is not to give a unified descriptive positive measure of vulnerability, which would claim to describe a person's or society's welfare, but rather, as in the spirit of poverty measurement, to provide a normative analysis, whereby all value judgments used to construct a measure are explicit, and which can be used as a tool to conduct analysis and design policy—to prioritize interventions, for example.[12] Furthermore, the section briefly comments on attempts to operationalize this concept.

Vulnerability can be defined as the magnitude of the *threat* of poverty, measured ex ante, before the veil of uncertainty has been lifted.[13] This can be compared to poverty itself, which is the magnitude of low welfare outcomes, observed without uncertainty; low welfare is defined as outcome levels below some accepted poverty line. The focus here is on exposure to the threat or the danger of low welfare outcomes, that is, downside risk, not just risk in general.

Let the vulnerability of a particular person be measured by

$$V^* = V(z,\mathbf{y},\mathbf{p})$$

where z is the poverty line, **y** is a vector of outcomes across n states of the world, and **p** is a vector of corresponding probabilities. It may be easiest to think of these outcomes as consumption levels, but such language will be avoided in an effort to stress that this measure is suitable to other well-being dimensions.[14]

Vulnerability is then a function of outcomes—a norm—and the probabilities linked to each outcome. Many functions could be imagined. To narrow this down for a measure, it is possible to define a number of desirable properties of a vulnerability measure. With a close parallel to well-known poverty axioms (see the annex in Sen 1997, for example) and definitions of risk (Rothschild and Stiglitz 1970), consider six desiderata:

- symmetry (only outcomes matter, and all states of the world are treated in the same way),
- focus (the focus is only on outcomes at or below the "norm"; those above are only valued as the norm),
- probability-dependent outcomes (in the measure, the impact of a change in the outcome in a particular state should only depend on the probability of that state),
- probability transfer (an increase in the probability for a better state at the expense of the probability of a worse state should not increase vulnerability),
- risk sensitivity (the presence of risk increases vulnerability), and
- scale invariance (the units in which z and y are measured do not matter).

Calvo and Dercon (2005) discuss the intuition behind these statements more thoroughly. They show that these six axioms are sufficient to obtain a narrow class of measures defined as

$$V^* = \sum_{i=1}^{n} p_i \, v\,(x_i)$$

where $x_i = \frac{\tilde{y}_i}{z}$, $v(.)$ is moœnotonically decreasing and convex and $\tilde{y}_i = \mathrm{Min}(y_i,z)$. (That is, y_i, but censored at z). This simply reads as the probability-weighted average of some convex function of outcomes, so that the worst states of the world get no lower weight (and higher, if strictly convex) than good states.

A number of measures have been used in recent research that could be compared to this result. Both Ligon and Schechter (2003), and Elbers, Gunning, and Kinsey (2003) take a utilitarian stance and view vulnerability as "low" expected utility, where "low" can be further specified by defining some minimum socially acceptable utility level. Ligon and Schechter's work uses a measure that may violate scale invariance, especially the focus axiom; thus, they do not focus on downside risk but on all risk for the welfare assessment, in line with expected utility. Their utilitarian (or "welfarist") view of vulnerability leads to some arguably peculiar normative results. For example, given the existence of serious downside risk, a person's vulnerability would be reduced by responding to the existence of that danger by increasing her outcomes in exceptionally good states of the world (for example, increasing the cash prize in the national lottery would then be part of a vulnerability-reducing policy).

Another set of measures were inspired by Ravallion (1988). Christiaensen and Subbarao (2004), Suryahadi and Sumarto (2003), Kamanou and Morduch (2004), and Chaudhuri, Jalan, and Suryahadi (2002) are recent examples. They all see vulnerability as expected poverty. Because poverty is usually measured by FGT indexes (Foster, Greer, and Thorbecke 1984), here vulnerability (V^{EP}) may be written as

$$V^{EP} = \sum_{i \forall y_i < z} p_i \left(\frac{z - y_i}{z} \right)^a \text{ where } a \geq 0$$

If $a > 1$, all the axioms thus far are satisfied, but not for $1 \geq a$. This is an important caveat, because the empirical literature resorts to both the probability of being poor ($a = 0$) and the expected shortfall ($a = 1$) with great frequency. For example, $0 < a < 1$ implies that increased risk will reduce vulnerability, while $a = 0$ would violate the probability transfer axiom. Moreover, even though $a > 1$ would secure all the axioms, it also proves to be a troublesome condition, because it imposes the condition that better outcomes will exacerbate the extent to which the individual dreads an increase in risk exposure, in spite of empirical evidence to the contrary (Ligon and Schechter 2003).

Two further axioms offer better alternatives: normalization (so that the measure is bounded between 0 and 1) and constant relative risk sensitivity (a proportional increase in the outcomes of all possible states of the world leads to a similar proportional increase in the certainty-equivalent outcome, implying, among other things, that better outcomes will reduce the extent to which the individual dreads an increase in absolute risk exposure).[15] A straightforward measure, satisfying all these axioms, is as follows:

$$V^*_\alpha = 1 - E[x_i^\alpha],$$

with, as before, $x_i = \frac{\tilde{y}_i}{z}$, and $\tilde{y}_i = \text{Min}(y_i,z)$, and where $0 < \alpha < 1$ and E is the expectation sign. The parameter α can be interpreted as a weight, reflecting risk sensitivity. Given outcomes, normalized by the poverty line and weighted by the risk sensitivity parameter, vulnerability is one minus the probability-weighted value of these normalized and weighted outcomes.

What has been obtained is a *measure of individual vulnerability,* a valuation ex ante of possible welfare levels, taking into account a poverty norm and risk sensitivity. As an individual measure, it provides a basis for comparison between the vulnerability of individuals. Vulnerability is distinct from poverty: a crucial distinction is the time at which it is measured, before or after the veil of uncertainty is lifted. But anyone who is poor with certainty ex post will also have (nonzero) vulnerability ex ante, because all possible outcomes are below the norm.[16] Similarly, all ex ante actions to minimize exposure to risk (such as entering into low-risk activities at the cost of low return) would be reflected in the overall valuation of vulnerability, and the focus is not just on risk but on all possible outcomes. For example, consider two individuals, one with a certain flow of outcomes at a level below the norm in each state of the world, and another individual, otherwise similar, but with some outcomes above the norm and some below in particular states of the world. Vulnerability measurement would provide a clear quantification of the relative position of these individuals, based on the threat of poverty. Admittedly, the approach is by necessity ignorant about whether the individuals themselves would judge the other's implied vulnerability higher or lower than his or her own.

A number of papers have tried to apply vulnerability as discussed above to data, although most appear to focus on the probability of being poor (expected headcount), with the drawbacks reported above. Furthermore, they tend to focus on reporting the figures that draw attention. As with poverty analysis, these headline-grabbing figures are less interesting and less helpful for policy design, even though they end up the only reported evidence. A more fruitful approach would be to construct profiles: finding the correlates of higher and lower vulnerability based on initial conditions, household and community histories, and policy measures. This type of application is still rare. One example is Ligon and Schechter (2003), who derive a vulnerability measure (albeit in the expected utility mode, assuming relative risk aversion, and not just focusing on downside risk) and regress it on certain characteristics using data from Bulgaria (table 5). They find that education substantially reduces vulnerability—for example, those with college education are on average 37 percent less vulnerable. Households in urban areas are (surprisingly) more vulnerable, while land holdings have no impact on vulnerability and owning farm animals reduces vulnerability. Possibly, in post-communist Bulgaria, the countryside can manage the vulnerability linked to change more easily. The sex of the head of household has no impact, while larger households are more vulnerable, although having more employed members or having members drawing a pension reduces vulnerability.

As with standard ex post poverty profiles, it should therefore be possible to generate multivariate vulnerability profiles for different contexts, and make statements about the relative differences in vulnerability between different types of households

TABLE 5.
Correlates of Vulnerability in Bulgaria in 1994, Based on Total Consumption

Variable	Coefficient	Standard error
Primary education	–0.0717	(0.0321)
Secondary education	–0.2356	(0.0354)
Post–secondary education	–0.3350	(0.0377)
Male headed?	–0.0300	(0.0256)
Age	0.0083	(0.0047)
Age squared	–0.0000	(0.0000)
Owns animals?	–0.1001	(0.0259)
Land cultivated (in hectares)	–0.0011	(0.0025)
Urban?	0.0758	(0.0262)
Number of pensioners in household	–0.1183	(0.0212)
Number of employed in household	–0.3095	(0.0237)
Family size	0.2426	(0.0137)

Source: Based on Ligon and Schechter 2003, table 2.

Note: These regressions also include province dummies. Details on variables and method in Ligon and Schechter (2003).

in different localities. However, one crucial part of the analysis has thus far been ignored: how to generate the possible outcomes in different states of the world, which is necessary for vulnerability measurement. This is not straightforward: a forecasting model for outcomes is needed, as is the necessary data to estimate or calibrate a distribution of future outcomes using only information available in advance.

In recent years, many researchers have been tempted to use the limited available data from a number of contexts for this purpose. Some use creative but rather glorious and ultimately unsatisfactory assumptions to exploit estimated and parameterized error distributions from cross-section data to derive distributions of potential outcomes, usually consumption (see, for example, Chaudhuri, Jalan, and Suryahadi 2002). Others use relatively short panel data sets to more carefully calibrate models to generate outcome distributions, although typically by necessity with relatively simple dynamics (for example, Ligon and Schechter 2003). Alternatively, a more dynamic structure was imposed in Elbers, Gunning, and Kinsey (2003). Ultimately, all these studies have to rely on backward-looking information while the purpose is to derive forward-looking outcome distributions—a problem very familiar to the time-series forecasting literature. And as in this literature, a careful Monte Carlo simulation study also showed that the appropriateness of different forecasting models used in the vulnerability literature will effectively depend on the underlying time-series properties of the outcome data, such as whether outcomes are following a nonstationary or a stationary process (Ligon and Schechter 2004).[17] If consumption or other outcomes are stationary, even a short panel or a cross-section may contain sufficient information for an appropriate forecasting model to determine vulnerability. But if outcomes are nonstationary, these models would be inappropriate.

This empirical issue is hard to address with short panels. Posing an even greater problem, if some of the processes described in the previous section are prevalent, such as the possibility that a shock permanently changes the underlying income process, stationarity would be violated, and it would be hard to detect such nonstationarity in very short panels. Overall, the best approach would be to develop careful dynamic models. More work is needed in this respect, but long panel data are typically missing. Does this mean that this endeavor is by necessity doomed? Not necessarily; the growth in good quality data sets for developing countries is impressive, and it is a direction worth considering further.[18]

Policy Implications and the Way Ahead

The presence of uninsured risk results in welfare losses.[19] For the poor, uninsured risk is a reason for substantial hardship. At present, many poor people are not offered opportunities to insure themselves against this hardship, while the support offered when shocks occur is often limited. Viewed in this way, public action to foster more insurance and mechanisms to protect the poor are justified. A further issue results from insurance and credit market failures: given their exposure to downside risk, the poor may enter into activities and asset portfolios with low risk, but also low returns. While this reduces their exposure to downside risk, it affects their long-term income and their ability to move out of poverty in the long run. Furthermore, shocks may have long-lasting effects: productive assets may be destroyed or sold off to survive, health may be undermined, or children may be taken out of school. These actions lead to a lower future income-earning potential for both the current and future generations. The result is higher poverty that may persist.

The presence of risk-reducing but low-return strategies on the part of households trying to reduce their vulnerability, as well as the occurrence of shocks with long-lasting effects, suggest that uninsured risk may lead to poverty traps: poverty persists due to market imperfections, the presence of risk, and the household's responses to it. Temporary support may prevent households from falling into the trap, and may also lift them out. In fact, given that market failures contribute to the existence of these traps, interventions may provide increases in efficiency, so that transfers focused on these groups may be productivity enhancing, without an efficiency-equity trade-off. This provides a strong justification for focusing aid on these problems, especially in the context of promoting broadly based growth. In fact, even in a growing economy, the processes of risk and vulnerability may keep these groups behind, because they cannot take advantage of new profitable opportunities, thus undermining the poverty impacts of growth.

This paper presents evidence supporting this view, but it could be argued that this is not sufficient evidence. The quantitative importance of these effects in different contexts needs to be established more firmly. More empirical work on the short- and long-term consequences of uninsured risk on poverty and growth in the developing world is a priority. The role insurance can play in promoting poverty reduction should not be overstated. If some forms of structural inequalities are the cause of persistent poverty, offering "full insurance of risk" to everyone would simply solidify these inequalities.[20]

Even with this proviso, the case for fostering better risk-focused social protection[21] seems strong, justifying public action and the allocation of budgetary resources to its provision. This does not, however, settle the issue of the form public action should take. State involvement is an obvious option, but encouraging nongovernmental organizations, local social institutions, and the private sector to provide more insurance and protection should be explored, too. A general state-run system of universal social insurance and substantial direct means-tested transfers might seem ideal from an equity point of view, but it is unlikely to be the most cost-effective system, because it would probably involve high administrative costs and possibly substantial incentive-related inefficiencies. In any event, informational requirements make this generally unfeasible in poor countries with limited budgets and administrative capacity. Still, it does not mean that public action cannot achieve substantial improvements in risk-related social protection, even given limited means.

Possible measures can be classified into two categories: first, ex ante measures that result in the poor and vulnerable taking action to reduce risk impact or taking out more insurance, before the veil of uncertainty has been lifted; second, ex post measures that provide transfers to the poor when they face bad shocks that remained uninsured. Ex ante measures would provide incentives and means to the poor to better protect themselves against hardship, perhaps through supporting self-insurance via savings, assisting income risk management by providing access to credit, supporting community-based risk sharing, and encouraging the introduction of insurance products tailored to poor contexts. Ex post measures would provide a genuine safety net, appropriately targeted to the poor but large enough in scale and coverage to provide broadly based social protection at some minimally accepted and feasible standard of living. It could be part of a more general welfare support system, or specifically targeted for risk-related hardship. These options are briefly discussed below.

New Insurance Products

In recent years, microfinance institutions and even insurance companies in developing countries have started to design and provide insurance products for low-income clients. Life and health insurance are most common. Nevertheless, relative to microcredit programs, insurance programs are typically still relatively limited. What scope is there for experimenting with and expanding insurance products? First, it is worthwhile to recall some of the main reasons for the lack of insurance to start with. Market-based insurance requires a high information environment while problems of adverse selection and moral hazard limit the extent to which insurance providers are willing to offer insurance. Problems with enforcement of payouts for claims undermine the willingness of clients to take out insurance. A possible solution for this credibility problem requires the establishment of reinsurance markets, but establishing these markets tends to be difficult and costly. Nonmarket insurance may benefit from a better information environment but there is no scope for insurance of important covariate or infrequent risks. Both market and nonmarket insurers solve some of the information problems they face by excluding certain groups and individuals from their arrangements.

Could micro-insurance—simple, low-cost insurance contracts, tailored to low-income clients—provide a way out? Such contracts need to overcome the same information and enforcement problems as market-based insurance, and the small scale of the contracts will make transactions costs high. Still, just as with micro-credit, it could provide a service to low-income clients who otherwise would remain rationed in the market, even if it would require substantial subsidies. It is nevertheless helpful to emphasize some differences with micro-credit provision. First, the enforcement problem in credit is faced by the loan provider, but in insurance, it is a problem for the client. Second, with credit, borrowers and lenders repeatedly interact during the repayment period, implying regular transactions and monitoring costs. For insurance, the information content of the regular payment of the premium is rather limited. The provider incurs only small transactions costs, because the insurance can be easily withdrawn when the premium is not paid; transactions costs are irregular and only high when a claim comes in. Finally, reinsurance is essential to keep the costs of insurance provision low, thus requiring regulation, high quality of actuarial data, and the certification of events to allow the reinsurance market to function.

The need for reinsurance and the costs of verification of claims imply that the types of risk that can be insured at relatively low cost are limited. Certain events may be easily verifiable, such as death or serious illness, so that life and health insurance might be obvious contracts to start with. Even in those cases there may be problems, however. To avoid adverse selection, certain groups would need to be excluded, based on disease (such as AIDS) or age—but these are the very groups that may suffer serious hardship without insurance. Reinsurance would require systems of certification—but what if in certain locations with poor institutions it may be easy to obtain false death or poor health certificates?

In general, surprisingly little research exists for micro-insurance, at least compared to the vast micro-credit literature. Additionally, little or no systematic evidence indicates how existing risk-sharing or other social institutions could be mobilized to provide a basis for more widespread insurance provision for different types of risk. The main requirement now is to obtain empirical evidence, thus highlighting the need for experiments combined with research, preferably in the form of "natural" micro-insurance experiments to evaluate its impact.

Alternative insurance products could also be promising. Weather-indexed bonds are one such example. A critical advantage is that claim verification is straightforward: a key source of losses is insured, not the loss itself.[22] Still, given the high covariance of rainfall and other climatic factors across regions and countries, the development of reinsurance markets covering large geographic areas would be particularly important. Whether products for weather or catastrophic risk can be introduced in some of the poorest countries remains to be seen, although some encouraging evidence is emerging (Skees et al 2004).

Promoting Self-Insurance through Savings and Micro-Credit

In addition to designing and supplying better insurance products for the poor, the poor can also be assisted to protect themselves. Substantial scope remains for more self-insurance, provided better savings instruments suitable for the poor can be offered (Dercon 2002). A key problem with existing self-insurance via assets is that such mechanisms tend to be risky and may be strongly covariate with incomes, limiting their effectiveness, while financial savings products are typically not tailored to the poor, offering low or negative returns, and involving prohibitive transactions costs.

As an area for subsidized intervention and regulation, self-insurance also does not suffer from the important informational problems affecting credit and standard insurance. Adverse selection and moral hazard are not issues, nor are there any serious reinsurance issues. The main issues are potentially high transactions costs and the need for credibility of the institution (Morduch and Sharma 2002). With few exceptions, such as SafeSave in Bangladesh, initiatives remain relatively thin on the ground. Most savings instruments within microfinance institutions still appear to be used primarily to access micro-credit—for example, as a means of developing reputation and commitment. Flexible savings instruments for precautionary purposes are usually not encouraged.

This does not mean that there is no further role for more standard micro-credit products. Increasing assets and incomes, which in turn allow savings to increase, offer a virtuous cycle to provide a buffer against future hardship. Furthermore, access to credit can serve as a means of insurance, allowing the poor to borrow in bad years against future incomes. Finally, because profitable sources of income, suitable for diversification purposes in an income risk management strategy, often involve important setup costs, small loans could have a very large impact on income risk exposure. Overall, however, this requires that microfinance institutions offer flexible products that allow the poor to enter into credit despite being faced with substantial risk. A possible solution would be to provide interlinked contracts, which typically offer more efficient outcomes than separate credit and specific insurance contracts; this is a standard solution for mortgage lending products in developed countries. An example would be to link credit with health insurance. More experimentation and research on such products is needed.

The Role of Targeted Transfers

Ex ante measures may provide substantial protection, but ultimately they cannot fully insure individuals and families. Informal mechanisms only offer limited insurance. Micro-insurance products will have to be simple, insuring only specific, highly observable risks, while high-risk groups may have to be excluded by design. The existence of certain risks, for example, catastrophic risks, can hardly be anticipated beforehand. Self-insurance fails if shocks happen to materialize in successive periods. All self-protection strategies require some outlay beforehand, at times high to guarantee the sustainability of the institution; the poorest households may not be able to afford such outlays, while credit to pay for insurance may not be available. Finally, the presence of uncertainty (the unknown unknowns) as distinct from risk also implies that household strategies and market-based products would fail in particular circumstances. In short, some ex post measures providing transfers to those affected by uninsured risk would always be necessary as part of a risk-related social protection system.

The scope and form of a transfer-based safety net would require an exhaustive discussion, beyond the reach of this paper. A few issues are relevant, however. For example, targeted support is probably the most efficient solution given limited means, but the potential errors of targeting bear caution, especially for those requiring support but excluded due to imperfections in the targeting design. Self-targeted programs may seem most attractive, where the design of the program ensures incentives for participation only by the target group and not by others, thus avoiding costly identification of the beneficiaries. Workfare programs such as food-for-work are often designed in such a way, but the return to the beneficiaries has to be kept low to ensure incentives for others not to participate. Coverage is typically not complete: certain groups may not be reached by such programs—for example, women that have to look after children may not find the time to take part. Alternative targeting schemes, such as allowing community leaders to select beneficiaries or schemes based on observed characteristics (such as nutritional status or livestock ownership), have their own costs and problems (Conning and Kevane 2002; Ravallion 2002). Who should be targeted for uninsured risk transfers is also not self-evident. In principle, an efficient safety net should arguably be most concerned with reaching those for whom protection will forestall poverty traps or persistence, via its effect on investment and activity choice. Given the problems of identifying those who are currently poor, it is unlikely that those most needing a safety net can be identified using any of the possible targeting methods.

The ex ante and ex post measures discussed above are relatively strictly focused on risk. However, at least as important would be to build risk-related dimensions into standard policy interventions. Just as risk is intrinsically linked to processes of income generation and asset formation, any program focused on income generation and asset formation should recognize these risk dimensions. Consider the following two examples.

Promoting modern inputs adoption.

Since the mid-1990s, the Ethiopian government has been promoting the adoption of modern input packages (such as fertilizer and high-yielding crop varieties), provided on seasonal credit with strict repayment enforcement, often involving local government officials. In the early years, with good rains, adoption increased rapidly because mean returns were high. However, after a series of poor harvests, repayment enforcement resulted in serious hardship in some areas and adoption flattened. Mean returns remain high in many areas, but in poor rainfall years, returns are low and possibly negative given the need to repay the credit. A credit product with some insurance element, such as weather-indexing, would surely be superior in this high climatic risk environment.

Conditional cash transfer programs.

In the 1990s, a number of programs were inspired by the Progresa program in Mexico, in which families received a cash transfer conditional on children enrolling and attending school. The incentive appears to have resulted in substantial increases in enrollment and other positive welfare effects. However, the program design ignores possible risk, while evidence in other settings has shown that school attendance may well be responsive to income shocks (Jacoby and Skoufias 1997). It has been suggested that even in the Progresa setting, a more efficient conditional cash transfer program would have included some element of "insurance" in which cash transfers could vary, for example, on the basis of local climatic and other circumstances.[23]

Whether particular programs focused on risk, or including some risk considerations, are effective must be determined empirically. The dearth of evidence at the moment leads to many possible interventions being reduced to standard safety nets. While in some settings this may be the most appropriate response, much more field-testing and experimentation with alternative programs, in the context of well-designed evaluations, would be worthwhile.

Notes

1. Risk can be viewed as the "known unknowns," while uncertainty is the "unknown unknowns."
2. Similar questions had been asked of the same households a decade earlier, see Dercon (2002) or the *World Development Report 2000/2001* (World Bank 2001, p. 140, table 8.2). The recall period was longer in Dercon (2002) so only the relative importance of shocks offers a suggestive comparison. The pattern is not dissimilar with one exception: the issue of taxation, land expropriation, and other "policy"-related problems were at that time the second most important category of problems reported, with at least 42 percent reporting taxation or forced labor and 17 percent reporting land expropriation problems.
3. In economics, the "consumption smoothing" and "risk-sharing" literature has thrived, and indeed work on developing countries has heavily influenced the mainstream research agenda. Surveys of this literature are found in Townsend (1995), Deaton (1997), Dercon (2002), and Morduch (2004).
4. Some caution is needed in using this information. If unobserved heterogeneity is correlated with the direct shock terms, what we may be picking up is not the impact of the shock, but some other characteristic, correlated with observing particular shocks. Arguably, we may then be measuring that unobserved characteristic and not the impact of the shock.
5. This is a straw man, set up to be destroyed in the rest of the paper, and "hard" evidence of this view is not easily found. However, it was prominent during the period of "social dimensions to adjustment" in the 1980s and 1990s, when it was considered necessary to set up temporary safety nets to cushion the possible hardship following retrenchment and public sector reform, as an afterthought in the context of stimulating growth as the key means to reducing poverty.
6. The fact that the expanding experimental literature on risk and preferences questions the validity of some of the underlying behavioral models for this analysis is not necessarily changing this view. Kahnemann and Tversky (1979) and some of their other work have shown that risk aversion may not be the appropriate concept, but that agents at any level of income do not like losses, leading to a concept of "loss aversion." Ideas of "safety

first," while seemingly not consistent with most experimental evidence, would also entail preference-led persistence in poverty.

7. The discussion of the evidence is based on Dercon and Hoddinott (2004).

8. BMI is defined as weight in kg, divided by the square of height in meters.

9. A poverty trap can be defined as an equilibrium outcome and a situation from which one cannot emerge without outside help, for example, via a positive windfall to a particular group, such as redistribution or aid, or via a fundamental change in the functioning of markets. Poverty traps are often conceptualized as caused by the presence of increasing returns to scale, although other mechanisms are possible, such as credit market failures or externalities. Dercon (2004c) provides a review of models relevant for poverty analysis, as does Barrett (2004).

10. Dercon (2004a) did not allow for the nonlinearities implied by multiple equilibria, as in more direct tests of poverty traps.

11. A possible source of confusion in the literature is the concept of "asset integration" (see, for example, Newbery and Stiglitz [1981]), arguing that risk preferences should be measured relative to final wealth levels. With imperfect credit and insurance markets, wealth is a *constraint* in the choice set and other constraints could be entered in assessing the behavior toward risk, but this is arguably different from assessing preferences before constraints on choices are considered.

12. There has obviously been a long debate about whether welfare measurement in economics can ever be devoid of value judgments, going back to Friedman and others. In the context of risk, economists typically use the "expected utility" framework, a weighted average of the satisfaction linked to each outcome, weighted by the probability of the state in which it would occur. It is used descriptively, as if decision making by households implies that they implicitly or explicitly maximize this. But even when using this as a descriptive concept for individual welfare, one has to enter the realm of normative economics, as one does when aggregating to obtain society-wide measurement. Poverty analysis, by focusing on specific welfare indicators, evaluated using a specific norm and aggregated by attributing weights to outcomes, is explicitly normative. Sen (2000) and his previous writings have clear discussions on these issues.

13. The rest of the analysis in this section is based on Calvo and Dercon (2005).

14. Recall the parallel with individual poverty measures that can be written as $P_i^*=P(z,y_i)$, but then only one outcome y_i needs to be considered. Aggregate poverty indexes that aggregate over P_i^* also aggregate over a vector of different y_i, but then aggregation is over individuals, not over states of the world (as it will be the case with V^*).

15. Alternatively, one could impose absolute relative risk sensitivity. See Calvo and Dercon (2005) for details.

16. So statements such as "person x is not vulnerable but outright poor" and "person y is vulnerable if she is not poor but . . ." are not statements that could be helpfully made using our concept, or at best reflect confusion about what is observed and when.

17. A stationary series can be understood as observations derived from a data-generating process that has stable mean and variance. In the context of this paper, this would mean that, for a particular household, the distribution of the outcome variable is identical in each period. A nonstationary series would not have this property. An example would be if consumption were to follow a random walk: that is, any shock has a permanent impact so that the best prediction of the current level is the previous period's level.

18. One issue ignored in this discussion is the time scale over which vulnerability is being measured—next year, in the next five years? In principle, prediction models can be constructed for different time spans, but again, the errors involved in these predictions will be dependent on the underlying properties of the series and the quality of the prediction model.

19. This section is partly based on Dercon (2004b), chapter 19.

20. Banerjee (2004) warned about another problem: providing more insurance in the form of protection against downside risk may provide incentives for more risk-taking so that the poor take on high return, risky investments. But this may undermine their access to credit markets, if moneylenders and banks need sufficient incentives for the borrower to repay in case the project fails. Social protection and safety nets may reduce these incentives, so the poor may become more excluded from credit markets. If they need access to these markets to grow out of poverty, they may become locked in long-term poverty because of social insurance such as the presence of a safety net. The empirical significance of this effect is unknown, but worth exploring.

21. The term "social protection" as used in this concluding section is rather narrow, and often qualified with "risk-focused." The term is used to focus on measures that support managing risk and the reduction of risk impact on the population and the poor in particular. Often, social protection is more broadly used to include as well the general or targeted welfare policies, including redistribution efforts and targeted transfers, without any risk focus. The paper does not try to argue that these broader social protection policies are not important (on the contrary), but rather, that there is much to be gained from concentrating on social protection with a specific risk-related vulnerability focus, as is done in the concluding section.

22. Developing weather insurance tailored to the poor may be less straightforward. It would require verifiable records on rainfall. But if the poor tend to live in marginal areas with limited agricultural wealth, few rainfall stations are likely to be available. Unless the local rainfall is highly covariate with rainfall in "richer" areas, rainfall insurance would not offer much protection.

23. Elisabeth Sadoulet, personal communication, March 2005.

References

Alderman, H., J. Hoddinott, and B. Kinsey. 2003. "Long Term Consequences of Early Childhood Malnutrition." Unpublished, Department of Economics, Dalhousie University, Halifax, Canada.

Alwang, J., P. Siegel, and S. Jorgensen. 2001. "Vulnerability: A View from Different Disciplines." Social Protection Unit, Human Development Network, World Bank, Washington, DC.

Banerjee, A. 2004. "The Two Poverties." In *Insurance against Poverty,* ed. S. Dercon, 59–75. Oxford: Oxford University Press.

Barrett, C. B. 2004. "Rural Poverty Dynamics: Development Policy Implications." Unpublished, Department of Applied Economics and Management, Cornell University, Ithaca, NY.

Barrett, C. B., and M. Carter. 2004. "The Economics of Poverty Traps and Persistent Poverty: An Asset-based Approach." Unpublished, Cornell University, Ithaca, NY.

Bigsten, Arne, P. Collier, S. Dercon, M. Fafchamps, B. Gauthier, J. W. Gunning, A. Isaksson, A. Oduro, R. Oostendorp, C. Patillo, M. Soderbom, F. Teal, and A. Zeufack. 2000. "Rates of Return on Physical and Human Capital in Africa's Manufacturing Sector." *Economic Development and Cultural Change* 48 (4): 801–28.

Binswanger, H. 1981. "Attitudes toward Risk: Theoretical Implications of an Experiment in Rural India." *Economic Journal* 91 (364): 867–90.

Bourguignon, F., C. Goh, and D. Kim. 2004. "Estimating Individual Vulnerability Using Pseudo-Panel Data." Policy Research Working Paper 3375, World Bank, Washington, DC.

Calvo, C., and S. Dercon. 2005. "Measuring Individual Vulnerability," Department of Economics Working Paper No. 229, Oxford University, U.K.

Chambers, R. 1989. "Editorial Introduction: Vulnerability, Coping and Policy," *IDS Bulletin* 20 (2): 1–7.

Chaudhuri, S., J. Jalan, and A. Suryahadi. 2002. "Assessing Household Vulnerability to Poverty from Cross-Sectional Data: A Methodology and Estimates from Indonesia." Discussion Paper 0102-52, Columbia University, New York.

Christiaensen, L., and R. Boisvert. 2000. "On Measuring Households Food Vulnerability: Case Evidence from Northern Mali." Working Paper 2000–05, Department of Agricultural, Resource and Managerial Economics, Cornell University, Ithaca, NY.

Christiaensen, L., and K. Subbarao. 2004. "Toward an Understanding of Household Vulnerability in Rural Kenya." Policy Research Working Paper No. 3326, World Bank, Washington, DC.

Conning, J., and M. Kevane. 2002. "Community Based Targeting Mechanisms for Social Safety Nets: A Critical Review." *World Development* 30 (3): 375–94.

———. 2004. "Why Isn't There More Financial Intermediation in Developing Countries." In *Insurance against Poverty,* ed. S. Dercon, 330–60. Oxford: Oxford University Press.

Das, J., S. Dercon, J. Habyarimana, and P. Krishnan. 2004. "When Can School Inputs Improve Test Scores?" Policy Research Working Paper No. 3217, World Bank, Washington, DC.

Dasgupta, P. 1993. *An Inquiry into Well-Being and Destitution.* Oxford: Oxford University Press.

Dasgupta, P., and D. Ray. 1986. "Inequality as a Determinant of Malnutrition and Unemployment: Theory." *The Economic Journal* 96 (384): 1011–34.

Deaton, A. 1997. *The Analysis of Household Surveys: A Microeconomic Approach.* Baltimore, MD: Johns Hopkins University Press.

Dercon, S. 1996. "Risk, Crop Choice and Savings: Evidence from Tanzania." *Economic Development and Cultural Change* 44 (3): 385–514.

———. 2002. "Income Risk, Coping Strategies and Safety Nets." *World Bank Research Observer* 17 (2) 141–66.

———. 2004a. "Growth and Shocks: Evidence from Rural Ethiopia." *Journal of Development Economics* 74 (2): 309–29.

———, ed. 2004b. *Insurance against Poverty.* Oxford: Oxford University Press.

———. 2004c. "Poverty Traps and Development: The Efficiency-Equity Trade-Off Revisited." In *Poverty, Inequality and Growth, Proceedings of the AFD-EUDN Conference 2003.* Paris: Agence Française de Développement.

Dercon, S., and L. Christiaensen. 2005. "Consumption Risk and Technology Adoption in Rural Ethiopia." Unpublished. Oxford University and the World Bank.

Dercon, S., and J. Hoddinott. 2004. "Health, Shocks and Poverty Persistence." In *Insurance against Poverty,* ed. S. Dercon, 123–36. Oxford: Oxford University Press.

Dercon, S., and P. Krishnan. 2000a. "In Sickness and in Health: Risk-Sharing within Households in Ethiopia." *Journal of Political Economy* 108 (4): 688–727.

———. 2000b. "Vulnerability, Seasonality and Poverty in Ethiopia." *Journal of Development Studies* 36 (6): 25–53.

Dercon, S., J. Hoddinott, and T. Woldehanna. 2005. "Vulnerability and Shocks in 15 Ethiopian Villages, 1999–2004." Unpublished, Oxford University.

Elbers, C., J. Gunning, and B. Kinsey. 2003. "Growth and Risk: Methodology and Microevidence." Tinbergen Institute Discussion Papers, 03-068/2, Tinbergen Institute, Amsterdam.

Eswaran, M., and A. Kotwal. 1989. "Credit as Insurance in Agrarian Economies." *Journal of Development Economics* 31 (1): 37–53.

Fogel, R. W. 1999. "Catching Up with the Economy." *American Economic Review* 89 (1): 1–21.

Foster, J., J. Greer, and E. Thorbecke. 1984. "A Class of Decomposable Poverty Measures." *Econometrica* 52 (3): 761–6.

Jacoby, H., and E. Skoufias. 1997. "Risk, Financial Markets and Human Capital in a Developing Country." *Review of Economic Studies* 64 (3): 311–36.

Jalan, J., and M. Ravallion. 2000. "Is Transient Poverty Different? Evidence from Rural China." *Journal of Development Studies* 36 (6): 338–57.

———. 2001. "Behavioral Responses to Risk in Rural China." *Journal of Development Economics* 66 (1): 23–49.

———. 2004. "Household Income Dynamics in Rural China." In *Insurance against Poverty,* ed. S. Dercon 107–23. Oxford: Oxford University Press.

Kahneman, D., and A. Tversky. 1979. "Prospect Theory: An Analysis of Decision Under Risk." *Econometrica* 47 (2): 263–91.

Kamanou, G., and J. Morduch. 2004. "Measuring Vulnerability to Poverty." In *Insurance against Poverty,* ed. S. Dercon, 155–75. Oxford: Oxford University Press.

Kochar, A. 1995. "Explaining Household Vulnerability to Idiosyncratic Income Shocks." AEA Papers and Proceedings, *American Economic Review* 85 (2): 159–64.

Ligon, E., and L. Schechter. 2003. "Measuring Vulnerability." *Economic Journal* 113 (486): C95–C102.

———. 2004. "Evaluating Different Approaches to Estimating Vulnerability." Social Protection Discussion Paper No. 0210, World Bank, Washington, DC.

Lokshin, M., and M. Ravallion. 2000. "Short-Lived Shocks with Long-Lived Impacts? Household Income Dynamics in a Transition Economy." Working Paper Series No. 2459, World Bank, Washington, DC.

———. 2005. "Lasting Local Impacts of an Economy-Wide Crisis." Policy Research Working Paper, World Bank, Washington, DC.

Martorell, R. 1999. "The Nature of Child Malnutrition and Its Long-Term Implications." *Food and Nutrition Bulletin* 20 (3): 288–92.

Morduch, J. 1990. "Risk, Production and Saving: Theory and Evidence from Indian Households." Working paper, Harvard University.

———. 1995. "Income Smoothing and Consumption Smoothing." *Journal of Economic Perspectives* 9 (Summer): 103–14.

———. 1999. "Between the State and the Market: Can Informal Insurance Patch the Safety Net?" *World Bank Research Observer* 14 (2): 187–207.

———. 2004. "Consumption Smoothing Across Space." In *Insurance against Poverty,* ed. S. Dercon, 38–56. Oxford: Oxford University Press.

Morduch, J., and M. Sharma. 2002. "Strengthening Public Safety Nets from the Bottom Up." Social Protection Discussion Paper No. 0227, World Bank, Washington, DC.

Narayan, Deepa, and Patti Petesch. 2002. *Voices of the Poor: From Many Lands.* New York, NY: Published for the World Bank, Oxford University Press.

Narayan, Deepa, Robert Chambers, Meera Kaul Shah, and Patti Petesch. 2000. *Voices of the Poor: Crying Out for Change.* New York, NY: Published for the World Bank, Oxford University Press.

Narayan, Deepa, Raj Patel, Kai Schafft, Anne Rademacher, and Sarah Koch-Schulte. 2000. *Voices of the Poor: Can Anyone Hear Us?* New York, NY: Published for the World Bank, Oxford University Press.

Newbery, D., and J. Stiglitz. 1981. *The Theory of Commodity Price Stabilization*. Oxford: Oxford University Press.

Pitt, M., M. Rosenzweig, and M. D. Hassan. 1990. "Productivity, Health and Inequality in the Intrahousehold Distribution of Food in Low Income Countries." *American Economic Review* 80 (5): 1139–56.

Ravallion, M. 1988. "Expected Poverty under Risk-Induced Welfare Variability." *The Economic Journal* 98 (393): 1171–82.

———. 2002. "Targeted Transfers in Poor Countries: Revisiting the Trade-Offs and Policy Options." Social Protection Discussion Paper No. 0314, World Bank, Washington, DC.

Rosenzweig, M., and H. Binswanger. 1993. "Wealth, Weather Risk and the Composition and Profitability of Agricultural Investments." *Economic Journal* 103 (416): 56–78.

Rosenzweig, M., and K. Wolpin. 1993. "Credit Market Constraints, Consumption Smoothing, and the Accumulation of Durable Production Assets in Low-income Countries: Investment in Bullocks in India." *Journal of Political Economy* 101 (2): 223–44.

Rothschild, M., and J. E. Stiglitz. 1970. "Increasing Risk I: A Definition." *Journal of Economic Theory* 2 (3): 225–43.

Sen, A. 1981. *Poverty and Famines. An Essay on Entitlement and Deprivation*. Oxford: Oxford University Press.

———. 1997. *On Economic Inequality.* Expanded edition with a substantial annex by J. E. Foster. Oxford: Clarendon Press.

———. 2000. *Development as Freedom*. Oxford: Clarendon Press.

Skees, J., P. Varangis, D. Larson, and P. Siegel. 2004. "Can Financial Markets be Tapped to Help Poor People Cope with Weather Risks?" In *Insurance against Poverty,* ed. S. Dercon, 422–51. Oxford: Oxford University Press.

Strauss, J., and D. Thomas. 1998. "Health, Nutrition, and Economic Development." *Journal of Economic Literature* 36 (2): 766–817.

Suryahadi, A., and S. Sumarto. 2003. "Poverty and Vulnerability in Indonesia Before and After the Economic Crisis." *Asian Economic Journal* 17 (1): 45–64.

Thomas, D., K. Beegle, E. Frankenberg, B. Sikoki, J. Strauss, and G. Teruel. 2004. "Education in a Crisis." *Journal of Development Economics* 74 (1): 53–85.

Townsend, R. M. 1995. "Consumption Insurance: An Evaluation of Risk-Bearing Systems in Low-Income Economies." *Journal of Economic Perspectives* 9 (Summer): 83–102.

UNDP (United Nations Development Programme). 2005. Human Development Reports. http://hdr.undp.org/reports/.

van de Walle, D., and K. Nead, eds. 1995. *Public Spending and the Poor: Theory and Evidence*. Baltimore: Johns Hopkins University Press.

Waaler, H. 1984. "Height, Weight and Mortality: The Norwegian Experience." *Acta Medica Scandinavia* (supp) 679: 1–56.

Waterlow, J. 1988. *Linear Growth Retardation in Less Developed Countries*. Nestle Nutrition workshop series Vol. 14. New York: Raven Press.

World Bank. 1993. *World Development Report: Investing in Health*. New York: Oxford University Press.

———. 2001. *World Development Report 2000/2001. Attacking Poverty.* New York: Oxford University Press.

Comment on "Vulnerability: A Micro Perspective," by Stefan Dercon

PAUL MOSLEY

Stefan Dercon's paper presents an admirable case for treating vulnerability as a component of poverty, and supports it with a great deal of new evidence on the persisting effects of income shocks and on what may be called the "pinning-in effects" of risk on the poor, deterring them from attempting the high-yield projects which might extract them from the poverty trap and thus perpetuating the vicious circle of poverty. I shall try to supplement his argument in relation to three of his themes: (a) the redefinition of poverty in the face of vulnerability considerations; (b) the impacts of vulnerability; and principally (c), the measures that may be taken to protect against it.

Vulnerability-Sensitive Poverty Definitions

Vulnerability, like poverty, can be evaluated both subjectively (for example, in terms of the interviewee's fears that she or he may be pushed below the poverty line during the next year) and objectively (for example, in terms of risk efficacy—the ratio of measurable risks, such as drought or ill-health, to assets).[1] The choice of indicator used to represent Dercon's vulnerability concepts, whether the "low expected utility" or "expectations of poverty" measure is used, makes a significant difference to the assessment of vulnerability, and in turn to the measured assessment of impact and to the actions taken to defend against it.

Causes and Impacts of Vulnerability

Let me try and illustrate immediately the impact that vulnerability has on people. One of the key reasons the concept of vulnerability is important is because awareness of

---

Paul Mosley is Professor of Economics, University of Sheffield.

Annual World Bank Conference on Development Economics—Europe 2006

TABLE 1.
Impact of Poverty and Vulnerability Measures on Behavior

	Indicator of Deprivation			
	Income poverty	**Vulnerability indicator[a]**	**Vulnerability (objective indicators only)**	**Vulnerability (subjective indicators only)**
Regression coefficient of deprivation indicator on risk aversion	0.000027 (1.34)	0.041** (4.46)	–0.000001 (–0.65)	0.03** (3.43)
Regression coefficient of deprivation indicator on physical investment	–0.000045 (0.65)	–0.102* (2.45)	–0.000061 (1.49)	–0.099* (1.99)

Source: Mosley and Verschoor 2005.

Note: Ordinary least squares analysis. T-statistics in parentheses. Sample: 296 farmers in Sironko and Bufumbo, eastern Uganda, surveyed in December 2001.

a. Measured using the components described in note 1 to this comment.

* significant at the 10 percent level.

** significant at the 5 percent level.

it helps us to understand behavior that material poverty on its own does not explain. In eastern Uganda between 2001 and 2003, Arjan Verschoor and I used experimental methods to measure attitudes toward risk, and to assess the impact of these attitudes on rural investment behavior.[2] Our estimates are presented in table 1. They suggest that risk aversion, and therefore investment, are responsive to vulnerability but not to income poverty.

These findings not only indicate a role for vulnerability in explaining behavior, but show that, as suggested above, the way it is measured is important for understanding the kinds of vulnerability that trigger changes in behavior.

I would like to take the theme of disentangling different kinds of vulnerability a step further. Beginning in table 1 in his paper, Dercon distinguishes between various risks afflicting Ethiopian peasant farmers according to their severity: the main ones are drought, death and illness of significant others, pests, crime, input prices, and political shocks. It is relevant for the construction of defenses against vulnerability to subdivide these further into shocks that arise from nature (for example, drought and pests) and shocks that arise from interpersonal relationship or its failure (these cut across Dercon's categories, but a part of "difficulty in obtaining inputs," a part of "crime" related to deception, a part of "political shocks," and a part of the risk associated with failure of collaborative enterprises and inability to access common property resources surely belong in here). We call these respectively natural and relational vulnerability. These pathologies of interpersonal relationship are important in the context of social protection because the appropriate defense against vulnerability, which is insurance, is not available in the case of situations of vulnerability that are relationally induced. In the essay by Wood (2003), exploitative interpersonal relationships between patrons and their clients (for example, labor-tenancy, tied in with rudimentary education and other protectional services) are represented as a "Faustian bargain" that vulnerable people may choose to protect themselves against risk, and in so doing lock themselves into activities with low rates of return. The key point is that although these social relationships and especially their going wrong (failures of trust) may be the fundamental cause of a person's being caught in a poverty trap, they lie behind several of the proximate causes listed in Dercon's table 1, rather than on the surface, and may therefore not be identified by the Ethiopian subjects as a cause of that vulnerability. And yet, awareness of this may be key to protection against vulnerabilities of this sort.

In some cases, there is an important gender dimension to this vulnerability. Females, probably more than males, may on committing themselves to a substantial act of entrepreneurship find themselves not only vulnerable to inability to service debt, but also cut off from traditional kin support and other mechanisms of informal insurance.[3] Many case study anecdotes are now available to illustrate the dynamics of poverty traps of this sort, and in particular the manner in which a transient shock can push a vulnerable household into long-term chronic poverty, reinforcing the argument about persistence of shocks in Dercon's own paper (Carter and May [1999]; Zimmerman and Carter [2003]; Hulme and Shepherd [2003]; and others) because there is a trade-off between commitment to entrepreneurship, or even the labor market, and informal mechanisms of insurance. Even the seeking of wage employment may cause social disapproval and social decapitalization, and this is one of the classic cases in which relational vulnerability reinforces a twist in the vicious circle of poverty.[4] Some of this evidence for this particular link in the long-term poverty trap is to be found in the context of industrialized as well as developing countries. Indeed, the case study I would like to quote (see box 1) to illustrate the general point is from Britain and is selected because it illustrates the three points (about gender, about institutionally enhanced vulnerability, and about the cross-cultural relevance of the concept) all together, and further because it leads into the final part of my story about institutional defenses against vulnerability. The passages in the box in italics are the ones where I feel that a consideration of the relational dimension of risk takes us beyond Stefan Dercon's exposition.

The essential point of box 1 is that where vulnerability is relational, in the shape of either short-term failures of trust or long-term exploitative relationships, the "therapy" required to protect against vulnerability goes beyond conventional risk-mitigation institutions and must be sought within the structure of the relationships themselves.

Institutions against Vulnerability

The particular institutions against vulnerability considered by Dercon are self-insurance, microfinance, micro-insurance, conditional cash transfers of the Progresa variety, and, in passing, the somewhat idealized concept of universal social protection. Within these we shall particularly concentrate on microfinance and micro-insurance.

Box 1. Case Study: Dressmaker and Clothing Retailer, Sheffield 5, United Kingdom

Black female single parent, in her 30s; educated to secondary level; had taken, at community college, a "black access course" in introductory business skills including letter writing and bookkeeping. Unemployed and on benefits until she received, in January 2001, a loan of £5,000 (about US$9,000) from SENTA (Sheffield Enterprise Agency), later topped up by a further £2,000 (about US$3,500). Approached and was refused a loan by a commercial bank "on grounds that she was unemployed, lacking capital, and lacking business experience."

The client initially opened, in one of the few ethnic-minority areas in Sheffield, a shop selling smart "street wear," appealing at that stage mainly to the black population. She expanded her market through advertising in clothes parties and free sheets distributed through people's doors. The business proved unexpectedly seasonal, with slumps in school holidays; nonetheless, it managed, with the help of judicious advertising guided by the SENTA mentor, to diversify into a broader market (basically the under-25 age group), and at its peak in September 2001, her market was 60 percent white and her turnover at an annual rate of £20,000 (about US$35,000) per year. A blend of mentoring and instinct—not, on her insistence, discussions with black traders in a similar position—had enabled her not only to grow fast, but also to jump the ethnic divide into a new market sector. Indeed, significantly for what was to come, her links with family and other members of the local black community loosened somewhat during this period. Speculatively, they may have been envious of her success at this time.

The business was then cut down by two burglaries, in October 2001 and January 2002, the second of which also involved some damage to the premises. The client has been pushed back below the poverty line, and is now trading "passively" from home, without the possibility of advertising from home or a shop outlet. The proximate cause of failure was not only the second burglary as such—the premises were insured—but that the insurance company involved had taken, at the time of writing, 12 months to assess the claim, and has paid out nothing so far. For all its fast growth, and its ability to withstand two shocks, the business did not have the "risk efficacy" to withstand the third shock.

Source: Lenton and Mosley 2005.

Microfinance, although often utilized to smooth consumption and therefore represented as a form of insurance (for example, Platteau and Abraham [1987]) is exposed, in the present context, to the criticism that it augments the debt-service obligations of very poor people and thereby their vulnerability in the event of a negative shock. In cases in which a dynamic microfinance sector is suddenly contami-

TABLE 2.
Performance Indicators and Possible Explanatory Factors in Bolivian Microfinance Organizations, 1997–2002

Indicator	ProMujer and CRECER	Other microfinance organizations
Well-being indicators (as of December 2002)		
Poor and destitute (%)	38.0	10.6
Without lowest level of education (%)	14.1	5.1
Asset value (US$)	421.6	924.4
Average annual sales (US$)	757.9	2,502.8
Performance indicators (annual average 1997–2002)		
Percentage growth of portfolio	24.7	5.7
Percentage growth of customer base	26.2	–5.3
Default rate (percent)	0.6	9.8
Return on assets (percent)	6.9	–1.9
Design characteristics		
Percentage female clients	98	57
"Internal account" for emergency loans	Yes	No
Loan modality	Village banks with solidarity groups	Solidarity groups, with the exception of FIE, Caja Los Andes, most of BancoSol, and the consumer-credit FFPs
Average loan size (US$)	134	901
Training services offered?	Yes: health, bookkeeping, legal services, and others	No (except for FIE)

Source: Marconi and Mosley forthcoming.

Note: FFP = *fondo financiero privado* (licensed nonbank financial intermediary); FIE = *Fondo de Inversiones Economicas.*

nated by imitative consumer-credit institutions and undermined by the collapse of a boom—such as in Bolivia between 1996 and 2000, but also applicable to a number of eastern European cases in the same decade—this increased vulnerability can have a macroeconomic dimension, thus linking with some of the other sessions in this conference. What is interesting is that we now have evidence concerning some of the ways in which this vulnerability can be mitigated by institutional design. During the Bolivian crisis, many microfinance institutions' clients, overwhelmed by an unmanageable burden of debt service, defaulted, reducing their levels of investment and, according to the argument presented in Marconi and Mosley (forthcoming) additionally aggravating the overall process of economic decline in the Bolivian economy—the microfinance sector as a whole behaved procyclically and augmented macroeconomic, as well as many people's microeconomic, instability. However, not all microfinance institutions behaved in this way: some, as illustrated by table 2, bucked the recession and retained high repayment rates. Of these, two, ProMujer and CRECER, were "village banks" targeted toward very poor women only, and offering a simple emergency-loan insurance mechanism through the organization's internal account,[5] offering supplementary training and mentoring services, an illustration of the "interlinked contracts" that Dercon approvingly mentions.

Both ProMujer and CRECER, uncontaminated by the general downward trend, bucked the recession and grew. This is a heartwarming story of the weak and more poverty-focused nongovernmental organizations (NGOs) outcompeting the more commercially oriented microfinance organizations. But it is also an illustration of the importance of institutional design: for ProMujer and CRECER used an integrated model of microfinance in defiance of the "minimalist" model (which offers credit only with no interlinked contracts, and is the model favored by aid donors and used by most of their competitors). It seems probable that the complementary services offered by ProMujer and CRECER created a quasi-family institutional loyalty among its clients, which persuaded nearly all of them to manage their indebtedness with more care in the boom, and treat their debts to the "parent" organization as senior to other debts. This loyalty in turn provided a tool for controlling the vulnerability of their clients, and prevented that vulnerability from growing and further contributing to the destabilization of the entire economy.

Turning to micro-insurance, Dercon argues that "there is surprisingly little research" on this theme. True enough, but the trickle of findings is beginning to swell now, and I would like to illustrate the relevance of some of this recent literature to his general argument.

The current structure of micro-insurance in the developing world is extremely patchy, heavily biased toward South Asia and toward health insurance, with only sporadic coverage in other regions. There are few insurance policies of any description available—except in Bangladesh, to which we shall come shortly—to cover the extreme poor, who stand most to benefit from them. And there are no insurance policies available in the whole of Africa for anyone, let alone poor people, to cover the risk listed in Dercon's sample of rural Ethiopians as the top priority—namely drought risks. This is more the pity because, as he mentions, it is not difficult to design weather insurance schemes that are almost free of moral hazards and can be very simply implemented (Hazell 1992; Mosley 2001; Skees et al 2004). To cover the second, third, and fifth most severe potential shocks mentioned in his sample (death or illness of a family member and crop disease), some micro-insurance policies now exist in East Africa (Cohen and Sebstad 2005), although they are available only to a limited extent to uncollateralized people in remote rural areas.

One reason for the limited development of micro-insurance is that the organizations that wish to supply this product (for the most part, NGOs) are often deficient in the kind of financial management capacities and contacts required for supplying it and often legally banned from supplying it, which makes a link-up with an interested commercial insurer essential—and an interested commercial insurer is hard to find because of the low volumes and high risks involved. So the history of successful micro-insurance is in the main the history of successful matchmaking between these two parties; some valuable examples are provided for East Africa in the symposium edited by Cohen and Sebstad (2005). Here, as in South Asia, the product that has taken off is health insurance, in many cases due to enlightened brokering by aid donors, as in the Foundation for International Community Assistance (FINCA) Uganda case (McCord 2005) between microfinance NGOs and private-sector health care insurers. But the existence of this brokering continues to be a rare exception; much more commonly, the poor remain without access to manageable insurance of any sort. A key priority for pro-poor field research is how to overcome this persisting institutional barrier.

There also exists a modest literature now on the impact of micro-insurance. We have found in relation to FINCA in Uganda and the Bangladesh Rural Advancement Committee (BRAC) (Mosley 2003) that the availability of health micro-insurance raises the investment rates of clients and induces a shift in their asset portfolios toward higher value investments (in particular, from working to fixed capital). It also provides some social capital externalities, including improved communication, in Bangladesh, between patients and health care providers, leading to an improvement in the quality of service. However, there was, in both of these samples, no evidence that the availability of micro-insurance stabilized expenditure. In Uganda, moreover, there was no evidence that it significantly increased the access of lower income clients to financial services. Research on the demand for micro-insurance services is still in its infancy and badly needed (although some early findings are summarized by Cohen and Sebstad [2005]). However, intuition suggests that product innovation of this kind as presently implemented is biased against the most vulnerable, precisely because of their aversion to risk as illustrated in table 1 in this comment.

In this situation, what may be required is explicit earmarking, in which a certain quota of micro-insurance contracts is reserved for the ultra-poor, as in the health insurance scheme operated by BRAC in Bangladesh (Halder and Mosley 2004). An alternative approach is provided by BRAC itself in the form of an interlinked contract of a different sort, in which an insurance function is provided, not by orthodox micro-insurance, but rather in the form of a minimum-risk transfer—namely food aid—leading to an interlinked sequence of services. Savings are linked with training in a specific skill, followed by a small loan for a low-input activity that uses that skill, such as poultry keeping, fish farming, or sericulture (Matin and Hulme 2003; Halder and Mosley 2004), followed by a larger loan—an escalator in which the insurance consists of limits imposed by the service provider on the client's choice of financial product. The general proposition, therefore, is that both microfinance and even micro-insurance are at risk of augmenting rather than restraining vulnerability, but that appropriate product design, specifically in the form of the interlinked contracts commended by Dercon, may be effective in counteracting this tendency.

In summary, various forms of decomposition of the concept of vulnerability and its causes can, I believe, help us better understand and operationalize the concept of vulnerability and defenses against it. A distinction between subjective and objective indicators of vulnerability is helpful for understanding what forms of vulnerability affect the spending patterns of the poor. A distinction between natural and relational forms of vulnerability helps to illustrate what kind of defenses against vulnerability the poor and their sponsors can erect. And a distinction between the empirical consequences of different design characteristics for microfinance and micro-insurance can help us to understand how effective those defenses can be in particular geographical contexts.

Notes

1. A great variety of methods are already used to assess subjective perceptions of vulnerability, sometimes using experimental methods to assess risk aversion, as in Mosley and Verschoor (2005) and sometimes imposing a fixed risk-aversion coefficient, as in Ligon and Schechter (2003). Mosley and Verschoor (2005) use a vulnerability index consisting of the following components: assets; memories and expectations of vulnerability; expectations of short-term income variations; perceived risk of entrepreneurial behavior; self-respect and perceived own status. The first of these components is objective, the others are subjective.
2. In passing, Dercon claims that the "emphasis on preferences is essentially misleading both as a complete theory of how risk causes poverty and as a guide to policy." Although he covers himself with the word "complete," attitudes to risk do, we claim, have significance in explaining escape from poverty, as documented in a small way by the correlations in table 1, and sometimes in a surprising way—the most vulnerable are not always the most risk-averse. These are the outliers from the pattern of table 1. Sometimes they are tempted, although their position is desperate (for one case study illustration, see Mosley [2004]) to risk everything on one wild gamble to retrieve a state of solvency.
3. As Diane Elson states (1999, p. 616): "Labour market institutions have typically been constructed on the assumption that women employees were secondary earners who would draw on the assets and earnings of men . . . to cushion them against risk. That is, labour market institutions have assumed that women have 'extended entitlements' which do not have the force of law, but are sanctioned by accepted norms about what is a legitimate claim . . . Women's very act of participating in the labour market, however, may weaken their extended entitlements, if it involves stepping outside what have been accepted as the normal roles for women. The possibility of earning an income of their own may empower them to make more decisions about their own lives—but it may also cut them off from support by male kin, leaving them on their own, and newly vulnerable to market forces." These remarks apply even more strongly to self-employed workers, as may be seen from the experience of the case study in box 1.
4. The following quotations from eastern Uganda illustrate: "Employers who are generally but not exclusively male, stated that it was easier to deal with male workers because there were 'fewer misunderstandings between men.' Many referred to the rumours and innuendo that would start in the village if a woman, and in a particular a married woman, worked for another man for payment. The few male employers that did hire female labourers generally hired women that were either widowed, separated, or divorced. On the supply side, men and women both stated that doing manual work for another was no better than begging, and was a reflection of a poor and 'disorganized' home. However, for a married woman, working for a male employer was considered particularly damaging, not only to her own reputation, but also the reputation of her husband. The concern was expressed in the following terms: 'when a wife goes for casual labour and is paid by another man, she is dissatisfied with her home and is seeking a new husband' " (Evans 1996, pp. 114–5).

In a similar vein Sarah Muzaki, in her 1998 dissertation about a close-by region of eastern Uganda, writes: "it was argued by some men and women that a true woman does not move too far unless she behaves like a loose dog. This saying is popularly used to define an unruly and immoral woman" (Muzaki 1998, p. 72).

5. The "internal account" of ProMujer and CRECER consists of a reserve fund financed by a surcharge on the interest rate, which may be used to make emergency loans to clients on the approval of the village committee.

References

Carter, M., and J. May. 1999. "Poverty, Livelihood and Class in Rural South Africa." *World Development* 27 (1): 1–20.

Cohen, Monique, and Jennefer Sebstad. 2005. "Reducing Vulnerability: The Demand for Microinsurance." *Journal of International Development* 17 (3): 397–475.

Elson, Diane. 1999. "Labor Markets as Gendered Institutions: Equality, Efficiency and Empowerment Issues." *World Development* 27 (3): 611–27.

Evans, Alison. 1996. "Agricultural Labour Markets and Rural Labour Markets in the Smallholder Sector of Uganda." Unpublished, School of African and Asian Studies, University of Sussex.

Halder, Shantana, and Paul Mosley. 2004. "Working with the Ultra-Poor: Learning from BRAC Experiences." *Journal of International Development* 16 (3): 387–407.

Hazell, Peter. 1992. "The Appropriate Role of Agricultural Insurance in Developing Countries." *Journal of International Development* 4: 567–81.

Hulme, David, and Andrew Shepherd. 2003. "Conceptualizing Chronic Poverty." *World Development* 31 (3): 403–25.

Kamanou, G., and J. Morduch. 2002. "Measuring Vulnerability to Poverty." Working paper, WIDER, Helsinki.

Lenton, P., and P. Mosley. 2005. "Community Development Finance Institutions and the Microeconomics of Escape from the Poverty Trap." Unpublished, University of Sheffield.

Ligon, E., and L. Schechter. 2003. "Measuring Vulnerability." *Economic Journal* 113 (486): C95–C102.

Marconi, R., and P. Mosley. Forthcoming. "Towards a Macroeconomics of Microfinance: Bolivia 1999–2004." *Journal of International Development.*

Matin, I., and D. Hulme. 2003. "Programs for the Poorest: Learning from the IGVGD Scheme in Bangladesh." *World Development* 31 (3): 647–65.

McCord, Michael. 2005. "Reducing Vulnerability: The Supply of Health Microinsurance in East Africa." *Journal of International Development* 17 (3): 319–27.

Mosley, P. 2001. "Insurance against Poverty? The 'New Generation' Agricultural Microinsurance Schemes." *Small Enterprise Development* 12 (1): 51–9.

———. 2003. "Microinsurance: Scope, Design and Assessment of Wider Impacts." *IDS Bulletin* 34 (4): 143–56.

———. 2004. "Severe Poverty and Growth: A Macro-Micro Analysis." Working Paper 51, Chronic Poverty Research Centre, Manchester, U.K.

Mosley, P., and Arjan Verschoor. 2005. "Risk Attitudes and the 'Vicious Circle of Poverty.'" *European Journal of Development Research* 17 (1): 59–88.

Muzaki, Sarah. 1998. "Gender in the Rural Informal Labour Market—The Case of Budadiri County, Mbale District." MA dissertation (Women and Gender Studies), Makerere University.

Platteau, J.-P., and A. Abraham. 1987. "An Inquiry into Quasi-Credit Contracts: The Role of Reciprocal Credit and Interlinked Deals in Small-Scale Fishing Communities." *Journal of Development Studies* 23 (4): 461–90.

Skees, J. P., P. Varangis, D. Larson, and P. Siegal. 2004. "Can Financial Markets be Tapped to Help Poor People Cope with Weather Risks?" In *Insurance against Poverty,* ed. S. Dercon, 422–51. Oxford: Oxford University Press.

Small Enterprise Development. 2001. Theme issue: Microinsurance. (Papers by Brown, McCord, Roth, Mosley, and Wright and Aleke-Dondo). 12 (1): 1–71.

Wood, G. 2003. "Staying Secure, Staying Poor: The 'Faustian Bargain.'" *World Development* 31 (3): 455–73.

Zimmerman, F., and Michael Carter. 2003. "Asset Smoothing, Consumption Smoothing, and the Reproduction of Inequality under Risk and Subsistence Constraints." *Journal of Development Economics* 71 (2): 233–60.

Comment on "Vulnerability: A Micro Perspective," by Stefan Dercon

RICHARD WILCOX

You may wonder why I am here speaking at a development economics conference when I manage project finance for the World Food Programme (WFP). The reason I am here is that we are developing an insurance project inspired by Stefan Dercon's work. We've based our work on Stefan's research.

In brief, what we hope to do in the fourth quarter of 2005 is to transfer Ethiopian weather risk to the international capital markets. To explain why we are doing this let me briefly go over the concept of humanitarian aid as insurance, explain the financial tool we intend to use, and outline the next steps in this effort.

What is the function of humanitarian aid from the perspective of the beneficiary? As Stefan has explained, weather shocks cause vulnerable populations uninsured income and asset losses. From the perspective of the beneficiary, we act as an insurance provider of last resort. The critical difference between insurance and emergency aid is that insurance provides contingency funding in the event of shock, whereas humanitarian aid seeks funding for assistance after the shock.

Essentially, the way this works is when there is a severe drought, we go and do needs assessments (in other words, we "loss adjust" the whole country just as an insurer would). Then, however, unlike an insurer who would have funds available, we go out and seek funds to aid in dealing with the needs that arise from these losses. In so doing we lose a lot of critical time.

This loss of time is crucial when trying to save livelihoods. Farmers, even in a severe drought year, know that prices at harvest time will be lower than later. Accordingly, if they will have to sell assets to purchase food, they need to secure this cash now. Moreover, everyone else is in the same situation, so the sooner the farmer gets assets to market the better the farmer's hope of getting a better price.

Dr. Richard Wilcox is Director of Business Planning, United Nations World Food Programme.

Annual World Bank Conference on Development Economics—Europe 2006

Contingency funding available immediately would be of far greater value to beneficiaries than aid coming in later. This contingency funding would be based on a contract that triggers a payout when there is a crisis, that is, at the time of harvest failure, and therefore, saves livelihoods. By creating this contingency funding based on a weather derivative, we are transferring risks from vulnerable populations to financial markets.

This shift from ex post emergency response to ex ante risk management consists of three important steps. First, we need to identify and quantify the systemic risk. In Ethiopia that is rainfall variation. In a largely rainfed agricultural economy such as Ethiopia's, everything correlates with rainfall. Rainfall variation also is an objective measure we can quantify in ways that the insurance market understands.

Next we have to price this risk. This costing of Ethiopia's exposure to rainfall variation is a very important step. As I said earlier, given our role as an insurance provider of last resort, the cost of this risk is critical information for an agency such as ours. It is also important information for the Government of Ethiopia and its donors. Donors de facto are reinsurance providers. That is the function their emergency budgets serve in cases of natural disasters in developing countries.

Accordingly, for the government and its donors to make informed decisions on how to structure their budgets—for what risks to establish contingency funding, what risks to transfer, which to retain—the price of the risk contains important information. With this information, emergency aid can be built into meaningful development portfolios. Until now these two parts of a meaningful development portfolio—investment and insurance protection—existed in isolation. With this new tool they can be brought together into one development budget.

The following is a brief explanation of the tool, the weather derivative underlying the risk management approach we are proposing to pilot in Ethiopia. An index is an objective and observable measure used to describe the variability in specific underlying components; for example, the Dow Jones Industrial Average is made up of 30 component stocks. Likewise, the Ethiopia rainfall index is built on 26 weather stations covering the country (minus the pastoral areas where necessary data is lacking), weighted for the types of crops grown in these areas and the relative importance of the respective areas for the vulnerable population. It is a verifiable index that correlates closely with the underlying economic impact and thereby creates an opportunity to manage this risk.

As you can see in figure 1, 1984, 1987, and 2002 were the historically worst years in Ethiopia. The contract we will write on this index will be designed to trigger a payout in these cases. As Stefan highlighted in his presentation, the quality of data is paramount. We have reviewed Ethiopia's weather data set and found it to be of sufficient quality to serve as a basis for a legally enforceable contract. In fact, Ethiopian weather data is of roughly the same quality as similar data from some European countries. We will have Ethiopia's data cleaned, that is verified, and within two weeks we hope that Ethiopia will be the first least developed country with an underwritable weather data set.

With this data we will then create financial protection based on the performance of a specified index in relation to a specified trigger. This contract then offers pro-

FIGURE 1.
Costs of Past Droughts Using Current Price and Population Levels

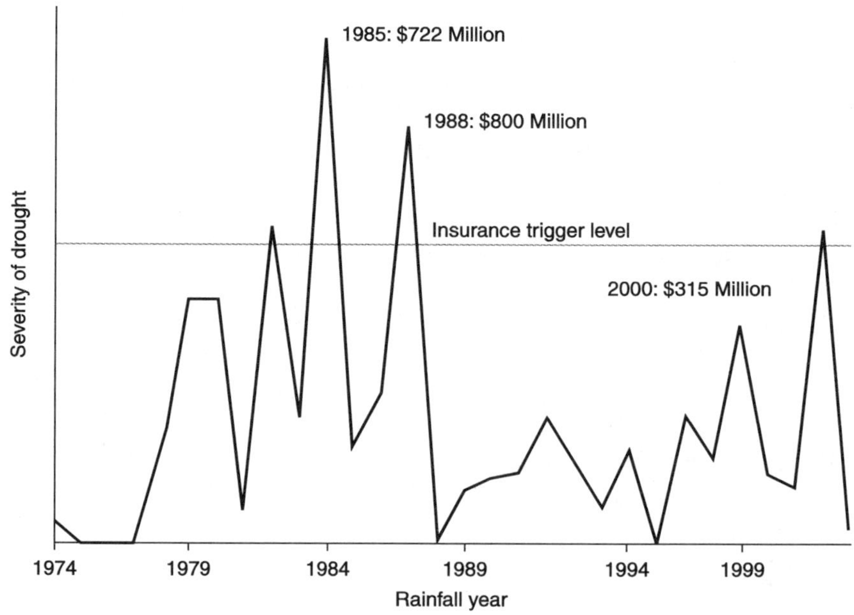

Source: WFP analysis 2005.

Note: Initial analysis is based on current WFP costs and includes 2.5 percent average annual population growth. From 1994 on, there is an 80 percent correlation between the rainfall index and WFP food needs data for Ethiopia.

tection against uncertain costs that result from index volatility through mitigating payments settled against the same index that has been determined to cause the losses. In a nutshell, what the Ethiopian index does is replicate the existing early warning system and use it as a basis for financing emergency relief operations in extreme years.

A sizeable weather risk market makes this possible. To date US$21 billion has been transacted in this market. The actors in this market, primarily the big reinsurers, are keen on the type of risk we are introducing. Much of their portfolios consist of weather risks in the northern hemisphere. Nobody has Ethiopian weather risk in their portfolio. The risks we are introducing, therefore, allow reinsurers to diversify their portfolios and we are confident that there will be interest in these risks.

The important thing is to get the incentives right. You can make a lot of mistakes, as surely we will, as long as you get the overall incentives right. Protection, that is, certainty of a payout, can give farmers the confidence allowing them to make better investment decisions on using higher yield, higher risk seeds, for example. For this to work the individual farmer would have to be directly connected to the insurance; in next year's pilot that is not what we are doing. We are only testing a tool at a macro level to see if it will work. In subsequent years, if successful, this tool can be extended all the way down to the individual farmer.

Weather insurance also provides beneficiary governments a workable system for handling their own exposure that they could take over in the future. Ultimately, the intention is to have this become a tool that the Ethiopian government itself can use to manage its weather risk.

Having this risk priced in international markets allows donors to quantify their exposure so that they can decide whether they want to retain or transfer these risks. Donors, by extension, act as reinsurers. That is what their emergency budgets do. With the information about the price of certain risks in the international markets, donors can make informed decisions about how to structure the protection they provide.

With a weather derivative, there is no moral hazard for the insured (in this case, WFP and Ethiopia's Disaster Preparedness and Prevention Commission) to distort needs. Payouts are determined by predefined deviations on an index. It is only variations in the underlying, objective measure—rainfall—that affects the payout.

So what are the next steps? In a couple of weeks we will be presenting the full model to our governing body. Then, over the course of the summer we will refine the model and prepare the contract. In November, we will take the Ethiopia drought insurance project to our board for approval. We have some indications from at least one major donor, so we are confident that we will be able to transact toward the end of this year before the Ethiopian agricultural season begins in March 2006.

Health Risks

Scaling Up Access to HIV Prevention, Treatment, and Care in Resource-Poor Settings: Challenges and Opportunities

JOEP M. A. LANGE

Communicable diseases remain the major cause of morbidity and mortality in resource-poor settings. Through both biological and social mechanisms, poverty greatly increases the vulnerability of people to many infectious diseases. In turn, the major infectious scourges, such as HIV/AIDS, tuberculosis, and malaria, perpetuate poverty and are an important contributor to negative economic and social development. HIV/AIDS is a case in point, because it primarily affects people in the prime of their lives, leading to losses in productivity and social cohesion. Its effects are most dramatic in Sub-Saharan Africa, where the situation is often aggravated by the fact that so many countries are suffering from weak or dysfunctional governance. The latter has contributed to a steadily progressive erosion of the public health sector in those countries. HIV/AIDS also fuels a tuberculosis epidemic. On one hand, we are dealing with greatly increasing demands on the public health sector, especially in countries hardest hit by the HIV/AIDS epidemic; on the other hand, that health sector is losing already scarce workers to HIV/AIDS. Likewise, the capacity of the education sector is weakened because of increased mortality of HIV-infected teachers.

In an era of globalization, the world cannot afford to ignore the health (and other) problems of developing countries. Humanitarian motives aside—which alone should be enough reason for action—the downward spiral of economic and social development in the poorest countries presents a recipe for global insecurity and instability. Despite the progress that has been made during the past few years in closing the "funding gap," implementation of effective interventions in countries has been lagging behind. There is great need for global leadership in the fight against HIV/AIDS and for a global action plan that takes a pragmatic approach, based upon the best of science and empirical evidence. The challenge is formidable, but the current momentum for the antiretroviral scale-up provides a unique opportunity to empower the poor and build sustainable health care systems in Africa and other resource-poor settings.

Joep M. A. Lange is Professor of Medicine, Center for Poverty-Related Communicable Diseases, Academic Medical Center, University of Amsterdam.

Annual World Bank Conference on Development Economics—Europe 2006

The human immunodeficiency virus (HIV), the causative agent of acquired immune deficiency syndrome (AIDS), creates havoc in many developing countries. Approximately 40 million people are now living with this virus, of which over 25 million live in Sub-Saharan Africa, and over 7 million in South and Southeast Asia (figure 1). Since the emergence of the epidemic in 1981, approximately 20 million people have died from HIV/AIDS and it has become the leading cause of death of individuals age 15–49 years in many of the countries concerned. In the hardest hit countries, such as Botswana and Swaziland, HIV prevalence rates in this age group approach 40 percent. In 2005, almost 5 million people became newly infected with HIV and over 3 million people died from HIV/AIDS. There is a rapidly growing epidemic in Eastern Europe and Central Asia, which was initially driven by intravenous drug users but is now spreading to other segments of the population (UNAIDS and World Health Organization 2005).

The HIV/AIDS epidemic is a humanitarian disaster on an unprecedented scale. But due to the "target population" of this disease and its invariably lethal nature if left untreated, it is much more than that. To quote Epstein, "The mortality and morbidity associated with AIDS make it unlike most other types of sickness and disease. Whereas most diseases prey largely on the very young, the old, or the weak, the way in which HIV is contracted and spread makes young adults, especially young women, the most vulnerable. As a result, in countries with high HIV prevalence, the socioeconomic consequences of high mortality among adults can be far-reaching, devastating households, families, and communities and eroding formal and informal mechanisms of social support" (Epstein 2004, p. 2). HIV/AIDS is a health emergency, but it is also a broad long-term development issue. Moreover, it is an important driver of the global tuberculosis (TB) epidemic (The Stop TB Partnership Annual Report 2004).

Apart from briefly discussing some of the abovementioned consequences of HIV/AIDS, this paper takes stock of interventions that could stem the epidemic and mitigate its impact, and of some of the obstacles that have to be overcome to achieve this.

Social and Economic Consequences of HIV/AIDS

HIV/AIDS is having a profound demographic impact, reversing gains in life expectancy and improvements in child mortality in many countries (Epstein 2004). Mortality among the population age 15–49 has increased manifold, even in countries with modest epidemics. In the absence of broad access to treatment, HIV/AIDS will result in radical changes in the structure of the population of hardest hit countries, with a striking gap in the productive and caregiver part of the population, leaving the young and old to cope alone, and reversing economic and social development.

The epidemic is increasingly feminized, especially in Sub-Saharan Africa, with young women being particularly vulnerable to acquiring HIV for biological, cultural, social, and economic reasons. In Sub-Saharan Africa, the peak HIV prevalence occurs at a younger age and at a higher rate among women than among men (UNAIDS and World Health Organization 2005). Infant and child mortality rates

FIGURE 1.
Adults and Children Estimated to be Living with HIV in 2005

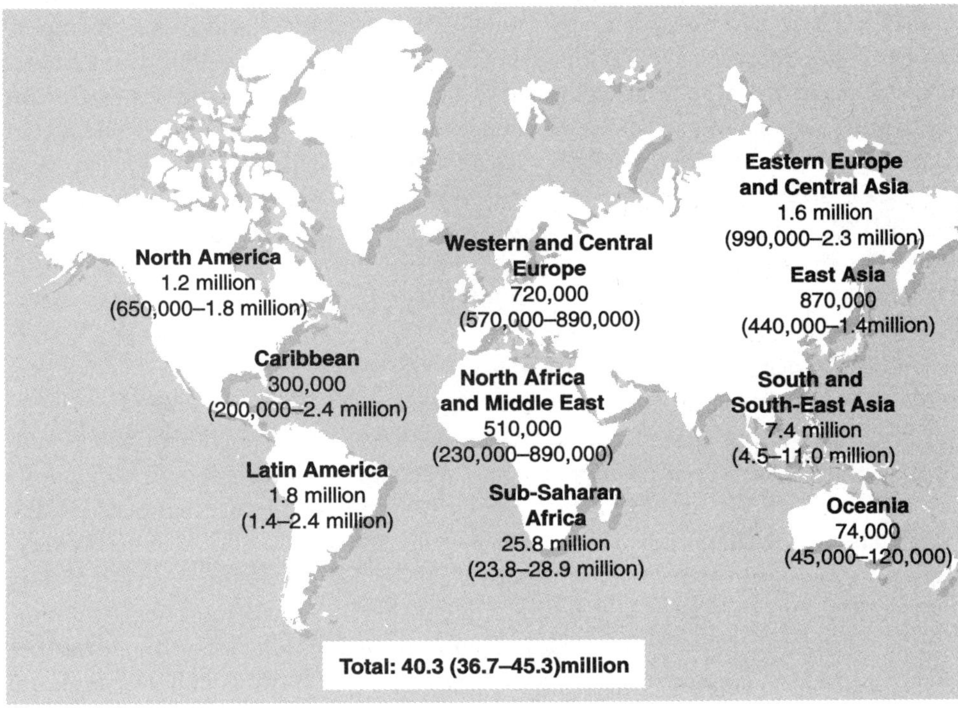

Source: UNAIDS and World Health Organization 2005.

go up because of HIV transmission from HIV-positive mothers during pregnancy, delivery, and breastfeeding, but also because mothers and fathers and other adults that could care for children die. There are currently more than 15 million AIDS orphans; in some countries, three-quarters of all orphans are AIDS orphans, stretching the limits of extended families, and contributing to the vicious cycle of inadequate education, poverty, and disease. At the household level, income declines as breadwinners fall ill and die, and as other household members are obliged to take time off from other productive activities to care for sick relatives. Simultaneously, households have to devote an increasing share of their income to health care and funerals.

The sector most directly affected by HIV/AIDS is the health sector. Demands have risen sharply because of HIV/AIDS, but already scarce health personnel are affected by the disease as well. Likewise, the capacity of the education sector is weakened because of increased mortality of teachers.

The impact of HIV/AIDS goes far beyond disruption of more or less tangible economic or administrative processes within households, businesses, or government agencies. It may disrupt the very fabric of society, leading to political instability and deteriorating security at the individual, community, and national level (Haacker 2004).

HIV/AIDS and Tuberculosis

Dual HIV/TB infections form an exceptional challenge. Worldwide, 14 million people are co-infected with these pathogens and TB is a leading cause of death among people living with HIV (Srikantiah et al 2005). HIV infection increases the risk of reactivating latent *M. tuberculosis* infection, placing HIV-positive persons at increased risk for developing TB (Bucher et al 1999). HIV infection also increases the risk of rapid TB progression after primary *M. tuberculosis* acquisition or reinfection (Daley et al 1992). TB may accelerate the progression of HIV disease via immune activation and is associated with a higher mortality and shorter survival in HIV-positive persons (Whalen et al 2000). The risk of TB increases as the HIV-related immune deficiency progresses; similarly, the highest mortality rates associated with TB occur in persons with the greatest immune deficiency (Shafer et al 1996). However, there already is a rapid increase in TB incidence soon after infection with HIV (Sonnenberg et al 2005). The presentation of TB in those with advanced HIV disease is often atypical, and a documented bacteriological diagnosis may be more difficult to make (Jones et al 1993). Concomitant treatment of HIV and TB also poses difficulties. Those with dual infections who initiate anti-HIV therapy (antiretroviral treatment) in advanced stages of HIV infection have a high rate of immune reconstitution disease, leading to considerable early morbidity and mortality (French, Price, and Stone 2004). There are overlapping drug toxicities (Lee 2003) and pharmacological interactions between anti-TB drugs and antiretroviral agents, considerably narrowing antiretroviral treatment choices in those who need concomitant treatment (De Maat et al 2003). It is no exaggeration to state that successful global control of TB very much depends on our ability to prevent and treat HIV infections.

Prevention of HIV Infections: Where Do We Stand?

Despite successes in curbing the HIV/AIDS epidemic in individual countries, global figures continue to grow. More people became infected with HIV in 2005 than in any previous year (UNAIDS and World Health Organization 2005). What drives the epidemic differs between and within regions and countries, but a common denominator is that it disproportionally strikes vulnerable and marginalized groups in the societies concerned: youth, women, sex workers, migrant workers, injecting drug users, homosexual men—those unable to protect themselves adequately against infection for a variety of social and biological reasons (UNAIDS and World Health Organization 2005). HIV is a virus, but inequity is at the roots of most of its spread. Condoms are highly effective at preventing sexual transmission of HIV, but only if they are available and used (Weller 1993). Even though condoms are effective, women are often in a difficult position to negotiate use by their male partners (Allen et al 1992). Needle exchange programs and substitution therapy for injecting drug users are effective at lowering HIV transmission rates within this population, but are often politically unacceptable in the very countries where the epidemic is fueled by intravenous drug use (UNAIDS and World Health Organization 2005).

It is clear that the world has to fight the current "prevention fatigue," and step up HIV/AIDS prevention efforts in a comprehensive and nondogmatic manner, but at the same time we should recognize that only an effective preventive vaccine can deliver a future without HIV/AIDS. Unfortunately, despite initial optimism, evolving scientific insights tell us that there is still a long way to go here. The major challenge is to develop immunogens that are capable of neutralizing primary HIV isolates from all genetic subtypes and regions of the world. The good news is that after many years of misguided and haphazard efforts, the global scientific community is now committed to a coordinated, collaborative, and systematic process to develop the vaccine (Coordinating Committee of the Global HIV/AIDS Vaccine Enterprise 2005). Yet, given the formidable scientific challenges that the design of an effective HIV vaccine poses, it is hard to predict if and when such a vaccine will be available. Thus, the development of alternative prevention technologies is urgently needed, especially those that would be "female-controlled" (that is, use of which would not require the consent of the male partner).

Since the early 1990s this need has driven the development of vaginal microbicides (Shattuck and Moore 2003). Unfortunately, first generation microbicides, all based on non–HIV-specific spermicides such as nonoxynol-9, in studies in high-risk populations led to more HIV-1 transmission at worst (Kreiss et al 1992), or were not effective at best (Van Damme et al 2002). The newest generation of vaginal microbicides under investigation utilizes classes of HIV-specific inhibitors that are also used for therapeutic purposes (Di Fabio et al 2003; Lederman et al 2004; Moore 2005), but clinical development is still at a very early stage. Likewise, oral antiretroviral pre-exposure prophylaxis (PREP) may also be effective in preventing sexual transmission of HIV (Tsai et al 1995), although recent animal studies seem to point at limitations of this approach, which may or may not be related to the specific drug utilized (Subbarao et al 2005). A number of PREP studies have been initiated in several high-risk populations across the globe, but unfortunately several have now been interrupted by ill-informed "activism," further delaying the search for female-controlled HIV prevention methods (Singh and Mills 2005; Lange 2005). The availability of female condoms may empower women, but their use ultimately still very much depends on consent of the male partner (Fontanet et al 1998). A recent randomized controlled study, conducted in South Africa, confirmed the finding of earlier observational studies that male circumcision may significantly reduce female-to-male transmission of HIV (Auvert et al 2005). Whether male circumcision could be introduced as a public health measure, reducing HIV transmission in all settings, remains uncertain at the moment.

The use of antiretrovirals for the prevention of mother-to-child transmission, introduced in 1994, has been highly successful. Unfortunately, as with the antiretroviral scale-up, cost and logistical considerations dictate widespread use of a suboptimal drug regimen in most developing countries, which, apart from limited efficacy, may also negatively affect future treatment outcomes for mothers (Jourdain et al 2004) and contribute to an increase in circulation and transmission of drug-resistant viruses (Jackson et al 2001; Eshleman et al 2001). Another issue that was initially downplayed in the exaltation about the success of short-course peripartum antiretroviral regimens in reducing mother-to-child transmission of HIV-1, is subsequent transmission via breastfeeding in populations where this practice is the norm and where formula feeding is not an alternative (Petra Study Team 2002). Infant-PREP during the period of breastfeeding may minimize this risk (Vyankadondera et al 2003).

Treatment of HIV Infections: Where Do We Stand?

The success of highly active antiretroviral therapy (HAART) is an illustration of the fact that in medicine quantitative insights can make a dramatic qualitative difference. Effective antiretroviral agents have been available since 1987 (Fischl et al 1987). First-generation antiretrovirals are still components of many antiretroviral drug regimens that are used today. The antiviral efficacy of HAART indeed is not only due to the appearance of drugs with new mechanisms of action, but primarily to using combinations of at least three anti-HIV drugs that inhibit viral replication to such an extent that development of viral drug resistance is smothered (provided the drugs have non-overlapping resistance patterns) (Lange 1997). The ability to measure the amount of virus in blood and other body compartments through molecular amplification techniques that became available in the mid-1990s has been of crucial importance in the realization that prior approaches of using one or two drugs could not suppress viral replication in a durable manner.

The introduction of HAART is one of the great success stories of modern medicine. Its impact on HIV-related morbidity and mortality (Palella et al 1988) can almost be compared to that of the introduction of penicillin on pneumococcal pneumonia half a century earlier. Those of us who have witnessed this turning point in the availability of therapeutic perspectives for people with HIV/AIDS cannot think about it without an immense feeling of satisfaction and gratitude. However, in contrast to pneumococcal infections, HIV infections are chronic and therapy is not curative. This implies that antiretroviral therapy, unlike a penicillin course, is a lifelong affair. This poses formidable challenges.

First is the problem of patient adherence: taking drugs according to prescription every day, again and again, proves difficult for many. Yet there are few diseases where strict adherence is as important as in HIV infection (Paterson et al 2000). Lapses may lead to rapid development of drug resistance, which not only undermines the efficacy of the current regimen, but—because of cross resistance among drugs—is also likely to compromise that of future regimens. Second, in 1998, after a few years of carefree prescribing, it became apparent that chronic use of antiretrovirals is often associated with development of chronic toxicity, such as the disfiguring lipodystrophy syndrome (Carr et al 1998). Use of particular antiretroviral agents in addition may lead to a rise of blood lipid levels to such an extent that an increased risk for cardio- and cerebrovascular morbidity and mortality may be cause for concern (Friis-Moller et al 2003; d'Arminio et al 2004). Particular antiretrovirals are toxic to mitochondria, the energy powerhouses of the cell, and may cause nerve and muscle damage and, in the worst case, deadly liver failure (Brinkman et al 1999). In summary, the success of HAART comes at a price. This should not cause us to lose sight of the fact that the benefits of HAART still far outweigh the disadvantages, but it has undoubtedly led to a certain reluctance to be very aggressive in starting antiretroviral therapy. Therapy is now generally initiated later in the course of infection than a few years ago and therapy guidelines have been modified accordingly (Yeni et al 2004).

The success of a particular antiretroviral regimen is directly dependent on the number of active drugs in that regimen. Unfortunately, there is a growing population of HIV-infected patients who harbor viruses with resistance to one or more currently available antiretroviral agents (Richman et al 2004). Usually the drug resistance mutations have been acquired during periods of suboptimally suppressive therapy, but patients may also be infected with drug-resistant strains (Little et al 2002). For a substantial proportion of patients it has become difficult or impossible to constitute antiretroviral drug regimens that will give sufficient and durable suppression of viral replication. Somewhat surprisingly, these people are often still doing better on "failing" drug regimens than without antiretrovirals. Viral resistance mutations may be associated with loss of viral fitness—they may make the virus less virulent. In such cases, despite the virological failure, decline of immune function may be relatively slow (Deeks et al 2001). Nevertheless, apart from dealing with chronic toxicity, finding ways to treat patients with drug-resistant viruses today is the major challenge of antiretroviral therapy. Fortunately, over the past few years patient adherence has been made easier by the development and appearance of greatly simplified regimens, comprising only a few pills a day. Single-pill, once a day fixed-dose combinations (FDCs) of first rate HAART regimens are being developed. Dealing with hepatitis virus co-infections forms an additional and increasing challenge in the HIV-infected population. Substantial proportions of patients have co-infections with either hepatitis C or hepatitis B virus. In the developed world, the relative contribution of liver-related mortality to mortality of HIV-infected subjects has risen greatly in the HAART era (Bica et al 2001; Macias et al 2002). This may be explained partially by a decline in traditional opportunistic disease manifestations, but is also due to the fact that the prolonged survival of HAART recipients allows the natural history of the hepatitis virus infections to take their course.

Obstacles to Scaling Up Antiretroviral Treatment

It was unbearable that the benefits of HAART were initially restricted to just a tiny proportion of those infected, that is, those living in the developed world. In light of the devastation HIV was causing in developing countries, pressure grew to make HAART available there, too. Since 2000 this has culminated in a number of important developments. Political commitment to include antiretroviral treatment as an essential component of the fight against HIV/AIDS increased substantially, both on an international and national level (United Nations General Assembly on HIV/AIDS 2001). Impressive price reductions for antiretrovirals for the poorest countries were negotiated between UNAIDS and research-based drug companies, followed by

TABLE 1.
Obstacles to Scaling Up Access to Antiretroviral Therapy

Insufficient political commitment
Cost of care, including antiretrovirals
Lack of infrastructure and expertise
Lack of a common agenda and leadership in implementation

Source: Author.

further price reductions of a number of drugs through generic competition. The World Health Organization (WHO) included antiretrovirals in the Essential Medicines list and formulated guidelines for the development of a public health approach to treatment of HIV infections in resource-poor settings (World Health Organization 2002). New and substantial funding mechanisms, such as the World Bank's Multicountry AIDS Program; the Global Fund to Fight AIDS, Tuberculosis and Malaria (GFATM); and President Bush's Emergency Plan for AIDS Relief (PEPFAR) were established. And lastly, through its "3 by 5" initiative, WHO set the target to have 3 million people in resource-poor settings on antiretroviral therapy by the end of 2005 (World Health Organization 2003).

Due to the increases in resources, in global and national commitment, and the effect of WHO's targetsetting, the numbers of people in resource-poor settings who receive HAART have increased substantially over the past years. The number of people receiving antiretroviral therapy in low- and middle-income countries has tripled since the end of 2001. Despite such progress, the reality is that at best one in ten Africans and one in seven Asians that need to be treated with antiretrovirals to prevent them from dying from AIDS within the next year or two were receiving this therapy in mid-2005. At the end of 2005 we are not only still far from meeting the "3 by 5" aim, with an estimated 1 million instead of 3 million of the targeted people receiving antiretrovirals, but the number of new HIV infections taking place in 2005 approached 5 million, 3.2 million of those occurring in Sub-Saharan Africa. From these figures it is clear that current efforts to rapidly expand and sustain antiretroviral therapy will be severely undermined without a more effective concomitant prevention effort (UNAIDS and World Health Organization 2005).

Apart from the dramatic shortfall in HIV prevention, there are other considerable obstacles to providing effective HIV therapy to all of those in need, as listed in table 1 and discussed here.

Insufficient Political Commitment

In some of the hardest hit countries, such as South Africa (with over 5 million HIV-infected people), governments fail to recognize the scope and urgency of the problem, and may even exhibit erratic and counterproductive attitudes at the highest level that block the action that is so urgently needed. This applies to both prevention and treatment. In the Russian Federation, where HIV incidence is high but prevalence is still so low that there is an opportunity to stem the emerging epidemic by rational government action, the national leadership is remarkably silent and passive about HIV/AIDS and its repressive attitudes actually fuel new infections (UNAIDS and World Health Organization 2004).

Cost of Care, Including Antiretrovirals

Health care budgets of Sub-Saharan African countries are generally extremely low, with annual per capita spending often being less than US$20. The annual cost of even the cheapest available HAART regimen for the poorest countries currently is around US$150, and in many settings this low price is theory rather than reality. This implies that for a long time the HAART scale-up will be dependent on substantial contributions from the international donor community. Middle-income countries form a specific problem, because they do not qualify for the same drug price reductions as the least developed countries, making some governments reluctant to initiate large antiretroviral treatment programs. However, we should also recognize the fact that governments make choices, and can only applaud the shining example of Brazil, where the government, after succumbing to pressure from civil society, has managed to provide effective universal free access to HAART for its HIV-infected population. In Brazil, domestic generic medicine production and the resulting increased bargaining power with research-based drug companies (through being able to credibly use the mechanism of compulsory licensing) have led to significant price reductions of antiretrovirals (Teixeira, Vitoria, and Barcarolo 2004). Similar engagement and pressure from civil society is lacking in many African countries.

Cost considerations have favored widespread use of a particular generic HAART FDC in Sub-Saharan Africa. In light of the emergency situation and the drive to put as many people as quickly as possible on treatment, this is understandable, but the long-term costs of this "cheap" choice should not be ignored. In the developed world, nobody today would initiate HAART with this specific drug combination. Although the short-term tolerance of the FDC in question is generally good, after a few years of treatment a majority of people, due to one of the components of the regimen, will develop a disfiguring syndrome of body fat redistribution, with complete loss of facial fat (Brinkman et al 1999; Van der Valk et al 2004). Apart from the avoidable human suffering this will cause, it will certainly have a negative impact on antiretroviral uptake and it would be wiser to spend a bit more money on better HAART regimens.

Lack of Infrastructure, Lack of Expertise

Even before the HIV/AIDS epidemic, the public health sector in Sub-Saharan Africa was very much underresourced, with limited possibilities to diagnose, prevent, and treat many of the diseases that abound, including those of noninfectious origin such as hypertension, diabetes mellitus, and stroke. Because of poor working conditions and low salaries, retainment rates of doctors and nurses in the public sector in many

Sub-Saharan countries are appallingly low (UNDP 2004). The HIV/AIDS epidemic has not only greatly increased demands on an already malfunctioning health sector, but also further attenuated the work force by its lethal effect on infected health care workers. Among the already low numbers of health care workers available, few have expert knowledge about the treatment of HIV infection. This situation exists in a number of Asian countries as well (Treat Asia 2004).

Lack of a Common Agenda and Leadership in Implementation

It has taken the world a long time to arrive at its current level of commitment to fight HIV/AIDS, but we are not where we should be yet. The HIV/AIDS epidemic represents a challenge of immense complexity and asks for an exceptional response. To paraphrase Jean-Francois Rischard, it is one of those inherently global problems that is getting out of hand in an exponential way, while the traditional way that human institutions work is along a linear time scale (the clash between "dog years" and "bureaucratic years") (Rischard 2002). Despite the increased sense of urgency regarding the tackling of HIV/AIDS and the increased resources for it, we still do not have the undisputed global leadership and common agenda with a clear division of tasks that is so needed to cope with the "implementation gap." In fact, in many countries, donors and technical assistance agencies are falling over each other, often in clear competition.

No single existing organization, institution, or program is fit to fill the leadership gap. Multilateral organizations such as WHO and the World Bank have pivotal roles to play, but certainly in the case of WHO, are inherently unable to deliver what is unrealistically expected of them, because of lack of resources, the inability to bypass an ineffective public sector, and the multisectorality that is required for an effective response. GFATM, although it can boast considerable successes (Severe et al 2005), unfortunately suffers from insecurity of long-term adequate funding prospects. Moreover, despite the intention to involve multiple stakeholders and delivery mechanisms and bypass government dominance, it has thus far been unable to channel money to the private sector that could make a pivotal contribution to scaling up access to antiretroviral therapy in Sub-Saharan Africa (figure 2) (GFATM 2005). A further limitation is that GFATM functions solely as a funding mechanism and has no implementation and technical assistance capacity. This may be fine or even preferable in situations in which there is sufficient competence and implementation capacity on the recipient's side, but this may often not be the case—another reason why better coordination among agencies involved in the scale-up is necessary. PEPFAR, which represents the largest financial commitment by a single nation toward an international health initiative ever, takes a different approach. It builds partnerships between organizations and institutions that can provide technical assistance on one hand and a number of developing country governments, organizations, and institutions on the other hand. In the short time that PEPFAR has been operational, it has been able to put approximately 400,000 people on antiretroviral therapy (USAID 2005). At the same time, it must be acknowledged that PEPFAR, driven by current

FIGURE 2.
Global Fund—Direct Recipients of Committed Grants, Sub-Saharan Africa as of June 15, 2005

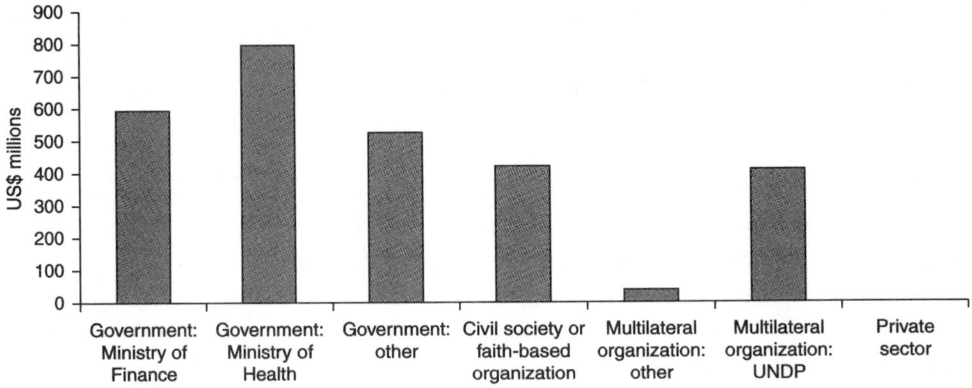

Source: www.theglobalfund.org.

U.S. unilateralism, operates in relative isolation from the other global players, and thus far has only paid lip service to building public-private partnerships in countries. Finally, although EU countries contribute considerable amounts of money to the global effort to fight HIV/AIDS, the EU is invisible because of fragmentation.

Overcoming the Obstacles

If it took a large concerted global effort, with clear divisions of tasks and accountability, to eradicate smallpox (Fenner et al 1988), how can it take less than that to tackle the infinitely more complex challenge of bringing HIV/AIDS under control? A disease that thrives on the many wrongs of societies: poverty, inequality, stigma, for which unfortunately there is no simple fast fix; a disease, that, if treated, entails lifelong care, requiring sustainable and effective health systems; a disease that mainly affects those in the prime of their lives, further contributing to poverty and undermining an effective response. The very magnitude, multisectorality, and complexity of the effort that is needed are obstacles to the global leadership, coordination, planning, and coalition building that are also direly needed.

We cannot afford to continue to do business as usual. We cannot afford not to treat those who need to be treated with antiretrovirals. We cannot afford to continue to debate the relative merits of prevention versus treatment. This is a false dichotomy. Mathematical modeling, comparing a range of scenarios through 2020, shows that our best option is to scale up treatment and prevention jointly. This strategy, as compared to either more treatment-centered or prevention-centered strategies, will lead to the lowest number of new infections, the highest number of deaths averted, and in the long term could also lead to dramatic reductions in resource needs for antiretroviral treatment (Salomon et al 2005).

We need massive training of health care workers to make them more effective in fighting HIV/AIDS, but in the short term we can never train enough of them to deal with the tasks required. We therefore also need to explore novel mechanisms of care delivery by nonphysicians, such as community-based observed therapy (Farmer et al 2001). Above all, we need to retain the health care workers that have been trained. Thus, we need to recognize economic realities on the ground, bypass government restrictions on remuneration of those working in the public sector, and offer them worthwhile career prospects. The eventual cost of not doing so will be far higher than immediate implications for health care budgets. We also need to make far more use of the skills and capacity available in the private health care sector—which is a major contributor to health care delivery in Sub-Saharan Africa—and should not exclude it from receiving donor money for the fight against the major communicable diseases.

The principle of "what works" should prevail over the questionable notion of what constitutes an "ideal society." Why are billions of dollars invested in the telecom, beverage, and oil industries in Sub-Saharan Africa and not in the health industry? Could it be that oil and telecom are allowed to make a profit? Why is it that we are always talking about the problem of drug distribution when there is virtually no place in Africa where one cannot get a cold beer or a cold Coca-Cola? Martin Wolf catches it in one sentence: "The sight of the affluent young of the west wishing to protect the poor of the world from the processes that delivered their own remarkable prosperity is unutterably depressing" (Wolf 2004, p. 320). Why is so little effort directed at building sustainable financing mechanisms for health care for the masses? Currently the richest quintile of the population in Sub-Saharan Africa profits far more from public sector services than the poorest quintile (Preker et al 2005), whereas the money of the former should contribute to the establishment of robust health insurance schemes. Why isn't part of the GFATM funds or other donor money used to kick start these?

The current "vertical approach" to scaling up antiretroviral therapy has been criticized for draining away scarce health sector resources for other diseases, but people should realize that by nature of the chronicity and manifold manifestations and ramifications of the disease, a vertical HIV treatment program rapidly becomes a horizontal program. I like to believe that the current momentum for the antiretroviral scale-up provides a unique opportunity to empower the poor and build sustainable health care systems in Africa and other resource-poor settings.

References

Allen, S., J. Tice, P. Van de Perre, A. Serufilira, E. Hudes, F. Nsengumuremyi, J. Bogaerts, C. Lindan, and S. Hulley. 1992. "Effect of Serotesting with Counseling on Condom Use and Seroconversion among HIV Discordant Couples in Africa." *British Medical Journal* 304 (6842): 1605–9.

Auvert, B., A. Puren, D. Taljaard, E. Lagarde, R. Sitta, and J. Tambeku. 2005. "Impact of Male Circumcision on the Female-to-Male Transmission of HIV." Paper presented at Third IAS Conference on HIV Pathogenesis and Treatment. Rio de Janeiro, Brazil. July 24–27.

Bica, I., B. McGovern, R. Dhar, D. Stone, K. McGowan, R. Scheib, and D. R. Snydman. 2001. "Increasing Mortality Due to End-Stage Liver Disease in Patients with Human Immunodeficiency Virus Infection." *Clinical Infectious Diseases* 32 (3): 492–7.

Brinkman, K., J. A. Smeitink, J. A. Romijn, and P. Reiss. 1999. "Mitochondrial Toxicity Induced by Nucleoside-Analogue Reverse-Transcriptase Inhibitors is a Key Factor in the Pathogenesis of Antiretroviral Therapy-Related Lipodystrophy." *Lancet* 354 (9184): 1112–5.

Bucher, H. C., L. E. Griffith, G. H. Guyatt, P. Sudre, M. Naef, P. Sendi, and M. Battegay. 1999. "Isoniazid Prophylaxis for Tuberculosis in HIV Infection: A Meta-Analysis of Randomized Controlled Trials." *AIDS* 13 (4): 501–7.

Carr, A., K. Samaras, S. Burton, M. Law, J. Freund, D. J. Chisholm, and D. A. Cooper. 1998. "A Syndrome of Peripheral Lipodystrophy, Hyperlipidemia and Insulin Resistance in Patients Receiving HIV Protease Inhibitors." *AIDS* 12 (7): F51–8.

Coordinating Committee of the Global HIV/AIDS Vaccine Enterprise. 2005. "The Global HIV/AIDS Vaccine Enterprise: Scientific Strategic Plan." *Public Library of Science Medicine* 2 (2): 111–21.

Daley, C. L., P. M. Small, G. F. Schecter, G. K. Schoolnik, R. A. McAdam, W. R. Jacobs Jr, and P. C. Hopewell. 1992. "An Outbreak of Tuberculosis with Accelerated Progression among Persons Infected with the Human Immunodeficiency Virus: An Analysis Using Restriction-Fragment Length Polymorphisms." *New England Journal of Medicine* 326 (4): 231–5.

d'Arminio, A., C. A. Sabin, A. N. Phillips, P. Reiss, R. Weber, O. Kirk, W. El-Sadr, S. De Wit, S. Mateu, K. Petoumenos, F. Dabis, C. Pradier, L. Morfeldt, J. D. Lundgren, and N. Friis-Moller. 2004. "Cardio- and Cerebrovascular Events in HIV-Infected Persons." *AIDS* 18 (13): 181–7.

Deeks, S. G., T. Wrin, T. Liegler, R. Hoh, M. Hayden, J. D. Barbour, N. S. Hellmann, C. J. Petropoulos, J. M. McCune, M. K. Hellerstein, and R. M. Grant. 2001. "Virologic and Immunologic Consequences of Discontinuing Combination Antiretroviral Drug Therapy in HIV-Infected Patients with Detectable Viremia." *New England Journal of Medicine* 344 (7): 472–80.

De Maat, M. M., G. C. Ekhart, A. D. Huitema, C. H. Koks, J. W. Mulder, and J. H. Beijnen. 2003. "Drug Interactions between Antiretroviral Drugs and Co-Medicated Agents. *Clinical Pharmacokinetics* 42 (3): 223–82.

Di Fabio, S., J. Van Roey, G. Giannini, G. van den Mooter, M. Spada, A. Binelli, M. F. Pirillo, E. Germinario, F. Belardelli, M. P. de Bethune, and S. Vella. 2003. "Inhibition of Vaginal Transmission of HIV-1 in Hu-SCID Mice by the Non-Nucleoside Reverse Transcriptase Inhibitor TMC120 in a Gel Formulation." *AIDS* 17 (11): 1597–1604.

Epstein, B. G. 2004. "The Demographic Impact of HIV/AIDS." In *The Macroeconomics of HIV/AIDS*, ed. Markus Haacker. Washington, DC: International Monetary Fund.

Eshleman, S. H., M. Mracna, L. A. Guay, M. Deseyve, S. Cunningham, M. Mirochnick, P. Musoke, T. Fleming, M. Glenn Fowler, L. M. Mofenson, F. Mmiro, and J. B. Jackson. 2001. "Selection and Fading of Resistance Mutations in Women and Infants Receiving Nevirapine to Prevent HIV-1 Vertical Transmission (HIVNET 012)." *AIDS* 15 (15): 1951–7.

Farmer, P. E., F. Leandre, J. S. Mukherjee, M. Claude, P. Nevil, M. C. Smith-Fawzi, S. P. Koenig, A. Castro, M. C. Becerra, J. Sachs, A. Attaran, and J. Y. Kim. 2001. "Community-Based Approaches to HIV Treatment in Resource-Poor Settings." *Lancet* 358 (9279): 404–9.

Fenner, F., D. A. Henderson, I. Arita, Z. Jezek, and I. D. Ladnyi. 1988. *Smallpox and Its Eradication.* Geneva: World Health Organization.

Fischl, M. A., D. D. Richman, M. H. Grieco, M. S. Gottlieb, P. A. Volberding, O. L. Laskin, J. M. Leedom, J. E. Groopman, D. Mildvan, and R. T. Schooley. 1987. "The Efficacy of Azidothymidine (AZT) in the Treatment of Patients with AIDS and AIDS-Related Complex: A Double-Blind Placebo-Controlled Trial." *New England Journal of Medicine* 317 (4): 185–91.

Fontanet, A. L., J. Saba, V. Chandelying, C. Sakondhavat, P. Bhiraleus, and S. Rugpao. 1998. "Protection against Sexually Transmitted Diseases by Granting Sex Workers in Thailand the Choice of Using the Male or Female Condom: Results from a Randomized Controlled Trial." *AIDS* 12 (14): 1851–9.

French, M. A., P. Price, and S. F. Stone. 2004. "Immune Restoration Disease after Antiretroviral Therapy." *AIDS* 18 (12): 1615–27.

Friis-Moller, N., C. A. Sabin, R. Weber, A. d'Arminio Monforte, W. M. El-Sadr, P. Reiss, R. Thiebaut, L. Morfeldt, S. De Wit, C. Pradier, G. Calvo, M. G. Law, O. Kirk, A. N. Phillips, and J. D. Lundgren. 2003. "Combination Antiretroviral Therapy and the Risk of Myocardial Infarction." *New England Journal of Medicine* 349 (21): 1993–2003.

GFATM (Global Fund to Fight AIDS, TB, and Malaria). 2005. www.theglobalfund.org.

Haacker, Markus. 2004. "HIV/AIDS: The Impact on the Social Fabric and the Economy." In *The Macroeconomics of HIV/AIDS,* ed. Markus Haacker. Washington, DC: International Monetary Fund.

Jackson, J. B., G. Becker-Pergola, L. A. Guay, P. Musoke, M. Mracna, M. G. Fowler, L. M. Mofenson, M. Mirochnick, F. Mmiro, and S. H. Eshleman. 2001. "Identification of K103N Resistance Mutation in Ugandan Women Receiving Nevirapine to Prevent HIV-1 Vertical Transmission (HIVNET 012)." *AIDS* 14 (11): F111–5.

Jones, B. E., S. M. Young, D. Antoniskis, P. T. Davidson, F. Kramer, and P. F. Barnes. 1993. "Relationship of the Manifestations of Tuberculosis to CD4 Cell Counts in Patients with Human Immunodeficiency Virus Infection." *The American Review of Respiratory Disease* 148 (5): 1292–7.

Jourdain, G., N. Ngo-Giang-Huong, S. Le Coeur, C. Bowonwatanuwong, P. Kantipong, P. Leechanachai, S. Ariyadej, P. Leenasirimakul, S. Hammer, and M. Lallemont. 2004. "Intrapartum Exposure to Nevirapine and Subsequent Maternal Responses to Nevirapine-Based Antiretroviral Therapy." *New England Journal of Medicine* 351 (3): 229–40.

Kreiss, J., E. Ngugi, K. Holmes, J. Ndinya-Achola, P. Waiyaki, P. L. Roberts, I. Ruminjo, R. Sajabi, J. Kimata, and T. R. Fleming. 1992. "Efficacy of Nonoxynol 9 Contraceptive Sponge Use in Preventing Heterosexual Acquisition of HIV in Nairobi Prostitutes." *Journal of the American Medical Association* 268 (4): 477–82.

Lange, J. M. A. 1997. "Current Problems and the Future of Antiretroviral Drug Trials." *Science* 276 (5312): 548–50.

———. 2005. "We Must Not Let Protestors Derail Trials of Pre-Exposure Prophylaxis for HIV." *Public Library of Science Medicine* 2 (9): 833–4.

Lederman, M. M., R. S. Veazey, R. Offord, D. E. Mosier, J. Dufour, M. Mefford, M. Piatak, J. D. Lifson, J. R. Salkowitz, B. Rodriguez, A. Blauvelt, and O. Hartley. 2004. "Prevention of Vaginal SHIV Transmission in Rhesus Macaques through Inhibition of CCR5." *Science* 306 (5695): 485–7.

Lee, W. M. "Drug-Induced Hepatotoxicity." 2003. *New England Journal of Medicine* 349 (5): 474–85.

Little, S. J., S. Holte, J. P. Routy, E. S. Daar, M. Markowitz, A. C. Collier, R. A. Koup, J. W. Mellors, E. Connick, B. Conway, M. Kilby, L. Wang, J. M. Whitcomb, N. S. Hellmann, and D. D. Richman. 2002. "Antiretroviral Drug Susceptibility and Response to Initial Therapy among Recently HIV Infected Subjects in North America: A Study from the Acute

Infection and Early Disease Research Program (AIEDRP)." *New England Journal of Medicine* 347 (6): 385–94.

Macias, J., I. Melguizo, F. J. Fernandez-Rivera, A. Garcia-Garcia, J. A. Mira, A. J. Ramos, J. M. Rivera, and J. A. Pineda. 2002. "Mortality Due to Liver Failure and Impact on Survival of Hepatitis Virus Infections in HIV-Infected Patients Receiving Potent Antiretroviral Therapy." *European Journal of Clinical Microbiology and Infectious Disease* 21 (11): 775–81.

Moore, J. P. "Topical Microbicides become Topical." 2005. *New England Journal of Medicine* 352 (3): 298–300.

Palella, F. J., K. M. Delaney, A. C. Moorman, M. O. Loveless, J. Fuhrer, G. A. Satten, D. J. Aschman, and S. D. Holmberg. 1988. "Declining Morbidity and Mortality among Patients with Advanced Human Immunodeficiency Virus Infection." *New England Journal of Medicine* 338 (13): 853–60.

Paterson, D. L., S. Swindells, J. Mohr, M. Brester, E. N. Vergis, C. Squier, M. M. Wagener, and N. Singh. 2000. "Adherence to Protease Inhibitor Therapy and Outcomes in Patients with HIV Infection." *Annals of Internal Medicine* 133 (1): 21–30.

Petra Study Team. 2002. "Efficacy of Three Short-Course Regimens of Zidovudine and Lmivudine in Preventing Early and Late Transmission of HIV-1 from Mother-to-Child in Tanzania, South Africa, and Uganda (Petra Study)." *Lancet* 359 (9313): 1178–86.

Preker, A. S., and J. C. Langenbrunner, eds. 2005. *Spending Wisely, Buying Health Services for the Poor.* Washington, DC: World Bank.

Richman, D. D., S. C. Morton, T. Wrin, N. Hellmann, S. Berry, M. F. Shapiro, and S. A. Bozzette. 2004. "The Prevalence of Antiretroviral Drug Resistance in the United States." *AIDS* 18 (10): 1393–401.

Rischard, J. F. 2002. *High Noon: 20 Global Issues, 20 Years to Solve Them.* Oxford: The Perseus Press.

Salomon, J. A., D. R. Hogan, J. Stover, K. A. Stanecki, N. Walker, P. D. Ghys, and B. Schwartländer. 2005. "Integrating HIV Prevention and Treatment: From Slogans to Impact." *Public Library of Science Medicine* 2 (1): 50–6.

Severe, P., P. Leger, M. Charles, F. Noel, G. Bonhomme, G. Bois, E. George, S. Kenel-Pierre, P. F. Wright, R. Gulick, W. D. Johnson Jr, J. W. Pape, and D. W. Fitzgerald. 2005. "Antiretroviral Therapy in a Thousand Patients with AIDS in Haiti." *New England Journal of Medicine* 353 (22): 2325–34.

Shafer, R. W., A. B. Bloch, C. Larkin, V. Vasudavan, S. Seligman, J. D. Dehovitz, G. DiFerdinando, R. Stoneburner, and G. Cauthen. 1996. "Predictors of Survival in HIV-Infected Tuberculosis." *AIDS* 10 (3): 269–72.

Shattuck, R. A., and J. P. Moore. 2003. "Inhibiting Sexual Transmission of HIV-1 Infection." *Nature Reviews. Microbiology* 1 (1): 25–34.

Singh, J. A., and E. J. Mills. 2005. "The Abandoned Trials of Pre-Exposure Prophylaxis for HIV: What Went Wrong." *Public Library of Science Medicine* 2 (9): 824–7.

Srikantiah. P., E. Charlebois, D. V. Havlir. 2005. "Rapid Increase in Tuberculosis Incidence Soon after Infection with HIV—A New Twist in the Twin Epidemics." *Journal of Infectious Diseases* 191 (2):147–9.

Sonnenberg, P., J. R. Glynn, K. Fielding, J. Murray, P. Godfrey-Faussett, and S. Shearer. 2005. "How Soon after Infection with HIV Does the Risk of Tuberculosis Start to Increase? A Retrospective Cohort Study in South African Gold Miners." *Journal of Infectious Diseases* 191 (2): 150–8.

Subbarao, S., R. Otten, A. Ramos, E. Jackson, D. Adams, C. Kim, S. Bashirian, J. Johnson, M. Monsour, R. Janssen, L. Paxton, A. Greenberg, and T. Folks. 2005. "Chemoprophylaxis with Oral Tenofovir Disoproxil Fumarate Delays but Does Not Prevent Infection in Rhesus Macaques Given Repeated Rectal Challenges of SHIV." 12th Conference on Retroviruses and Opportunistic Infections. Boston, MA. February 22–25.

Teixeira, P. R., M. A. Vitoria, and J. Barcarolo. 2004. "Antiretroviral Treatment in Resource-Poor Settings: The Brazilian Experience." *AIDS* 18 (suppl 3): S5–S7.

The Stop TB Partnership Annual Report 2004. 2005. World Health Organization, May.

Treat Asia. 2004. "Special Report: Expanded Availability of HIV/AIDS Drugs in Asia Creates Urgent Need for Trained Doctors." Bangkok, Thailand.

Tsai, C.-C., K. E. Follis, A. Sabo, T. W. Beck, R. F. Grant, N. Bischofberger, R. E. Benveniste, and R. Black. 1995. "Prevention of SIV Infection in Macaques by (R)-9-(2-phosphonylmethoxypropyl) adenine. *Science* 270:1197–9.

UNAIDS and World Health Organization. 2004. *AIDS Epidemic Update: December 2004.* Geneva.

———. 2005. *AIDS Epidemic Update: December 2005.* Geneva

UNDP (United Nations Development Programme). 2004. *Human Development Report 2004: Cultural Liberty in Today's Diverse World.* New York, NY: UNDP.

United Nations General Assembly on HIV/AIDS. 2001. "Declaration of Commitment HIV/AIDS, Global Crisis—Global Action." New York.

USAID. 2005. *www.usaid.gov*/our_work/global_health/aids/pepfarfact.html.

Van Damme, L., G. Ramjee, M. Alary, B. Vuylsteke, V. Chandeying, H. Rees, P. Sirivongrangson, L. Mukenge-Tshibaka, V. Ettiegne-Traore, C. Uaheowitchai, S. S. Karim, B. Masse, J. Perriens, and M. Laga. 2002. "Effectiveness of COL-1492, A Nonoxynol-9 Vaginal Gel, on HIV-1 Transmission in Female Sex Workers: A Randomized Controlled Trial." *Lancet* 360 (9338): 971–7.

Van der Valk, M., M. Casula, G. J. Weverling, K. van Kuijk, B. van Eck-Smit, H. J. Hulsebosch, P. Nieuwkerk, A. van Eeden, K. Brinkman, J. Lange, A. de Ronde, and P. Reiss. 2004. "Prevalence of Lipoatrophy and Mitochondrial DNA Content of Blood and Subcutaneous Fat in HIV-1-Infected Patients Randomly Allocated to Zidovudine- or Stavudine-Based Therapy." *Antiviral Therapy* 9 (3): 385–93.

Vyankadondera, J., S. Luchters, E. Hassink, N. Pakker, F. Mmiro, P. Okong, P. Kituuka, C. Ndugwa, N. Mukanka, A. Beretta, M. Imperiale Jr, E. Loeliger, M. Giuliano, and J. Lange. 2003. "Reducing Risk of HIV-1 Transmission from Mother to Infant through Breastfeeding Using Antiretroviral Prophylaxis in Infants (SIMBA Study)." 2nd IAS Conference on HIV Pathogenesis and Treatment. Paris, France. July 13–16.

Weller, S. C. 1993. "A Meta-Analysis of Condom Effectiveness in Reducing Sexually Transmitted HIV." *Social Science and Medicine* 36 (12): 1635–44.

Whalen, C. C., P. Nsubuga, A. Okwera, J. L. Johnson, D. L. Hom, N. L. Michael, R. D. Mugerwa, and J. J. Ellner. 2000. "Impact of Pulmonary Tuberculosis on Survival of HIV-Infected Adults: A Prospective Epidemiologic Study in Uganda." *AIDS* 14 (9): 1219–28.

Wolf, M. 2004. *Why Globalization Works.* New Haven and London: Yale University Press.

World Health Organization. 2002. "Scaling Up Antiretroviral Therapy in Resource-Limited Settings: Guidelines for a Public Health Approach." WHO, Geneva, Switzerland.

———. 2003. "Treating 3 Million by 2005: Making it Happen." WHO, Geneva, Switzerland.

Yeni, P. G., S. M. Hammer, M. S. Hirsch, M. S. Saag, M. Schechter, C. C. Carpenter, M. A. Fischl, J. M. Gatell, B. G. Gazzard, D. M. Jacobsen, D. A. Katzenstein, J. S. Montaner, D. D. Richman, R. T. Schooley, M. A. Thompson, S. Vella, and P. A. Volberding. 2004. "Treatment for Adult HIV Infection: 2004 Recommendations of the International AIDS Society USA Panel." *Journal of the American Medical Association* 292 (2): 251–65.

Comment on "Scaling Up Access to HIV Prevention, Treatment, and Care in Resource-Poor Settings: Challenges and Opportunities," by Joep M. A. Lange

FRANÇOISE NDAYISHIMIYE

As Professor Lange said, Human Immunodeficiency Virus (HIV), which is the causative agent of Acquired Immune Deficiency Syndrome (AIDS), is now devastating the world, especially in Sub-Saharan Africa. It is an unprecedented humanitarian disaster. The HIV/AIDS epidemic has social and economic as well as medical and physical impacts, with the added dimension of deteriorating security at the individual, community, and national levels.

Seroprevalence is still rising, particularly among the female population. Owing to a lack of infrastructure and resources, the capacity of the health sector is declining. We know today that only 10 percent of resources are in Africa, where 90 percent of people living with AIDS need treatment. This epidemic is perpetuating poverty because of rising mortality rates among productive people and the education sector, and also because of increasing demands on the public health sector.

Professor Lange's paper underlines the exceptional challenge posed by the co-infection of HIV and tuberculosis. In fact, this co-infection causes the highest HIV mortality rate in developing countries.

The world cannot afford to ignore these health problems and poverty in developing countries. Ignoring these issues in this era of globalization may cause global insecurity and instability. A rapid but long-term plan is needed to fight this epidemic. A huge gap exists between needs and interventions in the North and South. The world must not only find a way to bridge this gap but it must also find a correct response to the epidemic as well as a way to save the millions of lives that are being lost, especially in developing countries. This situation can be changed by providing antiretroviral treatment for those in need.

Françoise Ndayishimiye is NGO liaison, Secrétariat Exécutif Permanent du Conseil National de lutte contre le SIDA, Bujumbura, Burundi. Numbers of people in treatment have been updated to reflect circumstances as of February 2006.

Annual World Bank Conference on Development Economics—Europe 2006

Burundi's Commitment to Fighting AIDS

In Burundi, 25,000 people need treatment; however, only 6,400 people with HIV currently have access to treatment. Access to treatment programs is financed mainly by the Global Fund to Fight AIDS, Tuberculosis and Malaria (GFATM), and the World Bank Multicountry AIDS Program (MAP); and limited support is provided by the Clinton Foundation, Heineken, and other international NGOs. The lack of human resources and infrastructure throughout the country creates a enormous gap. Burundi is a best case scenario in Africa, but with our limited resources we will not go far if the developed world is not willing to support our initiative.

Burundi is a small country in central East Africa. The population is approximately 7 million, with a seroprevalence rate of 6.0 percent in rural areas and 10.4 percent in urban areas. The political will to fight HIV/AIDS has grown over the last few years. The Burundi government, with its limited funds, has, since 1999, budgeted a small amount to fight AIDS (Therapeutic Solidarity Fund against AIDS). A specific ministry for fighting AIDS was created, and a Permanent Executive Secretariat of the National AIDS Council has been put in place. Burundi overcame the debate on "prevention" versus "treatment," and the country is committed to providing a comprehensive package (prevention, treatment, care, and support) to those in need.

Today, Burundi is mobilizing all treatment capabilities. Many parties are involved in fighting this devastating disease, and antiretroviral (ARV) treatment is now free for HIV/AIDS patients. There are 25 treatment sites providing ARV treatment: 8 public sector sites treating 2,550 people; 3 private sector sites treating 350 people; and 5 associations and 14 religious NGOs treating 3,500 people. Associations of people living with HIV/AIDS are increasing their involvement in the fight against the disease, including the provision of access to treatment programs. Such associations' health structures are the largest and the highest quality treatment providers. More than 62 percent of people on ARV treatment in Burundi are treated through associations. Unfortunately, the private sector is underdeveloped and must be motivated by the government to increase its willingness and commitment to fight the epidemic, and the public sector is facing a lack of well-trained, motivated doctors and health care workers.

The treatment programs must be scaled up. Decentralization of services is now one of the main aims of the government to allow access to treatment for all. The current 25 treatment sites are located in 10 of the 17 provinces, with planned coverage of all provinces by the end of 2006. Many people are being saved by the decentralization of services and the collaboration among government, private sector, and civil society, including agricultural workers, professionals, teachers, business directors, military personnel, drivers, and others. The Association Nationale de soutien aux Seropositifs et Sideens (ANSS), an association led by people living with HIV/AIDS, is treating approximately 1,700 people with ARV and is providing a comprehensive package of services. The treatment program is complemented by counseling, adherence programs, home visits and care, and nutritional programs, especially for the poorest people. The people supported by these programs are doing as well as those living in developed countries, and mortality and morbidity rates among them have decreased.

Although adherence is adequate and the results are positive, the sustainability of good programs is entirely dependent on external willingness to support the poorest countries, such as Burundi.

The Efficiency of the Association-Driven Care and Treatment Model

The association-driven care and treatment (ADCT) model involves associations in ARV treatment. Its efficiency results from prioritizing the quality of care of patients and the commitment to provide a comprehensive package of services (prevention, treatment, care, and support). In association clinics, the treatment model includes prevention, medical care, psychosocial care, adherence follow up, nutritional care, and so on. The associations derive their models from the AIDS Empowerment and Treatment International network (AIDSETI).

AIDSETI is formed by 21 associations from 14 developing countries. These associations are doing well, but they are underfunded. Volunteer work is strong now, but our hope is that the success of these associations will lead to their gaining full support. Six associations from Burkina Faso are finally expanding their programs with the World Bank Treatment Acceleration Program (TAP); one association in Burundi is supported by MAP, which is financed by the World Bank and GFATM; another association in Ethiopia is supported by the Centers for Disease Control; and one in Kenya is supported by AIDSFONDS. The success of this model has boosted advocacy to develop additional programs.

These associations are successful because the comprehensive package of services they provide closely follows the World Health Organization (WHO) guidelines, which include

- counseling and voluntary testing services,
- medical and biological follow-up for HIV-positive individuals,
- consultation to assess and encourage future adherence to treatment,
- baseline biological follow-up tests,
- prophylaxis and treatment of opportunistic infections,
- antiretroviral treatment,
- psychosocial and nutritional support, and
- regular follow-up visits to evaluate treatment success and side effects.

People living with HIV/AIDS have also played a major role in the success of the ARV treatment programs. As a trained doctor, and being HIV positive myself, I am closely involved in the success of the ADCT model. I have known my HIV status for 10 years and have been involved in programs fighting HIV for 12 years. I helped found the Burundi Network of People Living with HIV/AIDS, and with my colleagues, I created Greater Involvement of People living with AIDS (GIPA) Center in Burundi. GIPA is helping to mainstream HIV prevention and treatment in development programs through businesses, ministries, NGOs, and UN agencies. Today I am in charge of helping civil society organizations access MAP financial support through the Secretariat of the National AIDS Council. As a member of the board of GFATM,

I support access to treatment for all, and I also advocate for the ADCT model to be used in many countries.

Many of us living with the virus or with AIDS have been willing to help and are capable of being active players in the fight against the epidemic. Our role cannot continue to be one of always being helped and supported as the beneficiary. We said *no.* We are *not* the burden of the world, we are not the problem, we are a part of *the solution.* We are at our best when we are involved. We decided to be in the front of the fight to preserve those who are still HIV negative and to support those already infected. We just need the space to do so. We have to be the front line of the fight as actors rather than beneficiaries; however, to achieve this we need access to treatment, and we have to be healthy so that we can support the fight. We need the support of political leaders and donors.

Why are we unable to treat all the people who need it?

- Many people still do not know they are infected because they have not been tested.
- Stigma in some regions remains a barrier to testing and treatment.
- Lack of access to treatment is a barrier to voluntary testing.
- Services are often unavailable outside cities.
- The public sector is not equipped with sufficient material and human resources, especially in rural areas.
- Resources to expand capacity of interventions are unavailable.
- It is feared that sustainable treatment programs cannot be made available.
- The world's willingness is limited. The promise of $10 billion from the United States has been a slogan rather than a reality. The "3 by 5" program was a dream that was not achieved. GFATM is facing resource mobilization limits, but the world cannot afford to keep losing thousands of lives because the price might be extraordinarily high.

In some countries the financial situation is very precarious. In Burundi, only two major funders, MAP and GFATM, support the treatment program, and those programs are limited by time. The national effort is not sustainable in a situation characterized by the high burden of the disease, by high poverty, and by 12 years of internal political insecurity. Programs such as the President's Emergency Plan for AIDS Relief and others do not consider Burundi a priority. The strengthening of the health care system is still a dream. Doctors still have very low salaries (US$60 per month) and prefer to be refugees in European countries where their diplomas are not even recognized but where they can at least earn a survival salary. The continuous brain drain from Africa to Europe and the humanitarian refugees in Europe may be a problem in tomorrow's world.

This Is the Time for Action

As Professor Lange said, we need to act now—the world cannot afford to ignore the health problems in developing countries, the consequences of which will be unbelievable tomorrow. At this 2005 ABCDE conference, we have to propose solutions to this problem, because it is seriously related to the progress of development. There will be no development without healthy people, and there are no healthy people without resources for a life-long care program. Let's consider the problem today, because the solution is in our hands. Let's find a sustainable way of supporting action; let's have the real willingness to take this seriously. And finally, let's take the budget used for war and use it to save and treat people instead. If there is no will to save people today, tomorrow it will be too late, and development will be hard to attain.

A Private Company's Contribution to Scaling Up Access to HIV Prevention, Treatment, and Care in Resource-Poor Settings: The Heineken Example

HENK RIJCKBORST

In March 2000, five big pharmaceutical companies started the Accelerated Access Initiative, offering HIV antiretroviral drugs to a number of developing countries for 10 percent of the regular price of these drugs in Western countries. In the months afterward, nothing happened with that offer. Many of the countries in Sub-Saharan Africa (SSA) did not have enough management capacity within their public health systems to purchase the drugs and to provide access to HIV seropositive people who needed such treatment. For this reason, Professor Joep Lange, president-elect of the International AIDS Society, made a plenary speech during the World AIDS Conference in Durban, South Africa, in July 2000, in which he beseeched especially the mining and brewing industries in SSA to use their medical infrastructure to provide antiretroviral treatment (ART) to their employees and dependents. (ART in this context is synonymous with HAART [Highly Active Anti Retroviral Treatment] as used in Professor Lange's paper.) Soon after the conference, we had a first meeting with Professor Lange in the Heineken head office in Amsterdam.

Heineken is an international brewing group employing more than 70,000 people all over the world in more than 120 breweries, 20 of which are located in SSA, employing approximately 7,000 people. Heineken has been present in the Democratic Republic of Congo (DRC) since 1935, so it has a long relationship with the African continent. According to previous Belgian and French colonial laws, employers had to pay for and organize a medical care package for their employees and dependents.

In 2000, Heineken employed 14 doctors, 40 medical assistants and nurses, a pharmacist, and numerous other medical staff to deliver medical care to about 40,000 people, the majority of whom (28,000) were children. The doctors were well trained and the brewery clinics simple but adequately organized and equipped, aiming to deliver a good quality medical care package.

Henk Rijckborst is Director, Heineken International Health Affairs, Amsterdam, the Netherlands.

Annual World Bank Conference on Development Economics—Europe 2006

In September 2000, representatives of General Management, Marketing, Human Resources, Corporate Affairs, and Health Affairs established a committee to prepare a proposal for Heineken's Executive Board (EB) to provide ART for free to its employees in SSA Operational Companies (OpCos). In mid-2001, the complete EB accepted a leadership role to act in accordance with the proposals made by the HIV policy committee and on September 1, 2001, Heineken started to provide ART in Rwanda and Burundi, later followed by Heineken OpCos in DRC, Republic of Congo (Brazzaville), Ghana, and Nigeria—15 sites total. The EB demanded that only high quality programs be undertaken, and that the program act on a low-profile basis, so as not to misuse its ART/HIV policy as a competitive advantage.

Was it not somewhat strange that a private business group substituted for what governments normally must do? We have to realize that providing ART in countries such as Rwanda and Burundi in the absence of high-tech hospitals and laboratories to monitor patients was completely new in 2001. Heineken contracted with Pharm-Access International (PAI), a Dutch nongovernmental organization (NGO) to provide technical assistance, to organize the training of doctors and laboratory staff, to organize the supply of drugs, and to upgrade the laboratories attached to the clinics by investing in modern lab equipment for all sites.

I will not explain in detail how implementation of the ART policy took place. However, I will make some summarizing comments. It was hard work and not a glamorous story at all. More than 6,000 people have accepted Voluntary Counseling and Testing (VCT) during the first three years of the program, over 400 of whom proved to be HIV seropositive. Today more than 200 people need treatment and are receiving ART.

Overall adherence to this ART therapy is better than 90 percent, which is very high and no drug resistance has been identified to date. Together with PAI, Heineken Health Affairs has proven that it is possible to provide ART in resource-poor settings.

Further goals were achieved, too. One other demand of the EB was to become active in promoting delivery of such therapy by other private sector colleagues. Numerous presentations on many occasions have been made to business audiences. Nowadays, several private sector colleagues in industry and banking are providing ART in SSA. Learning effects have been shared by presenting papers, and together with PAI, Stop Aids Now, and Boston University, a qualitative analysis of acceptance of VCT in Rwanda was conducted.

Five years ago we could not imagine working in partnership with NGOs; international bodies (International Labor Organization, UNAIDS, the World Bank, International Finance Corporation, the Global Fund to fight AIDS, Tuberculosis and Malaria); aid organizations such as the German GTZ, World Economic Forum/Global Health Initiative; the Dutch government (Ministry of Foreign Affairs/Development Cooperation); private investors in Africa; and many more. Working in partnerships with mutual respect has made us part, as a private business group, of the global network to fight HIV/AIDS (and malaria and TB). An equally important aspect is that accepting our responsibility toward our employees by offering them ART for free was possible and successful and that we as a representative of the private sector can play a modest but active role in the scaling-up to HIV prevention and treatment.

Never will the private sector deliver ART to large numbers of people, because we have a primary focus on our own employees; but we have already adapted our program in such a way that we will try to move our laboratory equipment to general and private clinics so that people other than those in our workforce will have the possibility of gaining access to treatment, thus delivering services to the wider community. An important role in organizing this effort is performed by the Dutch Ministry of Foreign Affairs, PAI, and (Anglo-)Dutch international corporations such as Unilever, Royal Dutch/Shell, Celltell, and Heineken International.

The Heineken Company has saved about 60 lives thanks to our HIV/AIDS treatment policies—not many, seeing that the HIV epidemic costs over 6,000 lives in SSA every day. However, I prefer not to diminish this accomplishment too much: for 60 families it is most important that there is a father who earns a salary allowing children to go to school and to enjoy a family life.

What did the program mean for Heineken internally? For the Health Affairs department it meant hard work—this is not simply distributing tablets to patients. It is monitoring them, auditing clinics and laboratories, training doctors, organizing bi-weekly teleconferences during which medical specialists from Europe discuss difficult cases presented by doctors from 15 sites, and, sometimes, suffering from frustration.

For Heineken's EB and General Management it means that HIV/AIDS, the number one cause of death among our workforce in SSA in the late 1990s, has become "manageable" even with regard to cost. HIV-seropositive people continued to work and Heineken dared to invest over 350 million euro (about US$425 million) in African breweries in SSA during the last four years.

Let us not forget that preventing diseases is important but that people need an income to live. Labor, and especially high-skilled labor, is important for Africa. Investing in Africa is as important as providing aid. A critical comment I would like to raise is the fact that so much money is currently going to SSA for HIV/AIDS projects and that everybody needs a success story; but this is heavily influencing the labor market for doctors and medical assistants. Doctors are leaving their countries and are moving to Botswana, which has received hundreds of millions of dollars. We are also currently losing medical staff because of higher payment elsewhere by aid organizations. This is not a serious matter in normal labor market conditions, but for us, for some time, it has been a problem. Training to work with ART, working according to strict protocols, reporting, computer literacy, and the ability to read and communicate in English in francophone countries are conditions that only few medical staff can comply with. We cannot change our remuneration policies for medical staff, which are based on international job-grading systems such as that provided by the Hay Group, without disturbing the remuneration system for other jobs. This adds an extra challenge to training doctors and nurses on HIV treatment.

Another challenge will be our role or responsibility toward HIV/AIDS in Asia and Eastern Europe: we do not know enough about the spread of the epidemic there and let us recognize that enormous language and cultural barriers have to be overcome. From this perspective, we have to realize how easy it is to work together with Africans, which is further eased by their ability to speak English or French.

In a short paper like this it is difficult to present the sensitive and difficult issue of ART and our corporate responsibilities in a fully balanced manner. I would like to make one final comment: do not ask why a company has an HIV policy, but ask why it lacks one.